PREVENTION'S
Quick and Healthy
LOW-FAT COOKING

FEATURING

ALL-AMERICAN

FOOD

EDITED BY JEAN ROGERS, FOOD EDITOR, **PREVENTION** MAGAZINE HEALTH BOOKS

RODALE PRESS, EMMAUS, PENNSYLVANIA

Copyright ©1995 by Rodale Press, Inc.
Illustrations copyright ©1995 by Mary Bergherr
Photographs copyright ©1995 by Rodale Press, Inc.

Front Cover: Grilled Breast of Chicken with Tomato-Basil Relish (page 92), Rainbow Vegetable Coleslaw (page 83) and Blueberry Peach Honey Shortcakes (page 286).

Cover Photography: Tad Ware & Company, Inc.

ISBN 0–87596–235–1 hardcover
ISBN 0–87596–237–8 paperback
ISSN 1064–7503

2 4 6 8 10 9 7 5 3 1 hardcover
2 4 6 8 10 9 7 5 3 1 paperback

OUR MISSION

We publish books that empower people's lives.

RODALE ✣ BOOKS

Prevention's Quick and Healthy Low-Fat Cooking

Editorial and Design Staff

Editor: Jean Rogers

Contributing Writers: Mark Golin, Cathy Perlmutter, Patricia Miller

Book and Cover Designer: Debra Sfetsios

Book Layout: Tad Ware & Company, Inc.

Illustrator: Mary Bergherr

Photographer: Studio 3

Food Stylist: Judy Tills

Assistant Food Stylist: Janice Cole

Recipe Development and Coordination: Janice Cole

Recipe Development: Colleen Minor, Deidre Schipani

Nutritional Consultant: Linda Yoakam, M.S., R.D.

Editor, Prevention *Magazine:* Mark Bricklin

Prevention *Magazine Health Books*

Editor-in-Chief, Rodale Books: Bill Gottlieb

Executive Editor: Debora A. Tkac

Art Director: Jane Colby Knutila

Research Manager: Ann Gossy Yermish

Copy Manager: Lisa D. Andruscavage

Contents

Introduction

You know how much sense a low-fat diet makes in terms of your health. A light and lean diet gives you a better shot at avoiding the killer diseases that plague our country, such as heart disease, some types of cancer, diabetes and a host of ills associated with being overweight in general.

It might never have occurred to you, however, that cutting fat also makes cents. What trims your middle may also fatten your wallet, according to a study done at Columbia University in New York City.

When 291 people were put on a cholesterol-lowering diet for nine months, those who followed it best saw their food bills go down—by $.75 to $1.10 a day. Researchers assessed food costs with random phone calls to participants both before the diet began and three, six and nine months after the diet. For three days, people detailed what they had eaten in the previous 24 hours, and scientists compared their responses to what those same people were consuming at the beginning of the study.

A savings of $.75 a day may sound insignificant. But as with most things, a cumulative effect sets in that very quickly makes it worthwhile. And that $.75 is a per-person figure, so a family of four could reap a savings of $3 a day. At the end of a year, we're talking $1,000 that you can use to go on a holiday, buy a treadmill or otherwise treat yourself, points out study leader Thomas A. Pearson, M.D., Ph.D., professor of epidemiology at Columbia.

Many people think that low-fat cooking involves unusual, expensive ingredients. But if you think about the cost of the leanest, lowest-fat foods—beans, grains, fruits, vegetables, chicken and such —the idea of cutting fat and cutting costs at the same time is pretty logical and pretty easy.

The recipes in this edition of *Prevention's Quick and Healthy Low-Fat Cooking* should have a familiar ring to them. We've chosen all-American favorites and given them nutrient makeovers. In their new, improved form, they can go a long way toward trimming your personal profile and beefing up your bank balance. Give them a try. You know what you've got to gain—and what you've got to lose.

Jean Rogers

JEAN ROGERS
Food Editor, *Prevention* Magazine Health Books

THE
FAT-FIGHTING
EDGE

HEALTHY HABITS–NOW AND FOREVER

America is the land of plenty—plenty of burgers, plenty of pizza, plenty of apple pie. The result for too many of us is extra pounds that sap our energy and threaten our health. Clearly, the excess weight has to go, but getting rid of it is never easy. Even when you are successful, those unwanted pounds have a way of picking up your scent like a pack of bloodhounds hot on your trail. Before you know it, they've once again got you surrounded.

So how do you lose those dogs—er, pounds—once and for all? You've got to change your scent. Become a new person. Become a person who no longer leads an overweight lifestyle with its overweight habits. And the trick is to do it without taxing your willpower, without subjecting yourself to undue deprivation and without adding rules and regulations that you can't wait to be rid of.

In other words, you have to create a new lifestyle that you can follow long enough to have it become second nature. You want a friend that hangs around for the rest of your life, guarding you against ever gaining weight again.

UNDERSTAND THE BASICS

Does the phrase "look before you leap" ring a bell? You can't make an honest commitment to do something unless you have some idea of what is required. So let's go through the healthy-lifestyle facts of life.

The first fact of life is that you can't lose 30 pounds in a month. Nor would you want to. After all, the goal isn't just to lose weight; it's to keep the pounds off permanently. And most experts agree that you have the best chances of doing that if you take a gradual approach—dropping no more than one pound a week.

The second fact of life is that in order to lose that pound a week, you need to establish a daily deficit of 500 calories. That requires some combination of the right foods and the right exercise. Most weight-loss experts favor a program in which you cut 200 calories of fat (roughly 22 grams of fat) from your daily diet and burn off 300 calories through exercise to achieve the magic number. (When it comes to diet, it's actually better to count grams of fat instead of calories.)

And the third fact of life is that the first two facts are useless unless you follow them consistently and maintain them long after excess pounds are gone. That means being comfortable with the changes you make and not demanding more of yourself than you are prepared to give.

FAT FACTS

The average American's diet is approximately 40 percent fat. And because fat calories are more readily converted into body fat, those kinds of calories are the first ones you want to reduce. But the question is, by how much?

Diet experts advocate a fat intake of no more than 25 percent of total calories. What does that really mean? Well, for a woman to maintain a weight of 130 pounds, for instance, she should take in about 1,600 calories a day. If only 25 percent of those calories come from fat, that's 400 calories' worth. Since each gram of fat is good for 9 calories, that's an upper level of 44 grams of fat a day. If you are a 160-pound woman eating 2,000 calories a day (at the 40 percent fat level), you're currently consuming about 89 grams of fat. To reach a streamlined 130, you need to figure out how to be satisfied with 45 fewer grams of fat per day. But not all at once.

As we mentioned before, to jump onto the pound-a-week weight-loss wagon, you need to cut 500 calories a day: 200 from your daily intake and 300 through exercise. With exercise making its hefty contribution, all that is really required to get the weight-loss wagon rolling is that you bid farewell to approximately 22 grams of fat per day.

After a certain amount of time, your 22-gram fat deficit, along with exercise, can slim your body to a point where it functions so efficiently that you stop losing weight. At this point, having become used to the dietary changes you've made, you can then go ahead and cut your fat intake far enough to reach a fat budget that corresponds to your dream maintenance weight.

While sheer instinct may tell you to grit your teeth and cut all the fat in sight, hoping your willpower holds out, that is the last thing you should do. "Completely eliminating your problem foods may set you up for failure," says Judith S. Stern, Sc.D., professor of nutrition and internal medicine at the University of California, Davis. "You have to determine what those foods are and find ways to replace them if you can't control your appetite for them."

Diane Hanson, Ph.D., a lifestyle specialist at the Pritikin Longevity Center in Santa Monica, California, thinks of it as leveraging your food choices: "doable changes that make a big difference. For example, if two or three tablespoons of blue-cheese dressing at lunch are dumping 16 or 24 grams of fat onto your daily intake, a small packet of low-fat dressing brought from home can shave off the grams and still leave you satisfied."

The concept of food substitutes is nothing new. But what makes them so exciting now is the ever-growing selection of low-fat products that are on the market. The difference between a regular meat lasagna entrée and a low-fat one translates into a fat savings of 7 grams. A nonfat, fruit-filled breakfast pastry can save you 16 grams of fat if you substitute it for the "real thing." Suddenly, dropping your fat intake for life doesn't look like such hungry work.

But whatever you drop should be dropped for good. So choose carefully or the pounds will return.

Before you lull yourself to sleep with visions of breakfast-pastry weight loss, remember this: At some point you're going to have to sweat. A study conducted by Drs. Susan Kayman, William Bruvold and Judith Stern at the University of California found that 90 percent of the participants who kept the weight off exercised regularly.

THE EXERCISE EQUATION

"To my mind, exercise has been undervalued with respect to weight loss," says Dr. Hanson. "As a matter of fact, when you look at what determines the continuation of a healthy lifestyle, exercise turns out to be the biggest behavioral driver."

It helps you look good and feel even better. It gives you a sense of accomplishment and mastery over your situation. "Current research is even showing that exercise may enhance your preference for fruits and vegetables," says Dr. Hanson.

Even if you already like veggies, exercise serves another important purpose. When you lower your calorie intake, your body, with an instinct for survival, slows down its metabolic rate and conserves energy. Exercise turns up the furnace so you become more efficient at burning fat. And, to drop a pound a week, you want that furnace stoked to the tune of 300 calories burned a day.

How you accomplish that goal is a matter of what you like to do. But the good news is that even a brisk, 45-minute walk will do the trick. But the real trick is to do it every day.

MAKE THE COMMITMENT

The difference between losing weight—and losing weight for good—is commitment: a truly motivated desire not only to change but also to maintain that change. You can think of your commitment as a lifetime contract with yourself. Of course, we've all cheated on some of our vows to become better, more effective or slimmer. In most cases, the problem isn't our willpower but our initial commitment. It just wasn't strong enough.

Before starting your new, lighter life, you need to make sure that you're revved and ready to do it and that the contract you make with yourself is so strong the Supreme Court—or a tempting éclair with your name on it—couldn't break it. Here's how to really, pardon the expression, commit yourself.

Choose the right moment. "It's not easy to begin a program during complicated periods in your life," says Kelly D. Brownell, Ph.D., professor of psychology at Yale University. "Divorce, an illness in the family, problems at work—those are all things that can sap your energy and make your environment less supportive for the changes you want to make."

Of course, some people thrive on complications. A divorce, for example, may be just the motivating kick one person needs to make big changes as part of a whole new lifestyle. "The thing you need to consider," says Dr. Brownell, "is how you respond to complications. If stress, worry and a frantic pace erode your eating plan, making serious lifestyle changes in the midst of what's currently happening may be a mistake."

And you don't want to look just at the present. If you're due for "stormy weather" in the upcoming weeks and months, you may want to bide your time and embark on your new lifestyle once things calm down and the sun comes out again.

Choose the right commitment. Do you want to lose a certain number of pounds or do you want to lose the bad habits that made you overweight to begin with? While those two goals may seem to be heads and tails of the same coin, the side that lands up after the toss can make all the difference between pounds gone forever and pounds gone for an all-too-brief amount of time.

"If you find yourself fantasizing about the moment when you've lost the weight and your diet is over, you're going to have problems," says Dr. Brownell. "At the point when you've finally reached that all-important number on the scale, there's a chance that your motivation to continue your healthy lifestyle may decrease, leaving you right back where you started."

So to make the commitment that will keep those pounds away forever, focus on the changes you plan to make. "Change your view of success," suggests Dr. Hanson. "Rather than making weight loss your goal, make lifelong health your goal. Rather than getting up each morning and heading for the scale, wake up and notice how much better you feel."

"I also find it helpful to think of overweight as a chronic condition," adds Dr. Brownell. "Just as diabetes requires constant maintenance lest it get serious, maintaining your ideal weight requires a lifetime of healthy eating and exercising practices."

Choose the right reason. "Some people lose weight because their husbands or wives want them to," says Jerome Brandon,

Ph.D., an exercise physiologist from Georgia State University and member of the American College of Sports Medicine. "The problem is that they make the effort to lose weight for someone else rather than because they themselves were personally motivated to do it. And eventually they will get tired of doing it."

So do it for yourself and not for someone else.

GET PREPARED

Every great journey begins with a great deal of preparation. How far would Christopher Columbus have gotten if he'd just awakened one morning, kissed his wife and headed out to discover the New World without the proper clothes, food, transportation or navigational equipment?

Changing your life is not much different from making a journey. In both cases, the most disappointing thing that can happen is that you have to give up because of difficulties you weren't prepared for. So no matter how charged up you are to start your new life, take some time to make the following preparations.

Educate yourself. If you're going to make lifestyle changes that you expect to practice for the rest of your life, you'd darn well better believe in them. And the best way to believe in something is to know beyond a shadow of a doubt how it works and, more importantly, why it works.

"First, when it comes to weight loss, there are scientific reasons for why it's best to eat and exercise a certain way," says Dr. Hanson. "If you understand how your body is designed to work, you'll believe in what you're doing and not be so inclined to give it up when the results are not happening as quickly as you want."

Second, by not understanding their body's own weight-loss mechanisms, people often select popular methods that doom them to failure. Then they blame themselves—when they never really had a chance. "You may think that the more calories you deprive yourself of, the faster you'll lose weight, and that's initially true. But if you don't realize that the body slows down its fat-burning furnace when calories are suddenly reduced, you're ultimately in for a big disappointment," says Dr. Hanson. "The only thing that will happen over time is that you'll be hungrier, less inclined to continue your program and still not sure why you aren't maintaining the initial weight loss."

So start out right by getting the facts. Know without a doubt that what you are doing is right and will eventually provide you with the results you want regardless of how things appear to be going on a day-to-day basis.

Find substitutes for eating. "When talking to patients, I often ask them why they overeat, why are they doing something that they know is ultimately harmful," says Dean Ornish, M.D., director of the Preventive Medicine Research Institute in Sausalito, California, and author of the best-selling *Eat More, Weigh Less.* "And the answer often is that it helps to get them through the day. They may feel alienated or isolated, and eating helps them deal with the pain. One patient described how food temporarily fills the void and numbs the pain."

According to Dr. Ornish, change is not brought about solely by focusing on new behaviors such as changing your eating habits and exercising. You need to address the underlying reasons for your behaviors. Otherwise, the problem remains and will eventually sabotage all your good intentions and commitments.

If some form of mental stress is behind your eating problem, you'll need to find a nonfattening substitute. Relaxation techniques and spending more time with friends are both great alternatives that are far lower in calories than a banana split.

Remove roadblocks. Visualize the changes you want to make, then visualize all the things that could keep you from doing them. "It could be that you are unwilling to start exercising," says Dr. Brownell. "But if you dig a little deeper, you may find that the reason is that you are embarrassed to be seen exercising."

If that is the case, then starting your new lifestyle by taking out a membership at the trendy new health club that everyone is going to would probably be a mistake. That membership card will get about as much use as a coupon good for five free pro-wrestling lessons.

Instead, acknowledge your fear and create an environment that guarantees privacy—maybe a stationary bike in your bedroom or an early-morning walk.

The same thing goes for food. If you know in your heart of hearts that you will never give up apple pie, then don't say you will and set yourself up for failure. Create a new recipe that makes apple pie less fattening.

Get support. "If you look at the factors that predict successful, permanent weight loss, social support ranks near the top of the list," says John Foreyt, Ph.D., director of the Nutrition Research Clinic at Baylor College School of Medicine and coauthor of *Living without Dieting.* "I'd go so far as to say it is absolutely critical."

When starting your new lifestyle, Dr. Foreyt insists that you make a public commitment, but not for the normal reasons. "It's not that you want to force yourself into a situation you can't back down from because everyone knows about it. What you are actually doing is making an assertive appeal for people's help and understanding."

In his book, Dr. Foreyt outlines four levels of support, each with its own special purpose. "First there's your family. They're going to need to get used to your new lifestyle. It may be that certain foods have to be kept out of the house. Compromises on family time may need to be made when your exercise or other activities conflict with family plans."

The second level is composed of close friends. "Everyone should have someone they can call when temptation rears its ugly head," says Dr. Foreyt. "Even one really good friend can make the difference in a crisis."

The third and fourth levels involve support groups and your doctor. "Support groups are the perfect place to get advice and encouragement from people experiencing the same things you are," notes Dr. Foreyt. "And your doctor gives you information and feedback and helps you monitor your progress."

For some people, maintaining all four levels of support is not necessary. But Dr. Foreyt still maintains the need for some form of social support, even for loners. And more importantly, the kind of support you solicit needs to be specific.

"You don't want people giving you negative support," says Dr. Foreyt. "While someone pointing out your mistakes may work in the short run, it isn't motivating over the long haul. So you want to be very direct about asking people to say something positive about your accomplishments."

Find a monitoring system that works. "Your actual weight is the least important thing you can monitor," says Ronette Kolotkin, Ph.D., director of behavioral programs at Duke University's Diet and Fitness Center and coauthor of *The Duke University Medical Center Book of Diet and Fitness.* "Instead, I always encourage people to keep a diary not just of food and exercise but also of any important behavioral problems they encounter, such as rapid eating in certain situations or a tendency to binge at particular times."

At the end of each week, Dr. Kolotkin suggests that you study your diary as if you were a weight-loss professional studying someone else's case history. What advice would you give the patient?

A one-year follow-up study conducted by Dr. Kolotkin found that people who monitored food intake, exercise and motivation were more successful than those who monitored weight only.

Paying daily homage to the bathroom scale is a dicey proposition for two reasons. First, your body weight is in constant flux. Up a pound today, down two tomorrow. A momentary gain in water weight may have you on the floor in despair despite the fact that the overall picture is improving.

Second, because your new lifestyle of healthy food and exercise is constantly trimming the fat while boosting the lean, a scale may show no change in weight even though you are getting slimmer and more toned by the minute. "That's why I always encourage people to wear form-fitting clothing," says Dr. Kolotkin. "As you lose weight, or even as your body composition changes, you'll get feedback every time you need to have your clothes taken in a bit. You'll constantly be aware of what your body is doing by the way your clothes fit."

Plan for trouble. "I always tell people that they can expect to slip," says Dr. Kolotkin. "It will happen. And the difference between moving on and just plain giving up has to do with having some strategy to deal with momentary failure."

There are two ways you don't want to react to a temporary backslide. On one hand, you don't want to be cavalier: "Oh well, I ate that box of doughnuts, but I'll worry about it tomorrow." On the other hand, you don't want to overreact: "Oh no, this is the end! How can I go on after eating my weight in doughnuts? I'm no good."

"You've got to be rational," says Dr. Kolotkin. "The first thing to do is acknowledge exactly what happened. 'I was at a party, lost control and ate 5,000 calories.' Don't overemphasize or underemphasize what occurred. Next, put it into perspective. 'Over the last six months, I've made some great changes; I've exercised regularly, eaten right and made serious progress. Compared with what I've achieved, this one incident is hardly a catastrophe. I don't feel great about it, but it also isn't the end of the world.'"

Next comes action. A good general doesn't waste time dwelling on defeat. Instead, he immediately plots a course of action that will take him back on the road to victory. "That does not mean you should exercise twice as long tomorrow to make up for today's mistake," says Dr. Kolotkin. "That's a lot like punishing yourself.

Instead, you want to take steps to ensure that what happened does not happen again."

If you found yourself bingeing on a bag of chips lying wantonly open in the kitchen, you may want to purge your house of binge foods. If you stopped exercising for a week because of scheduling difficulties, spend some time arranging things so that it doesn't happen again. "Then get right back into your program," says Dr. Kolotkin. "Set two alarm clocks so that you can't avoid waking up and exercising. Meet a friend for lunch who will make sure you eat the right foods. Write out a meal plan."

In other words, make your lifestyle changes foolproof and inescapable for the next few days just to get yourself back on track. Dr. Kolotkin finds that it takes most people only three days to turn around a negative incident.

Learn from past mistakes. What went wrong the last time you tried to lose weight? "When I ask people that, I'll normally get an unproductive answer like they started eating again," says Dr. Kolotkin. "But you need to look at the underlying reasons. Was the diet you placed yourself on too restrictive? Did you find your meal plans were falling apart because you were often pressed for time and had to eat whatever was available?"

Take some time to dig deep and honestly analyze what went wrong.

Create an environment that makes change easy. Weight loss and lifestyle change are so often looked at as matters of sheer willpower. But why make things tough when you can make them easy? "I call it environmental engineering," says Dr. Hanson, "and it's really where you make changes in your environment that make it easier to succeed."

Environmental engineering is a powerful yet simple concept. If you find yourself getting hungry at 3:00 each afternoon and the only thing available is a candy machine down the hall from your office, don't put yourself in the position of having to fight the urge to merge with a chocolate bar. Instead, reach into your desk and pull out the apple that you brought along for just such a moment.

That idea can be applied to all areas of your life. And once you've determined why you've failed in the past, you can set up your new environment to help avoid past mistakes. "When I encounter people who have a problem with after-dinner eating, I often suggest that they get a small refrigerator for beverages and keep it in the den," says Dr. Kolotkin. "That way, even if they are thirsty, they don't need to enter the kitchen and be tempted by an open refrigerator."

As for exercise, did your last walking program peter out after a week because you never seemed to have clean socks, batteries for your personal stereo or rain gear? Get equipped. Keep everything where you can get at it immediately. Keep an extra pair of walking shoes in your car for impromptu opportunities. Make it so easy on yourself that you can't possibly fail.

TAKE ACTION

You're ready to get started. But at what pace? Do you purge all the fat from your diet, change your eating habits and throw yourself into a daily exercise program at one fell swoop? Or should you ease into a lifestyle change like you ease into a hot tub—making a few food substitutions, exercising a couple days a week, getting comfortable?

When making your decision, don't think about how fast you want to lose weight. The real question is which technique makes it easier to assimilate changes that you can keep for life?

"If you're looking to make permanent lifestyle changes, my feeling is that incorporating them slowly makes them easier to get used to," says Dr. Kolotkin. "It's less overwhelming. The goals seem more attainable if you go step-by-step rather than full force."

Dr. Kolotkin experienced the power of small changes firsthand in working with a woman who, at age 45, had never exercised and was so out of shape that a flight of stairs would leave her winded and grasping the banister for support. When she started her program, five minutes on a stationary bike was all she could do. "But rather than dwell on the thought that five minutes was not a very big or important change, she embraced the notion of small, gradual changes and took pride in the fact that she was actually exercising at all," says Dr. Kolotkin. "And gradually, over the following months, as she got comfortable with one level of exercise, she increased it. She's now been in four walking marathons!"

Of course, Dr. Kolotkin is quick to admit that gradual change means gradual results, sometimes too gradual for some people. "It's not as exciting or motivating to make small changes and so some people resist it, thinking that they'll never get where they want to be.

"But then I remind them that they tried cutting calories too quickly in the past and found the diet too restrictive to continue.

Although they did lose some fast weight, in the end they went back to their old habits and gained it back."

On the other hand, if you like big, exciting changes, you've got an ally in Dr. Ornish. According to him, comprehensive changes can make people feel so much better so quickly that rather than being overwhelmed by the changes, they are instead strongly motivated to continue.

So which is right for you? Part of the answer lies with your doctor and your current situation. Big dietary changes may be within your capability, but if you haven't been exercising regularly, too much activity too fast could be dangerous.

The second part of the answer has to do with your own mental makeup. Do big challenges bring out the best in you or do you find them intimidating? What's worked for you in other situations? Remember, the only right answer here is the one that's right for you.

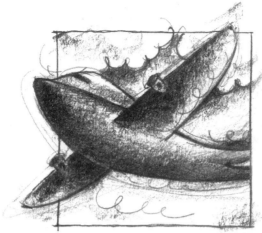

CHAPTER 2

EATING
LIGHT IN THE
REAL WORLD

BEST BETS FOR HEALTH WATCHERS

You're cruising down the interstate when breakfast beckons. It's fast food or nothing, but can you refuel on such fare without taking a detour around your healthy diet?

You're cooling your heels at the airport between flights. Hunger strikes as you catch a whiff of just-baked cookies. A transgression can send you into a tailspin, but can you resist?

Situations like these can be challenging for health-conscious people. But no matter how difficult a situation, choices are usually available—some better than others.

The key in these circumstances is to make choices actively, not passively, says Sachiko St. Jeor, Ph.D., professor of nutrition at the University of Nevada School of Medicine. "You don't have to be a victim of your environment," Dr. St. Jeor says. "You can take control."

With those words of inspiration in mind, we decided to explore some real diet danger zones to find good, better and best choices. Here are some ideas that may help you make informed food choices in any situation.

FAST-FOOD BREAKFAST

Good: *Pancakes.* A decent choice in any fast-food restaurant, assuming you hold the butter or margarine and go easy on the syrup. At Hardee's, which offers the most diet-friendly pancakes by fast-food standards, three 'cakes contain 280 calories and just 2 grams of fat (6 percent of calories). McDonald's pancakes aren't bad either, with 245 calories and 4 grams fat (15 percent of calories) in three.

Better: *McDonald's fat-free apple bran muffin.* Only 180 calories, no fat. Add a glass of orange juice (about 60 calories and no fat in 6 ounces), and 8 ounces of 1 percent milk (about 110 calories and 2 grams fat), and you have a pretty nutritious, low-fat breakfast for 350 calories, says Dr. St. Jeor.

Best: *A bowl of nonsugary cereal.* McDonald's serves up Cheerios (¾ cup for 80 calories and 1 gram fat) and Wheaties (¾ cup for 90 calories and 1 gram fat)—either of which provides about 15 to 30 percent of the daily quota for iron and vitamins A and C. Pour on the 1 percent milk, and the total calorie count is still under 200—plus you meet about a third of your daily calcium requirement.

FAST-FOOD CHICKEN SANDWICHES

Good: *Arby's Lite Roast Chicken Deluxe or Wendy's Grilled Chicken Sandwich.* Here are two sandwiches worth clucking about. Arby's has 276 calories and 7 grams fat (23 percent of calories). Wendy's chicken sandwich is close, with 290 calories and 7 grams fat (22 percent of calories).

Better: *Chick-Fil-A Chargrilled Chicken Sandwich.* This East Coast chain offers one lean chicken, with just 17 percent of calories from fat (258 calories, 4.8 grams fat). If you have high blood pressure, however, take note: This sandwich may be low in fat, but it's high in sodium, with 1,121 milligrams.

Beware: A chicken sandwich by any other name could be a fat trap. Burger King's Chicken Sandwich, for example, will set you back 700 calories, with 54 percent of those calories from fat.

McDonald's McChicken (470 calories and 25 grams fat), Wendy's Breaded Chicken (450 calories, 20 grams fat) and Arby's Grilled Chicken Deluxe sandwiches (430 calories, 19.9 grams fat) aren't much better, with about 40 to 48 percent of calories from fat.

CINEMA FARE

OK: *Red licorice.* Red Vines, for example, by American Licorice Company, has only 140 calories and no fat in seven licorice sticks. Trouble is, we're talking empty calories here; red licorice has virtually no nutrient value.

Better: *Nonbuttered popcorn.* Only 55 calories, about 100 milligrams sodium and about 3.1 grams fat per cup for oil-popped corn. The problem is, who can stop at a cup? Most theaters serve up popcorn by the gallon, which makes fat, calorie and sodium totals soar.

Best: *Eat before the film.* "Remind yourself that movies last just two hours, and you can go that long without food," says Dr. St. Jeor. "Get into watching the movie as a pure experience, without shoveling down food you can't see or really enjoy."

MIDAFTERNOON SNACKS

Good: *Low-fat, low-sugar dried cereal.* Cheerios or mini shredded wheat will do. These cereals are not just low in fat but also are nutrient-fortified.

Also good: *Prunes.* Seven prunes contain about 140 calories, no fat and 4 grams of dietary fiber.

Best: *Instant bean soup.* Packaged in individual serving cups—and available in a wide variety of flavors—instant bean soups are easy to take to the office. Just add boiling water or add cold water and heat in the microwave. Two good choices are a black bean soup made by Fantastic Foods and a couscous tomato minestrone made by Nile Spice. Both are rich and tasty—and can really satisfy an appetite for about 200 calories and 1 gram or less of fat. Nutritionist Evelyn Tribole, R.D., author of *Healthy Homestyle Cooking*, points out that many such soups are high in vitamins (including C and A), minerals like iron, complex carbohydrates and fiber.

AIRPORT FOOD

Good: *Sushi.* It's becoming as all-American as bagels. In airports, stick with the kind with the cooked fish filling (like those with crabmeat) or vegetable filling to avoid risk of parasites, says Judith

S. Stern, R.D., professor of nutrition and internal medicine at the University of California, Davis. A full serving of vegetable sushi contains about 365 calories and just 1 gram fat.

Better: *Nonfat frozen yogurt.* Four ounces of Honey Hill Farms Ghirardelli Chocolate flavor, for example, contains 115 calories, no fat and, as a bonus, 110 milligrams of calcium—a boon for the bones. (Skip the "mix-ins" like chopped candy and nuts.)

Even better: *A steaming cup of decaf café latte (made with skim milk).* A café latte is mostly hot milk, with a little espresso floated on top. You sate your appetite and do your bones a favor calciumwise (264 milligrams in 7 ounces for less than 80 calories and less than half a gram of fat).

Best: *Take a fitness walk through the terminal.* You can chart your course and ensure that you don't get lost by picking up a map of the terminal at the information desk. Tip: Wear a fanny pack or backpack so you can stride more freely in your travels.

AIRPLANE MEALS AND SNACKS

Good: *Pasta entrées.* Meat entrées are usually greasy, notes Dr. Stern, while pasta entrées are generally lower in fat.

Better: *Fly American Airlines.* They're starting to routinely offer Weight Watchers frozen meals—the same kind you get in the supermarket—on many flights, without advance reservations.

Best: *Plan ahead.* Don't leave your in-flight food up to chance. Pack snack food—like fruit, a bagel or serving-size cereal—in your carry-on bag so you won't be tempted by the salted peanuts or smoked almonds, suggests John Foreyt, Ph.D., director of the Nutrition Research Clinic at Baylor College School of Medicine and coauthor of *Living without Dieting.* And don't forget to order a special low-fat meal in advance. A low-fat, low-cholesterol breakfast on United Airlines, for example, might include fresh fruit, an asparagus and egg-substitute frittata, mushroom ragout and a roasted tomato half. Talk about friendly skies!

Finally, drink lots of bottled water. It keeps you hydrated and reduces appetite.

MIXED DRINKS

Good: *Virgin (nonalcoholic) fresh-fruit daiquiris.* About 80 to 100 calories, with little or no fat. The standard recipe calls for about half a cup of fresh fruit (like strawberries, which contain roughly 30 calories), 2 ounces of a mixer called "sweet and sour" (a nonfat lemon-and-sugar drink, with about 50 calories) and a big scoop of ice.

Best: *Virgin Mary.* This spicy tomato-juice concoction is a boon in so many ways. It fills you with liquid; it's low cal—about 32 calories for a 6-ounce glass, with no fat; it's spicy, which satisfies taste buds; it provides some nutrition in the form of vitamin C; and finally, there's a great big celery stick to provide crunch appeal.

BURGERS IN DISNEYLAND

Good: *Turkey burger.* Served with lettuce, tomato and fat-free Thousand Island dressing on a honey wheat bun, it contains only 367 calories and 9.5 grams fat (23 percent of calories).

Best: *Veggie burger.* Same fat-free dressing and bun, with only 365 calories and 8 grams fat (19 percent of calories).

BALLPARK FARE

Good: *Check out the latest offerings.* It's a whole new ball game out there! Stadium concessionaires are innovating to appeal to the increasing numbers of female sports fans, says Matthew Bauer, media manager for Sportservice Corporation in Buffalo, the leading food supplier to ballparks across the country. Among the new offerings:

■ Rotisserie chicken, as an alternative to fried chicken, available at the new Texas Rangers Stadium in Arlington. (A great choice, as long as you remove the skin!) Also in several parks: grilled chicken served on a bed of greens.

■ The vegetarian burrito at Tiger Stadium in Detroit—loaded with julienned strips of zucchini, peppers and onions in a soft flour tortilla.

■ Fresh sliced-turkey sandwiches at Dodger Stadium in Los Angeles and other locales.

■ Frozen-fruit Popsicles, along with low-fat frozen yogurt, as an alternative to ice cream, available at Sportservice client stadiums, including Milwaukee County Stadium, Riverfront Stadium in Cincinnati, Comiskey Park in Chicago, Busch Stadium in St. Louis and Gateway Stadium in Cleveland.

Best: *Crudités.* At Dodger Stadium, they give it a more manly name (relish tray), but that's what it is—a plate loaded with fresh cucumbers, celery, carrots and radishes.

Beware: A less-fortunate new trend in stadium cuisine is the legion of waiters sent out with handheld computers who take your order at your seat and then deliver the food to you. Just say no! Stand up and go get it yourself. Walking burns calories!

CHINESE MEALS

Good: *A shared entrée of stir-fried vegetables and lots of steamed rice.* Chinese-food lovers reeled in shock when news stories revealed that many of their favorite dishes are loaded with fatty oils. And it's true: A typical serving of stir-fried veggies can contain 400 calories and anywhere from 6 to 18 grams of fat. But you can avoid some of the fat and still enjoy this flavorful cuisine by sharing an entrée. To appease your appetite, pile on the steamed rice.

Best: *Steamed veggies with chicken or shrimp.* Even if it's not on the menu, most cooks in Chinese restaurants can create a delectable steamed meal. Often, they serve it in a beautiful bamboo steamer. For flavor, sprinkle the food with soy sauce or ask for a brown sauce with scallions on the side to drizzle on top. In these entrées, light-meat chicken contains only about 175 calories and 5 grams fat, while shrimp is even leaner, with only about 22 calories and less than 1 gram fat.

RESTAURANT DESSERTS

Good: *Two forks.* That way you can share whatever dessert you order with a friend. "If you're used to eating dessert and you let yourself have just a bite or two, you'll be less likely to feel deprived and binge later," says Dr. Foreyt.

Better: *Decaf cappuccino (espresso with frothed skim milk).* Tribole suggests having it with a biscotti or two on the side. Many different companies are manufacturing biscotti—almond cookies designed for dipping. They're generally low in fat and calories. Some biscotti have only 30 calories and less than 1 gram of fat per cookie.

Best: *Sorbet.* This tangy juice-based dessert is mostly water. A half-cup of fruit sorbet, such as pineapple or peach, might provide about 120 calories and no fat.

CHOCOLATE-LOVERS' SUPERMARKET SNACKS

Good: *SnackWell's Devil's Food Cookie Cakes.* Deep, chocolate, cakey interior surrounded by a thin layer of marshmallow, then a dark chocolate coating—so sweet and rich, it's hard to believe they're fat-free. Drawbacks: Each hefty cookie contains about 50 calories, so you can't eat infinite amounts. They don't really offer vitamins or minerals either. And the leading ingredient is sugar.

Also good: *Chocolate Pudding Pops.* One pop (made by Jell-O) is only 79 calories, with 2 grams fat.

Special mention: *Chocolate-flavored low-fat yogurt.* Would you believe chocolate-raspberry yogurt? Chocolate-cherry? Chocolate-cappuccino? They're really, really chocolatey and contain only 200 calories for ¾ cup, with just 2 grams fat. They're put out by Whitney's of New York and are available in some parts of the country.

SEAFOOD ENTRÉES

Good: *Haddock.* Just 112 calories and 1 gram fat for every 3½ ounces (8 percent of calories from fat).

Best: *Lobster.* The winner and still champion. Steamed or boiled, it gets just 5 percent calories from fat. You get 98 calories and less than a gram of fat in 3½ ounces. You'll need to skip the melted butter, however—try cocktail sauce instead.

Beware: *Tuna salad.* Sorry, Charlie. A cup of tuna salad, with regular mayo, provides 380 calories and 19 grams fat (45 percent of calories).

MUNCHIES

Good: *Baked Bugles.* Unlike the regular Bugles product (with 150 calories and 8 grams fat per serving), the kind marked "Oven Baked" are relatively low calorie (90 calories for 42 Bugles) and low-fat (2 grams fat). But like the regular product, they taste oily and crunchy. (The sodium's pretty high, though, at 300 milligrams per serving, and they don't offer many nutrients.)

Better: *Air-popped popcorn.* Three cups contain only 93 calories and a gram of fat, plus about 3 grams dietary fiber.

Better yet: *Fat-free (baked) potato chips or tortilla chips.* Guiltless Gourmet No-Oil Tortilla Chips contain 110 calories for 22 chips, a respectable 4 grams fiber and zero fat. Similarly, Louise's Fat-Free Potato Chips contain about 100 calories per ounce and no fat.

BEEF

Good: *Healthy Choice Extra-Lean Low-Fat Ground Beef.* Four ounces (uncooked) has 4 grams fat—that's about 28 percent of its calories. By comparison, four ounces of regular ground beef contains 30 grams fat (77 percent of calories).

Better: *Select-grade top and eye round.* With about 20 to 25 percent of calories from fat, this is a cut above all other supermarket-grade cuts.

Best: *New brands of beef that are raised to be low in fat through diet.* There are several, including Dakota Lean Meats. Most of the Dakota cuts—ranging from top sirloin to tenderloin to sirloin tips—average about 2.7 grams fat and 130 calories for every 4-ounce serving. That's a respectable 18 percent of calories from fat.

CHAPTER 3

SMART
CHOICES
FOR PARTIES
AND BETWEEN
MEALS

FUN SNACKS AND NIBBLES

Americans love to snack, whether it's at coffee break, after school, at parties or before bedtime. In the 1980s, many of us replaced breakfast, lunch and dinner with more relaxed all-day light eating or snacking and coined a new name for it—"grazing." But traditional party and snack foods are also traditionally high in fat, calories and sodium. Today's grazing requires a healthful, well-balanced "pasture" to browse through. In this chapter, you'll find creative, low-fat appetizers and finger foods to build an elegant party menu, as well as snacks for lunches, outings and casual get-togethers. And all of them will fit into your healthy eating—and easy living—plans.

SEVEN-LAYER SKINNY DIP

SERVES 20

*T*he original version of this dip is always the first to disappear at parties—and this low-fat twin will be, too! Serve it with home-made tortilla chips for "scooping."

> 1   *can fat-free refried black beans*
> 1   *cup nonfat sour cream*
> ½   *cup fat-free mayonnaise*
> 1   *teaspoon chili powder*
> 1   *teaspoon ground cumin*
> 1   *cup shredded fat-free Cheddar cheese*
> ½   *cup chopped scallions*
> ½   *cup sliced black olives*
> 1   *tomato, seeded and chopped*
> ½   *avocado, chopped*

Spread the refried beans over the bottom of a 9″ pie plate. In a small bowl, combine the sour cream, mayonnaise, chili powder and cumin. Spread this mixture over the beans. Then sprinkle on the Cheddar, scallions, olives, tomatoes and avocados. Chill until needed.

Chef's note: For easy homemade fat-free refried beans, rinse and drain your favorite canned beans and mash them with a fork or in a food processor.

Preparation time: 20 minutes

Per serving (2 tablespoons): 29 calories, 0.7 g. fat (20% of calories), 0.8 g. dietary fiber, no cholesterol, 139 mg. sodium.

RED PEPPER DIP

MAKES ABOUT 1 CUP

*R*oasted red peppers have an intriguing smoky-sweet flavor. Use fresh vegetables, Bagel Coins (page 25) or Sesame Wonton Chips (page 29) for dipping.

1 *jar (7 ounces) roasted red peppers, rinsed and drained*

½ *cup nonfat cream cheese*

2 *scallions, coarsely chopped*

1 *clove garlic, coarsely chopped*

1 *tablespoon lemon juice*

Place the peppers, cream cheese, scallions, garlic and lemon juice in a blender or food processor. Process until the mixture is thoroughly pureed.

Pour the mixture into a bowl and chill until needed.

Preparation time: 5 minutes

Per tablespoon: 10 calories, no fat (0% of calories), no dietary fiber, 1 mg. cholesterol, 43 mg. sodium.

Tangy Eggplant Dip

*W*hen the party's over, store any leftover dip in the refrigerator. It makes an excellent filling for Toast Cups (page 24), or warm it up and toss with pasta for a quick supper.

1   teaspoon olive oil
1   eggplant (1 pound), peeled and finely chopped
1   cup minced onions
1   cup finely chopped celery
1   can (14½ ounces) stewed tomatoes
2   tablespoons red wine vinegar
2   tablespoons currants
1   tablespoon capers, rinsed

Heat the oil in a large frying pan over medium heat. Add the eggplant, onions and celery to the pan. Cook, stirring, until the vegetables are soft and lightly browned, about 5 minutes. Add the tomatoes and break them into small pieces with a spoon. Add the vinegar, currants and capers. Reduce the heat to low and cook for 15 minutes more to blend the flavors.

Serve immediately or chill.

Preparation time: 15 minutes
Cooking time: 20 minutes

Per tablespoon: 6 calories, 0.1 g. fat (14% of calories), 0.1 g. dietary fiber, no cholesterol, 23 mg. sodium.

HERBED SALMON SPREAD

lthough the percentage of calories from fat is high in this recipe, this spread is lower in fat and calories than the usual spreads. And fat in salmon comes from polyunsaturated omega-3 oils, which are actually beneficial to your health. Serve this spread as a dip for tortilla chips or use as a filling for Toast Cups (below).

4   ounces cooked salmon, flaked
8   ounces low-fat herbed cheese, such as Boursin
¼   cup minced red onions
1   teaspoon dried dill
1   teaspoon lemon juice

In a medium bowl, blend the salmon, cheese, onions, dill and lemon juice. Place in a serving bowl and chill until ready to serve.

Preparation time: 10 minutes

Per tablespoon: 43 calories, 2.4 g. fat (50% of calories), no dietary fiber, 10 mg. cholesterol, 59 mg. sodium.

TOAST CUPS

MAKES 20

hese crisp bread cups make great containers for fillings such as Tangy Eggplant Dip (page 23) and Herbed Salmon Spread (above).

20   slices whole-wheat bread

Cut the crust off the bread slices. Coat both sides of the slices with no-stick spray. Press each slice into a muffin cup. Bake at 350° for 10 to 15 minutes, or until the toast cups are crisp and golden.

Preparation time: 5 minutes
Baking time: 15 minutes

Chef's note: Very fresh bread works best for the cups.

Per cup: 69 calories, 1.2 g. fat (15% of calories), 3.2 g. dietary fiber, no cholesterol, 178 mg. sodium.

BAGEL COINS

SERVES 9

*H*ere's a good way to turn day-old bagels into party fare or a bedtime snack. We've used Italian seasoning mix, but you can experiment with other herb blends.

>   2   *onion bagels, 4½" in diameter*
>   2   *teaspoons dried Italian seasoning*
>   2   *tablespoons grated Parmesan cheese*

Slice each bagel in half vertically. Starting with one half of one bagel, continue slicing vertically into ¼" coins (about 18 per bagel half). Repeat with remaining bagel halves for a total of about 72 coins.

Place the coins on a baking sheet and coat them with no-stick spray. Sprinkle with the Italian seasoning and Parmesan. Bake at 350° for 10 to 12 minutes, or until golden brown and crisp.

Preparation time: 5 minutes
Baking time: 12 minutes

Per serving: 44 calories, 0.8 g. fat (16% of calories), 0.3 g. dietary fiber, 3 mg. cholesterol, 70 mg. sodium.

CRISPY SWEET ONION RINGS

SERVES 10

*F*or the best onion rings ever, use Vidalia, Texas Sweet or Maui onions when they're in season.

2 *egg whites*
2 *large sweet onions, peeled*
2 *cups finely ground cornflake crumbs*
1 *teaspoon chili powder*

Coat a large baking sheet with no-stick spray.

In a large bowl, beat the egg whites until just foamy. Cut the onions crosswise into ¼″ slices and separate them into individual rings. Add the rings to the bowl and toss them with the egg whites to coat.

Mix the crumbs with the chili powder; place the crumbs on a sheet of wax paper. Roll the coated rings a few at a time in the crumbs. Place the crumb-covered rings on the prepared baking sheet. Bake at 375° for 15 minutes, until the outside is crispy and the onion is soft.

Preparation time: 15 minutes
Baking time: 15 minutes

Chef's note: To make cornflake crumbs, use a food processor or blender. Or place the cornflakes between two pieces of wax paper; with a rolling pin, crush the flakes until they become fine crumbs.

Per serving: 94 calories, 0.2 g. fat (2% of calories), 1 g. dietary fiber, no cholesterol, 219 mg. sodium.

POTATO CHIPS

SERVES 4

*P*urchased potato chips are loaded with fat, calories and sodium. But with this easy recipe, you can make your own healthier chips. For nice thin chips, use a mandoline, or manual slicing machine. The metal version can be very expensive, but good, inexpensive plastic mandolines are available at cooking stores. For a gourmet touch, try the new exotic blue or purple potatoes.

> 2 *Idaho potatoes*
> 2 *sweet potatoes*

Slice the potatoes as thin as possible (about 20 slices per potato) by hand, in a food processor or with a mandoline. Place 10 slices at a time on a microwave rack and microwave for 4 minutes, or until golden and crispy.

Watch the first batch carefully; cooking time depends on the moisture content of the potatoes. If after 4 minutes the potatoes are not crisp, continue cooking at 30-second intervals. Repeat for the remaining 7 batches.

Preparation time: 5 minutes
Microwaving time: 40 minutes

Chef's note: If you don't have a microwave, place a metal cooling rack on a baking sheet. Arrange the potato slices on the rack. Bake at 450° for 15 to 20 minutes.

Per serving: 66 calories, 0.1 g. fat (1% of calories), 1.8 g. dietary fiber, no cholesterol, 5 mg. sodium.

FRESH TOMATO SALSA
WITH HOMEMADE TORTILLA CHIPS

SERVES 8

*G*oat cheese gives this traditional salsa an unexpected twist. Enjoy it with easy-to-make tortilla chips.

1 cup chopped, seeded plum tomatoes (about 4)
½ cup chopped scallions, greens included
½ cup chopped fresh coriander
1 tablespoon lime juice
1 tablespoon grated lime rind
1 teaspoon olive oil
½ jalapeño pepper, seeded and finely minced
   (wear rubber gloves when handling)
1 tablespoon crumbled goat cheese
4 flour tortillas, 8″ in diameter

In a medium bowl, combine the tomatoes, scallions, coriander, lime juice, lime rind, oil and peppers. Just before serving the dip, sprinkle the goat cheese over the top.

Cut each tortilla into 8 wedges, using a knife or pizza cutter. Coat a baking sheet with no-stick spray. Place the wedges on the prepared baking sheet. Bake at 350° for 10 minutes, or until golden and crispy.

Preparation time: 10 minutes
Baking time: 10 minutes

Chef's note: Plum tomatoes are small and meaty with less juice and fewer seeds than regular tomatoes. Because they're frequently used in cooking, they're often called Italian tomatoes or Roma tomatoes.

Per serving: 16 calories, 0.5 g. fat (26% of calories), 0.2 g. dietary fiber, no cholesterol, 4 mg. sodium.

SESAME WONTON CHIPS

*F*or a change from potato and tortilla chips, try these homemade wonton chips. Use them for scooping up dips or crumble them as a garnish on soup.

> 20 *wonton skins*
> 2 *tablespoons sesame seeds, toasted*

Cut the wontons in half diagonally. Place the wontons on a baking sheet. Spray them with no-stick spray and sprinkle with the sesame seeds. Bake at 350° for 5 minutes, or until golden brown.

Preparation time: 5 minutes
Baking time: 5 minutes

Chef's notes: You'll find wonton skins at Asian grocery stores or in the produce or freezer section of your supermarket.

To toast sesame seeds, spread them in a shallow pan and bake at 350° until the seeds are a light golden brown. Stir the seeds occasionally during toasting.

Per chip: 14 calories, 0.2 g. fat (15% of calories), no dietary fiber, no cholesterol, 10 mg. sodium.

HAPPY O'S TRAIL MIX

Dried cranberries, or "craisins," add a tart tang and a splash of dark red to this high-energy, low-fat snack mix. Banana chips are thin, crisp, dried banana slices; you can find them in the dried fruit or buy-in-bulk section of your supermarket.

> 2 *cups round, whole-grain toasted oat cereal*
> ¼ *cup dried cranberries*
> ¼ *cup golden raisins*
> ¼ *cup crumbled banana chips*
> 1 *tablespoon peanuts*

In a medium bowl, combine the oat cereal, cranberries, raisins, banana chips and peanuts.

Preparation time: 5 minutes

Per ¼ cup: 49 calories, 1.2 g. fat (22% of calories), 0.2 g. dietary fiber, no cholesterol, 50 mg. sodium.

HONEY JACK POPCORN

MAKES 8 CUPS

Take this popcorn confection to the ballgame, add a prize and you'll think you're eating its packaged cousin!

> ¼ *cup honey*
> 1 *tablespoon molasses*
> 8 *cups air-popped popcorn*
> ¼ *cup chopped honey-coated nuts*

Combine the honey and molasses in a small saucepan; warm over low heat until thinned. Place the popcorn in a large bowl and cover with the honey mixture. Add the nuts and toss until coated.

Coat a large baking sheet with no-stick spray. Place the popcorn on the prepared baking sheet. Bake at 300° for 20 minutes, tossing after 10 minutes. Remove from the oven and cool.

Preparation time: 5 minutes
Cooking time: 1 minute
Baking time: 20 minutes

Per cup: 91 calories, 2.5 g. fat (24% of calories), 0.8 g. dietary fiber, no cholesterol, 3 mg. sodium.

GINGER AND SPICE PARTY MIX

MAKES 4 CUPS

Crystallized ginger gives an oriental twist to this low-fat version of a popular party snack.

   1   *cup crispy, waffle-shaped rice cereal*
   1   *cup crispy, waffle-shaped bran cereal*
   1   *cup crispy, waffle-shaped corn cereal*
   1   *cup small knot pretzels*
   1   *teaspoon pumpkin pie spice*
  ¼   *cup slivered crystallized ginger*

In a large glass microwave-safe measuring cup, combine the cereals and pretzels. Coat the mixture with no-stick spray and toss with the pumpkin pie spice to coat. Microwave for 1 minute. Cool the mixture and toss with the ginger.

Preparation time: 5 minutes
Microwaving time: 1 minute

Chef's note: If you don't have a microwave, heat the mix on a baking sheet at 325° for 5 minutes.

Per ¼ cup: 36 calories, 0.2 g. fat (5% of calories), 0.5 g. dietary fiber, no cholesterol, 88 mg. sodium.

ARTICHOKE BARS

*S*erve these quichelike bars at your next party or brunch. Low-fat cheese and fat-free egg substitute help trim the fat in this recipe.

> 1   *can (14 ounces) artichokes, rinsed, drained and minced*
> 1   *can (4 ounces) chili peppers, drained*
> ½   *cup fat-free egg substitute*
> ½   *cup dry bread crumbs*
> ½   *cup shredded low-fat Cheddar cheese*

In a medium bowl, combine the artichokes, peppers, egg substitute, bread crumbs and Cheddar, mixing thoroughly.

Coat an 8″ × 8″ baking pan with no-stick spray. Pour the mixture into the prepared pan. Bake at 350° for 25 minutes, or until the mixture is set. Cut into bars and serve warm.

Preparation time: 5 minutes
Baking time: 25 minutes

Per bar: 39 calories, 0.8 g. fat (16% of calories), 0.2 g. dietary fiber, 1 mg. cholesterol, 190 mg. sodium.

GRANOLA BARS

MAKES 24

*K*eep a pan of these crunchy low-fat bars handy for on-the-run breakfasts or after-school snacking. Using low-fat granola makes this treat much lower in fat than most purchased granola bars.

2   *egg whites*
2   *tablespoons honey*
½   *teaspoon ground cinnamon*
4   *cups low-fat granola cereal*

Beat the egg whites in a large bowl until soft peaks form.

Combine the honey and cinnamon in a small saucepan and warm over low heat. Add the warm honey mixture to the egg whites and beat until blended.

Fold the granola cereal into the egg whites until the cereal is completely coated. Press the mixture into a 13″ × 9″ baking pan. Make sure the mixture is evenly distributed to prevent burning.

Bake at 350° for 15 minutes, or until golden brown. Remove from the oven and cut into 24 squares before the bars cool. Cool and remove the bars from the pan. Store in an airtight container.

Preparation time: 10 minutes
Cooking time: 1 minute
Baking time: 15 minutes

Per bar: 121 calories, 4.3 g. fat (30% of calories), 0.8 g. dietary fiber, 3 mg. cholesterol, 51 mg. sodium.

10 Quick After-School Treats

These snacks are so quick and easy that kids can make them with an adult helper. (Or you can prepare the snacks ahead so they're ready when your children get home.) They're low in fat and full of the energy kids need for a pick-me-up after a day of school and play.

1. Yogurtcicles. For homemade yogurt pops, combine one 6-ounce can of fruit juice concentrate and two 8-ounce cartons of low-fat yogurt. Experiment with juice/yogurt combos such as pineapple or raspberry yogurt and orange juice. Fill small plastic drink cups half full of the yogurt mixture. Freeze for 1 hour or until a wooden stick will stand upright in the cup. Insert sticks and freeze until firm.

2. Trail Mix. Happy O's Trail Mix (page 30) is a great-tasting, easy-to-pack and easy-to-make snack mix. Or let kids concoct their own mix of cereal, dried fruits and nuts.

3. Apple-Raisin Wedges. Cut one apple into quarters and remove the seeds and membrane. Put a dollop of low-fat cream cheese in the center of each wedge. Sprinkle with raisins.

4. Yogurt Fruit Smoothie. In a blender, combine one 16-ounce can of fruit and the packing juice, one 8-ounce carton of low-fat yogurt and 1 cup of milk. Blend until smooth. Use your imagination to create tasty fruit/yogurt combinations.

5. Flying Saucers. Spread large or mini flavored rice cakes with low-fat or nonfat cream cheese. Eat plain or sprinkle with raisins or other dried fruit or sunflower seeds.

6. Granola Bars. The Granola Bars (page 33) make a super snack for after school or to pack in a lunch. For a variation, stir in ½ cup raisins or other dried fruit cut into small pieces.

7. Frozen Bananas. Peel a banana and insert a wooden stick in the thickest end. Wrap in plastic wrap and freeze until firm. Eat plain or dip in flavored, low-fat yogurt and sprinkle with chopped nuts or sunflower seeds.

8. Yogurt Parfait. In an 8-ounce cup, layer flavored low-fat yogurt with fresh fruit or berries. Start with the yogurt, add a layer of fruit, top with yogurt and sprinkle with granola.

9. Apple Snack. Place eight graham crackers in a plastic bag and seal with a twist tie. Crush graham crackers until they are coarse crumbs. Put a spoonful of crumbs in the bottom of a 6-ounce cup. Top with a spoonful of applesauce. Repeat layers until the cup is full, ending with a layer of graham cracker crumbs.

10. Banana Boat. Peel a banana and slice in half lengthwise. Spread one half with peanut butter and sprinkle with granola. Top with the other half and gently press the halves together. Cut into four chunks for easy eating.

COOL GARDEN PIZZA

—

*C*reate your own variations of this colorful appetizer by topping it with your favorite vegetable combinations.

> 1 *cup low-fat ricotta cheese*
> 2 *ounces goat cheese*
> 1 *clove garlic, minced*
> ½ *teaspoon red pepper flakes*
> ½ *teaspoon dried Italian seasoning*
> 1 *purchased 12" pizza crust, baked*
> 1 *sweet red pepper, finely chopped*
> 4 *scallions, finely chopped*
> 4 *mushrooms, finely chopped*
> 1 *carrot, finely chopped*

In a medium bowl, combine the ricotta, goat cheese, garlic, pepper flakes and Italian seasoning. Spread this mixture on the crust. Sprinkle the peppers, scallions, mushrooms and carrots evenly over the top. Chill until ready to serve.

Preparation time: 15 minutes

Chef's note: You'll find a variety of easy-to-prepare pizza crusts at your supermarket: refrigerated or frozen dough crusts, crusts from a mix or already prepared crusts such as foccacia. Whichever type you use, try to pick one that is low in fat. The fat content can vary widely from brand to brand.

Per slice: 68 calories, 1.6 g. fat (21% of calories), 0.3 g. dietary fiber, 5 mg. cholesterol, 99 mg. sodium.

PITA PARTY PIZZA

*P*ita rounds make perfect, ready-made pizza crusts. The feta cheese, spinach and Greek olives give this pizza a Mediterranean flair.

> 2 *whole-wheat pita rounds, 8" in diameter, uncut*
> 1 *box (10 ounces) frozen chopped spinach, thawed and squeezed dry*
> ½ *cup shredded nonfat mozzarella cheese*
> ¼ *cup crumbled feta cheese*
> ¼ *cup sliced Greek olives or black olives*
> 1 *tomato, seeded and chopped*
> ¼ *cup thinly sliced red onions*

Prick the pitas several times with a fork. Divide the spinach and spread it over the pitas. Divide the mozzarella, feta, olives, tomatoes and onions, and sprinkle them evenly over the spinach. Place the pitas on a baking sheet and bake at 400° for 10 minutes.

To serve, cut each pizza into eight slices.

Preparation time: 10 minutes
Baking time: 10 minutes

Per slice: 32 calories, 0.7 g. fat (19% of calories), 0.6 g. dietary fiber, 2.2 mg. cholesterol, 103 mg. sodium.

ROASTED GARLIC AND SMOKED TURKEY QUESADILLAS

*B*rown these Southwestern sandwiches in a skillet or on the grill at your next backyard party. The roasted garlic gives them a mild, sweet flavor.

> 1 *whole head garlic*
> 8 *ounces low-fat cream cheese*
> 16 *flour tortillas, 8" in diameter*
> 8 *ounces smoked turkey breast, shaved*
> 1 *sweet red pepper, diced*
> 2 *cans (4½ ounces each) sliced black olives, drained*

Place the garlic head on a square of aluminum foil and coat the garlic and the foil with no-stick spray. Wrap and bake at 475° for 30 minutes, or until the garlic is soft and golden. Remove the garlic from the foil and cut it in half crosswise. Squeeze the softened garlic from each half. Add the garlic to the cream cheese and blend.

Spread a tablespoon of the garlic cream cheese over an entire tortilla. Top one-half of the tortilla with ½ ounce of the turkey, 1 tablespoon of the peppers and 1 tablespoon of the olives, and then fold the tortilla in half. Repeat to make a total of 16 folded tortillas.

Place a large no-stick frying pan over medium heat until hot. Add the tortillas 2 at a time. Heat for 1 to 2 minutes on each side, or until golden.

Cut each quesadilla into 3 wedges and serve warm.

Preparation time: 10 minutes
Baking time: 30 minutes
Cooking time: 32 minutes

Chef's notes: You can purchase shaved turkey at the deli counter of your supermarket, or ask at the meat counter.

The garlic can be roasted ahead of time to halve your last-minute cooking time.

Per wedge: 55 calories, 2.2 g. fat (35% of calories), 0.3 g. dietary fiber, 3 mg. cholesterol, 117 mg. sodium.

SPINACH-STUFFED MUSHROOMS

MAKES 20

*D*on't be misled by the high percentage of calories from fat in these vegetarian treats. Each contains only 22 calories, so even a tiny amount of fat yields a deceptively high percentage. Serve these attractive and flavorful stuffed caps as an appetizer or as a garnish for chicken or turkey.

> ½ *cup minced onions*
> 1 *teaspoon olive oil*
> 20 *medium mushrooms*
> 1 *box (10 ounces) frozen chopped spinach, thawed and squeezed dry*
> ¼ *cup chopped toasted walnuts*
> 2 *tablespoons nonfat sour cream*

In a large frying pan over medium heat, sauté the onions in the oil for 2 minutes.

Remove and chop the stems from the mushrooms, setting the caps aside. Add the stems to the onions in the pan. Cook the onions and mushroom stems until soft, about 5 minutes. Add the spinach and walnuts and heat through. Take the pan off the heat and blend in the sour cream.

Coat an 8″ × 8″ baking pan with no-stick spray. Place approximately 1 tablespoon of the spinach mixture in each of the mushroom caps. Place the stuffed caps in the prepared baking pan and bake at 350° for 10 minutes, or until the caps are heated through.

Preparation time: 15 minutes
Cooking time: 10 minutes
Baking time: 10 minutes

Per cap: 22 calories, 1.2 g. fat (44% of calories), 0.7 g. dietary fiber, no cholesterol, 15 mg. sodium.

BASIL CHICKEN ROLLS

MAKES 24 ROUNDS

Make these elegant appetizers the day before the party and refrigerate them. Then just slice and serve the rolls on toothpicks or rounds of melba toast.

4   boneless, skinless chicken breast halves
    (3 ounces each)
4   ounces low-fat cream cheese
1   teaspoon prepared pesto
¼   cup chopped fresh basil
¼   cup chopped sweet red peppers
1   cup cornflake crumbs

Place the chicken breasts between sheets of wax paper and pound lightly until slightly thinned and of a uniform thickness. Remove the paper.

Combine the cream cheese and pesto in a small bowl. Spread 2 tablespoons of the mixture evenly over each breast. Sprinkle 1 tablespoon each of the basil and peppers over each breast and roll each of them up. Dredge the rolls in the crumbs to coat.

Coat a baking sheet with no-stick spray. Place the rolls on the prepared baking sheet and spray them with no-stick spray. Bake the rolls at 350° for 25 minutes, or until they are golden brown and firm to the touch.

Chill the rolls and then slice each into 6 pieces.

Preparation time: 15 minutes
Baking time: 25 minutes

Chef's note: Pesto is a mixture of fresh basil, olive oil, Parmesan cheese and pine nuts. Prepared pesto can be found in the refrigerator section of your grocery store. If pesto is not available, season the cream cheese with a teaspoon of dried basil.

Per round: 38 calories, 1.1 g. fat (26% of calories), 0.1 g. dietary fiber, 7 mg. cholesterol, 77 mg. sodium.

GRILLED APPLE AND TURKEY BITES

MAKES 16

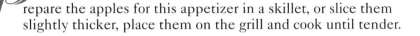

*P*repare the apples for this appetizer in a skillet, or slice them slightly thicker, place them on the grill and cook until tender.

> 1   *large apple, cored and cut into 16 wedges*
> 4   *slices (1 ounce each) cooked turkey breast*
> 16 *thin slices French bread*
> ¼   *cup Dijon mustard*

Coat a large frying pan with no-stick spray. Add the apples to the prepared pan and cook over medium heat until the apples are soft and lightly brown, about 3 minutes.

Quarter the turkey slices into 16 (2″) squares.

Toast the French bread until golden and spread with the Dijon mustard. Top each piece with a square of turkey and a slice of grilled apple.

Preparation time: 10 minutes
Cooking time: 3 minutes

Per piece: 65 calories, 1 g. fat (14% of calories), 0.6 g. dietary fiber, 5.2 mg. cholesterol, 145 mg. sodium.

MEATBALLS IN MAPLE MUSTARD SAUCE

*D*ijon mustard tempers the sweetness of the maple syrup in this low-fat variation of a party standard.

Meatballs

1	*pound lean ground turkey breast*
¼	*cup fat-free egg substitute*
1	*can (8½ ounces) water chestnuts, drained and chopped*
¼	*cup chopped scallions*
¼	*cup dry bread crumbs*

Maple Mustard Sauce

¼	*cup maple syrup*
¼	*cup defatted reduced-sodium chicken stock*
2	*tablespoons Dijon mustard*

To make the meatballs: Place the turkey, egg substitute, water chestnuts, scallions and bread crumbs in a large bowl. Blend thoroughly. Form the mixture into 30 (1″) balls.

Coat a baking sheet with no-stick spray. Place the meatballs on the prepared baking sheet. Bake at 400° for 15 minutes, or until no longer pink inside. Keep warm until ready to serve.

To make the maple mustard sauce: In a small saucepan, whisk together the maple syrup, stock and mustard. Cook over medium heat until the sauce simmers.

Preparation time: 10 minutes
Baking time: 15 minutes

Chef's note: To serve, place the meatballs in a chafing dish and coat with the sauce. Serve warm with toothpicks.

Per meatball: 46 calories, 0.3 g. fat (6% of calories), 0.7 g. dietary fiber, 10 mg. cholesterol, 33 mg. sodium.

RUMAKI

MAKES 60

*T*he classic version of rumaki calls for bacon and chicken livers, which are high in fat and cholesterol. This lighter version substitutes chicken breasts, pineapple and Canadian bacon, which is quite lean.

2	*boneless, skinless chicken breast halves (3 ounces each)*
¼	*cup low-sodium soy sauce*
20	*pineapple chunks*
20	*water chestnuts*
5	*slices Canadian bacon*

Cut the chicken breasts into nickel-size pieces, approximately 10 per breast. In a small bowl, marinate the chicken in 2 tablespoons of the soy sauce. In another small bowl, marinate the pineapple and water chestnuts in the remaining soy sauce. Let both marinate for about 15 minutes.

Cut the Canadian bacon lengthwise into 4″ × ¼″ strips. Wrap each water chestnut, pineapple or chicken piece with a bacon strip and secure with a toothpick. Coat a baking sheet with no-stick spray. Place the rumaki on the prepared baking sheet. Broil at 500° for 5 minutes, turning once. Serve warm.

Preparation time: 10 minutes plus 15 minutes marinating time
Broiling time: 5 minutes

Chef's note: Buy rectangular rather than round Canadian bacon to ensure that the meat strips will be long enough to wrap around the chicken, water chestnuts and pineapple.

Per piece: 13 calories, 0.2 g. fat (18% of calories), 0.2 g. dietary fiber, 2 mg. cholesterol, 43 mg. sodium.

Pear Slices with Smoked Trout and Basil

MAKES 20

A sophisticated and unusual combination of flavors—an appetizer ideal for an elegant cocktail, New Year's Eve or after-theater party.

  2 *medium pears, halved and cored*
  1 *tablespoon lemon juice*
  8 *ounces low-fat cream cheese*
  2 *ounces smoked trout, flaked*
  2 *tablespoons chopped fresh basil*
  1 *tablespoon grated lemon rind*
20 *small fresh basil leaves*

Slice the pear halves into wedges about ¼″ thick (about 5 slices per pear half). Place them in a medium bowl and toss to coat with the lemon juice. (This will prevent them from discoloring.)

In another medium bowl, combine the cream cheese, trout, chopped basil and lemon rind until thoroughly blended.

To serve, top each pear slice with a dollop of smoked trout cream cheese. Garnish with a fresh basil leaf.

Preparation time: 15 minutes

Chef's notes: A zester is a great little gadget for removing the intensely flavored citrus rind. Remove the rind before you squeeze the juice from the fruit. Be sure to grate off only the colored rind and avoid scraping deeply into the white, more bitter, layer beneath it.

For a really fancy presentation, put the cream cheese mixture in a pastry bag fitted with a star tip and pipe it onto the pear slices.

Per slice: 38 calories, 2.1 g. fat (47% of calories), 0.4 g. dietary fiber, 6 mg. cholesterol, 86 mg. sodium.

CHAPTER 4

OLD
FAVORITES...
AND LOTS
MORE

SOUPS AND SALADS

Each region of America boasts an incredible variety of fruits, vegetables, meat, poultry and seafood that have been adopted and adapted by the immigrants who settled this country. In the East, they dreamed up new ways to use clams and oysters; in the North, they turned to the Ojibwa for wild rice. The South melded the sweet and spicy flavors of the Caribbean with European dishes; in the West, they capitalized on a garden of fresh fruits and vegetables. And in the Southwest, they adopted fiery chili peppers to season dishes from eggs to stew. The soups and salads in this chapter make the most of regional ingredients and reflect America's ethnic diversity.

GRANDMA'S CHICKEN NOODLE SOUP

SERVES 4

*G*randma was right—chicken soup is good for just about all that ails us. This low-fat version has all the soothing qualities and rich flavor of her original recipe.

5	*cups defatted chicken stock*
1	*large onion, thinly sliced*
½	*cup sliced celery*
⅓	*cup sliced carrots*
3	*cloves garlic, minced*
½	*teaspoon dried thyme leaves*
⅛	*teaspoon ground pepper*
4	*boneless, skinless chicken breast halves (3 ounces each), cut into ½" pieces*
1	*tablespoon minced fresh parsley*
3	*ounces ribbon egg (no-yolk) noodles*

In a 4-quart saucepan, combine the stock, onions, celery, carrots, garlic, thyme and pepper. Bring to a boil over medium heat and cook for 3 minutes. Add the chicken and cook for 8 to 10 minutes, or until tender. Stir in the parsley.

While the chicken mixture is cooking, cook the noodles for 8 to 10 minutes in a large pot of boiling water. Drain. To serve, place the noodles in individual soup bowls and top with the hot soup.

Preparation time: 10 minutes
Cooking time: 23 minutes

Chef's note: Cooking the noodles separately keeps them from becoming soggy and overcooked.

Per serving: 185 calories, 1.8 g. fat (9% of calories), 1.2 g. dietary fiber, 34 mg. cholesterol, 638 mg. sodium.

CHILLED CUCUMBER BUTTERMILK SOUP

SERVES 4

*K*eep cool as a cucumber on a sultry summer day with this refreshing soup. Serve it in frosted mugs as an appetizer.

2   cucumbers, peeled, seeded and chopped
1   cup low-fat buttermilk
½   cup defatted chicken stock
2   tablespoons minced fresh parsley
2   tablespoons minced chives
1   teaspoon lemon juice

Place the cucumbers, buttermilk, stock, parsley, chives and lemon juice in a blender container. Blend on high speed for 20 to 30 seconds, or until smooth. Serve chilled.

Preparation time: 5 minutes

Chef's note: Chive blossoms are a lovely garnish for this soup.

Per serving: 48 calories, 0.8 g. fat (13% of calories), 1.6 g. dietary fiber, 2 mg. cholesterol, 127 mg. sodium.

BACKYARD GARDEN TOMATO SOUP

*H*omegrown tomatoes capture the essence of summer in this ripe-red soup. Use the bounty of your own garden or visit a nearby farmers' market for the freshest ingredients. If you hanker after that just-from-the-garden flavor this winter, canned tomatoes will give better flavor than fresh.

1	*tablespoon olive oil*
1½	*cups diced onions*
1	*sweet red pepper, diced*
2	*cloves garlic, minced*
4	*cups chopped fresh plum tomatoes or canned crushed tomatoes*
2	*cups water*
¼	*cup minced fresh basil*
2	*tablespoons minced fresh mint*

In a 4-quart saucepan, combine the oil, onions, peppers and garlic. Cook over medium-high heat for 1 minute; cover, reduce heat to low and cook for 5 minutes.

Add the tomatoes, water, basil and mint. Bring to a boil over medium heat and simmer, uncovered, for 15 minutes, or until the vegetables are just tender.

Preparation time: 10 minutes
Cooking time: 25 minutes

Chef's note: Mint and tomatoes make a beautiful pair. The sweetness of mint counteracts the natural acidity in tomatoes and eliminates the need for added sugar.

Per serving: 99 calories, 4.1 g. fat (34% of calories), 3.5 g. dietary fiber, no cholesterol, 19 mg. sodium.

MIDWESTERN VEGETABLE BARLEY SOUP

SERVES 4

*S*avor the flavors and ingredients of the heartland in this chunky soup. Turkey bacon adds a hint of smokiness without all the calories and fat of regular bacon.

⅓	*cup diced turkey bacon*
½	*cup chopped onions*
3	*large cloves garlic, minced*
1	*cup sliced celery*
¾	*cup sliced carrots*
1	*can (14 ½ ounces) no-salt-added tomatoes, chopped*
3½	*cups defatted chicken stock*
¼	*cup quick-cooking pearl barley*
1	*cup broccoli florets*

Coat a 4-quart saucepan with no-stick spray. Add the turkey bacon and onions; cook over medium heat for 2 to 3 minutes. Add the garlic and cook for 1 minute. Add the celery, carrots, tomatoes and stock. Cook over medium-low heat for 5 minutes.

Add the barley and cook for 5 minutes; add the broccoli and cook for an additional 5 minutes, or until the vegetables and barley are just tender.

Preparation time: 10 minutes
Cooking time: 20 minutes

Per serving: 145 calories, 3.2 g. fat (19% of calories), 4.7 g. dietary fiber, 9 mg. cholesterol, 468 mg. sodium.

APPLE CIDER PUMPKIN SOUP

SERVES 6

*C*elebrate autumn with this smooth, spicy cream soup. Pumpkin puree, low-fat evaporated milk and nonfat sour cream combine to form a creamy texture without the fat of heavy cream. It's lovely served as an appetizer for roast turkey or pork.

1	teaspoon canola oil
¼	cup minced shallots
1	teaspoon minced fresh ginger
1	can (16 ounces) pumpkin
2	cups apple cider
¾	cup defatted chicken stock
½	teaspoon pumpkin pie spice
¾	cup evaporated low-fat milk
¼	cup nonfat sour cream

Coat a 4-quart saucepan with no-stick spray. Add the oil, shallots and ginger; cook over medium heat for 2 minutes. Add the pumpkin, cider, stock and pumpkin pie spice. Bring to a boil and cook over medium-low heat for 10 minutes. Whisk in the milk and sour cream.

To reheat, warm over medium heat but do not boil.

Preparation time: 10 minutes
Cooking time: 15 minutes

Per serving: 112 calories, 2.2 g. fat (17% of calories), 1.5 g. dietary fiber, 5 mg. cholesterol, 107 mg. sodium.

CAULIFLOWER RED PEPPER SOUP

*R*oasted red peppers give this creamy soup its rosy red color. Serve it as a first course or with a salad for a light lunch or dinner.

1 *cup diced onions*
2 *teaspoons olive oil*
3 *cups coarsely chopped cauliflower*
2 *cups defatted chicken stock*
1 *jar (7 ounces) roasted red peppers, rinsed, drained and coarsely chopped*
  Pinch of black pepper
1 *cup 1% low-fat milk*
1 *tablespoon minced chives*

In a 2-quart saucepan over medium heat, sauté the onions in the oil for 1 minute. Add the cauliflower. Stir well, cover, reduce the heat to medium-low and cook for 5 minutes. Add the stock, red peppers and black pepper; bring to a boil over medium heat and cook, uncovered, for 10 to 12 minutes, or until the vegetables are tender. Let cool slightly and stir in the milk.

Pour one-half of the soup into a blender and blend on high speed until smooth. Repeat with the remaining soup. To serve, heat the soup until hot but do not allow the mixture to boil. Serve garnished with the chives.

Preparation time: 10 minutes
Cooking time: 20 minutes

Chef's note: Roasted red peppers are available in jars and are a handy substitute for home-roasted ones, which makes this soup quick and easy to prepare.

Per serving: 100 calories, 3.2 g. fat (27% of calories), 2.5 g. dietary fiber, 3 mg. cholesterol, 279 mg. sodium.

COUNTRY HERB SOUP

SERVES 4

*S*eason this soup with basil, chives and dill fresh from your backyard or patio garden.

> 1 *cup diced leeks*
> ¾ *cup diced onions*
> 3 *cloves garlic, minced*
> 2 *cups defatted chicken stock*
> 3 *new potatoes, peeled and diced*
> 2 *cups chopped fresh spinach*
> ½ *cup chopped fresh basil*
> ¼ *cup minced chives*
> 2 *tablespoons minced fresh dill*
> 1½ *cups 1% low-fat milk*

Coat a 3-quart saucepan with no-stick spray. Add the leeks, onions and garlic and cook over medium heat for 2 to 3 minutes. Add the stock and potatoes; bring to a boil over medium heat and cook for 10 minutes, or until the potatoes are tender.

Add the spinach, basil, chives and dill; cook for 5 minutes. Stir in the milk. Pour half of the soup into a blender container. Blend on high speed for 20 to 30 seconds, or until smooth. Repeat with the remaining soup. To reheat, warm over medium heat but do not boil.

Preparation time: 10 minutes
Cooking time: 20 minutes

Chef's note: For a fabulous garnish, float an edible nasturtium bloom in each soup bowl.

Per serving: 176 calories, 1.4 g. fat (7% of calories), 3 g. dietary fiber, 4 mg. cholesterol, 317 mg. sodium.

OJIBWA WILD RICE SOUP

SERVES 4

Ojibwa tribespeople still harvest wild rice from the lakes and rivers of Minnesota and Wisconsin. Lake and river wild rice tend to have longer grains than paddy-grown rice. For convenience and quicker cooking, we've used instant wild rice to give this soup its nutlike flavor.

> 1 teaspoon olive oil
> 3 cups sliced onions
> ¾ cup diced celery
> ½ cup diced carrots
> 3 cloves garlic, minced
> ½ cup instant wild rice, rinsed
> 6 cups defatted chicken stock
> 1 cup sliced mushrooms
> 1 teaspoon dried rosemary

Coat a 4-quart saucepan with no-stick spray. Add the oil, onions, celery and carrots. Cook over medium heat for 5 minutes, or until the vegetables begin to soften. Add the garlic, cook for 1 minute; then add the rice, stock, mushrooms and rosemary. Cook, partially covered, over medium heat for 15 to 20 minutes, or until the rice is tender.

Preparation time: 10 minutes
Cooking time: 30 minutes

Chef's note: Before using wild rice, rinse it in a sieve under cold running water until the draining water runs clear.

Per serving: 169 calories, 1.7 g. fat (9% of calories), 2.9 g. dietary fiber, no cholesterol, 735 mg. sodium.

Roasted Garlic Potato Soup

*T*wo whole heads of garlic! That may seem overpowering, but don't worry. Roasting mellows and sweetens the flavor of garlic and makes it quite delicate.

2	*whole garlic heads*
2	*teaspoons olive oil*
	Pinch of dried thyme
2	*cups sliced leeks*
4	*cups peeled, diced potatoes*
3½	*cups defatted chicken stock*
1½	*cups 1% low-fat milk*

Slice ½" off the top of each garlic head. Place the heads on a piece of aluminum foil, drizzle them with 1 teaspoon of the oil and sprinkle them with the thyme. Seal the foil and bake at 450° for 30 to 40 minutes, or until the garlic is soft. When cool, squeeze out the garlic and mash it to a paste.

Coat a 4-quart saucepan with no-stick spray. Add the remaining 1 teaspoon of the oil and the leeks and cook over medium heat for 2 to 3 minutes. Add the potatoes, stock and garlic. Bring to a boil over medium heat, reduce the heat to medium-low and cook for 20 to 25 minutes, or until the potatoes are tender. Stir in the milk.

To thicken slightly, place one-third of the soup in a blender container, blend on high speed for 15 to 20 seconds, or until smooth; stir into the remaining soup. To reheat, warm over medium heat but do not boil.

Preparation time: 10 minutes
Baking time: 40 minutes
Cooking time: 30 minutes

Per serving: 253 calories, 3.6 g. fat (13% of calories), 2.7 g. dietary fiber, 4 mg. cholesterol, 479 mg. sodium.

San Francisco Seafood Soup

*F*ennel and saffron complement the shrimp and fish in this soup from the Golden Gate city. Fennel lends a tinge of anise, while saffron adds a touch of golden yellow color.

1	*teaspoon olive oil*
1½	*cups diced onions*
1	*green pepper, diced*
3	*cloves garlic, minced*
3	*cups water*
1	*can (14½ ounces) no-salt-added tomatoes, chopped*
¾	*cup tomato juice*
½	*cup clam juice*
1	*teaspoon fennel seeds, crushed*
¼	*teaspoon saffron*
8	*ounces firm-fleshed fish, cut into ½" pieces*
4	*ounces peeled and deveined shrimp*

Coat a 4-quart saucepan with no-stick spray. Add the oil and onions and cook over medium heat for 2 to 3 minutes. Add the peppers and garlic and cook for 1 minute.

Add the water, tomatoes, tomato juice, clam juice, fennel seeds and saffron. Bring to a boil over medium-high heat, reduce the heat to medium-low and cook for 15 to 20 minutes, or until the vegetables are just tender.

Add the fish and shrimp. Cook for 3 to 5 minutes, or just until done. Do not overcook.

Preparation time: 10 minutes
Cooking time: 30 minutes

Chef's note: Any type of firm-fleshed fish works well in this soup, such as halibut, salmon, grouper or snapper.

Per serving: 154 calories, 2.3 g. fat (13% of calories), 2.5 g. dietary fiber, 75 mg. cholesterol, 312 mg. sodium.

PINTO BEAN TORTILLA SOUP

SERVES 4

*C*orn tortilla strips garnish this hearty soup with its south-of-the-border blend of flavors and ingredients. Whole pinto beans and refried pintos add texture and thicken the soup.

1	*teaspoon olive oil*
1¾	*cups diced onions*
3	*cloves garlic, minced*
⅓	*cup diced carrots*
2	*cans (15 ounces each) low-sodium pinto beans, rinsed and drained*
3	*cups fat-free refried beans*
1½	*cups defatted chicken stock*
1½	*cups water*
2½	*teaspoons mild chili powder*
2	*tablespoons minced fresh coriander*
3	*corn tortillas, cut into thin strips*
⅓	*cup shredded reduced-fat Monterey Jack cheese*

Coat a 4-quart saucepan with no-stick spray. Add the oil and onions and cook over medium heat for 2 minutes. Add the garlic and carrots and continue cooking over medium heat for 3 to 5 minutes, or until the vegetables begin to soften. Add the pinto beans, refried beans, stock, water and chili powder. Bring to a boil over medium-high heat; reduce the heat to medium-low and cook for 15 to 20 minutes longer, or until the vegetables are tender. Stir in the coriander.

While the soup is cooking, bake the tortillas at 425° for 4 to 5 minutes, or until crisp. To serve, ladle the hot soup into serving bowls and top with the Monterey Jack and tortilla strips.

Preparation time: 15 minutes
Cooking time: 30 minutes
Chef's note: Coriander is a delicate herb and should be added at the end of cooking for the best flavor.

Per serving: 418 calories, 5.1 g. fat (10% of calories), 3.1 g. dietary fiber, 7 mg. cholesterol, 797 mg. sodium.

Red Pepper Dip (page 22), Tangy Eggplant Dip (page 23), Potato Chips (page 27)

Fresh Tomato Salsa with Homemade Tortilla Chips (page 28),
Seven-Layer Skinny Dip (page 21)

Pita Party Pizza (page 37)

Backyard Garden Tomato Soup (page 48), American Harvest Loaf (page 252)

Seafood Chicken Gumbo (page 69)

61

Southwest Three Bean Salad (page 75)

62

Wild Rice Shrimp Salad (page 80)

Chicken Parmesan (page 90)

MIAMI BLACK BEAN SOUP

SERVES 4

*T*his thick, spicy vegetarian soup reflects its Caribbean heritage with cumin, red pepper flakes and jalapeño peppers. Lime juice adds depth to the flavor, and lime wedges make an attractive garnish.

1	*teaspoon olive oil*
1½	*cups diced onions*
1	*green pepper, diced*
4	*cloves garlic, minced*
3	*cans (15 ounces each) black beans, rinsed and drained*
2½	*cups vegetable stock*
2	*cups crushed tomatoes*
1½	*tablespoons lime juice*
1½	*teaspoons ground cumin*
½	*teaspoon crushed red pepper flakes (or to taste)*
1	*lime, cut into wedges*
⅓	*cup nonfat sour cream*
⅓	*cup diced sweet red, yellow or green peppers*
2	*tablespoons sliced jalapeño peppers (wear rubber gloves when handling)*

Coat a 4-quart saucepan with no-stick spray. Add the oil, onions, green peppers and garlic. Cook over medium heat for 3 to 4 minutes, or until the vegetables begin to soften. Add the beans, stock, tomatoes, lime juice, cumin and pepper flakes. Partially cover and cook over medium-low heat for 15 to 20 minutes, or until the vegetables are tender.

Place the lime, sour cream, sweet red, yellow or green peppers and jalapeño peppers in individual small bowls and pass separately.

Preparation time: 10 minutes
Cooking time: 25 minutes

Per serving: 244 calories, 3.6 g. fat (11% of calories), 14.6 g. dietary fiber, no cholesterol, 960 mg. sodium.

WILD MUSHROOM SOUP

SERVES 4

*A*lone or in combination, dried mushrooms such as shiitakes, cèpes, porcinis, morels and chanterelles have an intense woodsy flavor, so a few go a long way. The liquid remaining after you've soaked dried mushrooms also is very flavorful and can be used in the recipe or saved for other soups or sauces to add a mushroom flavor.

1	*ounce dried mushrooms*
1½	*cups hot water*
1	*teaspoon olive oil*
3	*tablespoons minced shallots*
3	*cloves garlic, minced*
8	*ounces fresh button mushrooms, coarsely chopped*
2	*tablespoons unbleached flour*
4	*cups defatted chicken stock*
3	*tablespoons quick-cooking pearl barley*

Place the dried mushrooms in a medium bowl and pour the water over them; let sit for 15 minutes. Strain the mushrooms, reserving the liquid. Coarsely chop the mushrooms. Strain the liquid through a coffee filter to remove any particles.

Coat a 4-quart saucepan with no-stick spray. Add the oil, shallots and garlic. Cook over medium heat for 1 minute. Add the dried and fresh mushrooms. Cover and cook over medium heat for 3 minutes. Add the flour and cook for 1 minute over medium heat, stirring constantly. Add the reserved mushroom liquid, stock and barley. Bring to a boil and cook over medium heat for 15 minutes, or until the mushrooms and barley are tender.

Preparation time: 5 minutes plus 15 minutes standing time
Cooking time: 20 minutes

Per serving: 118 calories, 1.6 g. fat (12% of calories), 2.3 g. dietary fiber, no cholesterol, 474 mg. sodium.

CAPE COD CLAM CHOWDER

SERVES 4

*N*ew England–style clam chowder features a cream rather than tomato base. Thick, smooth and creamy, this chowder is perfect for lunch or a light supper.

1	teaspoon olive oil
2	slices turkey bacon, finely diced
1¾	cups diced onions
2	tablespoons unbleached flour
¾	cup clam juice
¾	cup water
1½	cups peeled, diced potatoes
1½	cups 1% low-fat milk
1	tablespoon lemon juice
1	tablespoon minced fresh parsley
⅛	teaspoon hot-pepper sauce

Coat a 4-quart saucepan with no-stick spray. Add the oil and bacon and cook over medium heat for 3 to 5 minutes, or until the bacon begins to crisp. Add the onions, cook for 1 minute, then cover and cook for an additional 3 minutes.

Remove the cover and add the flour. Cook over medium heat, stirring constantly, for 1 minute. Add the clam juice, water and potatoes to the pot. Cook over medium heat for 5 to 8 minutes, or until the potatoes are tender. Stir in the milk, lemon juice, parsley and hot-pepper sauce. Bring to a boil and serve.

Preparation time: 10 minutes
Cooking time: 20 minutes

Per serving: 153 calories, 3.6 g. fat (20% of calories), 1.8 g. dietary fiber, 8 mg. cholesterol, 108 mg. sodium.

FRESH SALMON CORN CHOWDER

SERVES 4

*D*ill, red potatoes, corn and salmon add dashes of vivid color to this creamy soup. Be sure to use fresh dill—its flavor is more intense than dried.

12 *ounces salmon fillet*
2½ *cups water*
2 *tablespoons lemon juice*
¼ *teaspoon hot-pepper sauce*
1½ *cups diced onions*
⅓ *cup diced celery*
¼ *cup diced carrots*
4 *red new potatoes, unpeeled, diced*
2½ *cups 1% low-fat milk*
¾ *cup corn*
2 *tablespoons chopped fresh dill*
2 *tablespoons sliced scallions*

In a medium frying pan, combine the salmon, water, lemon juice and hot-pepper sauce. Bring to a boil over medium-high heat. Reduce heat to medium-low and simmer for 5 to 8 minutes, or just until the salmon begins to flake. Remove the salmon, reserving the liquid. Cut the salmon into bite-size pieces; set aside.

Coat a 4-quart saucepan with no-stick spray. Add the onions, celery and carrots and sauté for 1 to 2 minutes over medium heat. Add the salmon-poaching liquid to the vegetables and bring to a boil over medium heat. Add the potatoes and cook for 6 to 8 minutes, or until tender. Add the milk, corn, dill, scallions and reserved salmon. Cook for 2 to 3 minutes over medium heat, until hot. Do not allow the mixture to boil.

Preparation time: 10 minutes
Cooking time: 25 minutes
Per serving: 316 calories, 4.8 g. fat (13% of calories), 4.1 g. dietary fiber, 21 mg. cholesterol, 619 mg. sodium.

Seafood Chicken Gumbo

*F*ilé powder—ground sassafras leaves—gives gumbo authentic Creole flavor.

>   1 tablespoon canola oil
>   1 tablespoon unbleached flour
> 1½ cups diced onions
>   1 green pepper, diced
>   ¼ cup diced celery
>   1 can (14½ ounces) no-salt-added tomatoes, chopped
>   1 can (10 ounces) tomatoes with chilies, chopped
> 1½ cups water
>   8 ounces boneless, skinless chicken breasts, diced
>   8 ounces peeled and deveined shrimp
>   1 cup shucked oysters, drained and rinsed
>   ½ teaspoon filé powder (optional)
>   2 cups hot cooked rice

In a 4-quart saucepan, combine the oil and flour. Cook over medium heat for 3 to 5 minutes, stirring constantly, until the roux turns dark brown. Add the onions, peppers and celery and cook over medium heat for 3 to 4 minutes, or until the vegetables begin to soften.

Add the no-salt-added tomatoes, tomatoes with chilies and water to the pan; bring to a boil. Cook over medium heat for 10 minutes. Add the chicken and cook for an additional 4 to 6 minutes, or until the chicken is almost cooked through. Add the shrimp, oysters and filé powder and cook for 3 to 5 minutes, or just until the seafood is cooked through.

To serve, place rice in each bowl; top with gumbo.

Preparation time: 10 minutes
Cooking time: 30 minutes
Per serving: 152 calories, 4.6 g. fat (27% of calories), 1.6 g. dietary fiber, 96 mg. cholesterol, 330 mg. sodium.

SPICY PEANUT NOODLES WITH CHICKEN

SERVES 4

*P*eanut butter and red pepper flakes create a sweet-hot dressing for this oriental-style salad.

⅓ *cup soft tofu*

2 *tablespoons creamy peanut butter*

2 *tablespoons defatted chicken stock*

1 *tablespoon honey*

1 *tablespoon low-sodium soy sauce*

1 *tablespoon rice wine vinegar*

½ *teaspoon red pepper flakes*

6 *ounces linguine*

2 *boneless, skinless chicken breast halves (3 ounces each), cooked and cut into strips*

1 *sweet red pepper, diced*

½ *cup sliced scallions*

½ *cup chopped fresh coriander*

In a blender container, combine the tofu, peanut butter, stock, honey, soy sauce, vinegar and pepper flakes. Blend on high speed for 10 to 20 seconds, or until smooth.

Cook the linguine in a large pot of boiling water for 8 to 10 minutes, or until just tender. Rinse the linguine under cold water; drain. Toss the noodles with the peanut dressing, chicken, peppers, scallions and coriander.

Preparation time: 15 minutes

Chef's note: Grilled chicken enhances the flavor of this salad.

Per serving: 272 calories, 7 g. fat (23% of calories), 1.4 g. dietary fiber, 54 mg. cholesterol, 212 mg. sodium.

SPRING GREEN PASTA SALAD

SERVES 6

*B*asil, asparagus and spinach add three shades of garden-fresh green to this pasta side-dish salad.

Salad

8	ounces bow tie pasta
2	cups cut (1" pieces) asparagus spears, cooked
2	cups torn fresh spinach
1	can (15½ ounces) cannellini beans, rinsed and drained
½	cup chopped fresh basil
½	cup sliced scallions
¼	cup shredded Parmesan cheese

Dressing

6	tablespoons defatted chicken stock
2	tablespoons rice wine vinegar
1	tablespoon extra-virgin olive oil
1	tablespoon minced shallots
1	clove garlic, minced

To make the salad: Cook the pasta in a large pot of boiling water for 10 to 12 minutes, or until just tender. Rinse under cold water; drain.

In a large bowl, combine the pasta, asparagus, spinach, beans, basil and scallions. Toss gently.

To make the dressing: In a small bowl or blender container, combine the stock, vinegar, oil, shallots and garlic. Mix well.

Pour the dressing over the salad and toss gently. Place in a serving container, sprinkle with the Parmesan and serve.

Preparation time: 15 minutes
Cooking time: 12 minutes

Per serving: 248 calories, 5.4 g. fat (18% of calories), 5.6 g. dietary fiber, 36 mg. cholesterol, 274 mg. sodium.

SOUTHWEST CHICKEN CAESAR SALAD

SERVES 4

The chicken and croutons in this salad are seasoned with a feisty blend of cumin, chili powder and garlic for a southwestern flair.

2   teaspoons ground cumin
2   teaspoons mild chili powder
¼   teaspoon minced garlic
4   boneless, skinless chicken breast halves (3 ounces each)
2   cups cubed sourdough bread
¼   cup nonfat mayonnaise
¼   cup skim milk
1   tablespoon red wine vinegar
¼   teaspoon Worcestershire sauce
¼   teaspoon anchovy paste
1   clove garlic, minced
6   cups torn romaine lettuce
⅓   cup shredded Parmesan cheese
½   sweet red pepper, sliced
½   green pepper, sliced

In a small bowl, mix the cumin, chili powder and garlic. Sprinkle one-half of the seasoning mixture over the chicken breasts and let sit at least 15 minutes.

Coat a 15″ × 10″ jelly-roll pan with no-stick spray. Place the bread in a medium bowl; spray the bread with no-stick spray. Toss with the remaining seasoning mixture and bake in the prepared pan at 425° for 5 to 8 minutes, or until lightly browned and crisp.

In a small bowl, combine the mayonnaise, milk, vinegar, Worcestershire sauce, anchovy paste and garlic; mix well.

Grill or broil the chicken breasts for 6 to 8 minutes, or until the chicken is cooked through, turning once.

Cut the chicken on the diagonal into strips.

To serve: Toss the romaine lettuce with the dressing and Parmesan. Place on a platter and top with the chicken and croutons. Garnish with the red peppers and green peppers.

Preparation time: 10 minutes plus 15 minutes marinating time
Baking time: 8 minutes
Grilling time: 8 minutes

Per serving: 191 calories, 5.2 g. fat (25% of calories), 2.6 g. dietary fiber, 41 mg. cholesterol, 494 mg. sodium.

FRESH SPINACH BASIL SALAD

SERVES 4

This side-dish salad is a delightful way to incorporate vitamin-rich spinach into your everyday meals.

6   *cups torn fresh spinach*
½   *cup torn fresh basil*
2   *tablespoons orange juice*
1   *tablespoon rice wine vinegar*
2   *teaspoons extra-virgin olive oil*
1   *small clove garlic, minced*
2   *tablespoons (½ ounce) shaved Parmesan cheese (see note)*

In a large bowl, combine the spinach and basil. In a small bowl, combine the orange juice, vinegar, oil and garlic; mix well. Toss the spinach and basil with enough dressing to lightly coat the leaves. Place the greens on a platter and sprinkle with the Parmesan.

Preparation time: 5 minutes

Chef's note: To shave Parmesan cheese, use a vegetable peeler to cut small, thin strips of cheese. The cheese will have a distinctive appearance, and you'll get the most flavor from it.

Per serving: 59 calories, 3.5 g. fat (48% of calories), 2.3 g. dietary fiber, 2 mg. cholesterol, 125 mg. sodium.

CALIFORNIA CHEF'S SALAD

*A*rtichoke hearts give this traditional meal-in-a-bowl favorite a tangy new twist.

Salad

2	boneless, skinless chicken breast halves (3 ounces each)
6	cups torn mixed lettuce
2	ounces turkey ham, thinly sliced, cut into strips
2	ounces low-fat roast beef, thinly sliced, cut into strips
½	cup sliced onions
2	tomatoes, cut into wedges
1	can (14 ounces) quartered artichoke hearts, rinsed and drained
1	cup thinly sliced sweet red, green or yellow peppers
3	ounces reduced-fat Cheddar cheese, cut into strips

Thousand Island Dressing

¾	cup nonfat plain yogurt
3	tablespoons chili sauce
2	tablespoons sweet pickle relish

To make the salad: Grill or broil the chicken for 6 to 8 minutes, or until the chicken is cooked through, turning once. Cut the chicken into strips.

Place the lettuce on a serving platter; top with the turkey ham, beef and chicken. Arrange the onions, tomatoes, artichoke hearts, peppers and Cheddar over the salad. Serve with the dressing on the side.

To make the Thousand Island dressing: In a small bowl, combine the yogurt, chili sauce and pickle relish; mix well.

Preparation time: 15 minutes
Grilling time: 8 minutes

Chef's note: If you are pressed for time, substitute thinly sliced deli chicken breast for the grilled chicken. Look for sliced deli roast beef that has little fat around it or "marbled" through it.

Per serving: 269 calories, 6.7 g. fat (22% of calories), 2.2 g. dietary fiber, 48 mg. cholesterol, 820 mg. sodium.

SOUTHWEST THREE BEAN SALAD

SERVES 4

*A*n eye-catching red, white and black, this side dish will liven up grilled chicken or fish, fajitas or burgers.

1	cup canned black beans, rinsed and drained
1	cup canned kidney beans, rinsed and drained
1	cup canned Great Northern beans, rinsed and drained
⅓	cup diced red onions
¼	cup diced sweet red peppers
¼	cup minced fresh coriander
¼	cup defatted chicken stock
1½	tablespoons red wine vinegar
1	teaspoon olive oil
½	teaspoon mild chili powder
1	clove garlic

In a medium bowl, combine the black beans, kidney beans, Great Northern beans, onions, peppers and coriander; stir gently.

In a blender container, combine the stock, vinegar, oil, chili powder and garlic. Blend on high speed for 30 to 45 seconds, or until well-blended. Pour over the beans and toss gently. Let sit at least 15 minutes before serving to allow the flavors to mingle.

Preparation time: 10 minutes plus 15 minutes standing time

Per serving: 204 calories, 2.3 g. fat (9% of calories), 7.4 g. dietary fiber, no cholesterol, 442 mg. sodium.

GRILLED CHICKEN COBB SALAD

SERVES 4

*C*obb salads are as lovely to look at as they are to eat. The ingredients in this version are arranged like a wheel on a bed of different varieties of lettuce.

Dressing

6	*tablespoons tomato juice*
1½	*tablespoons red wine vinegar*
2	*teaspoons olive oil*
½	*teaspoon minced garlic*
½	*teaspoon Worcestershire sauce*

Salad

4	*boneless, skinless chicken breast halves (3 ounces each)*
4	*cups torn mixed lettuce*
1	*cucumber, thinly sliced*
⅓	*cup diced turkey bacon, cooked until crisp*
2	*tomatoes, cut into wedges*
½	*avocado, sliced*
1½	*tablespoons (½ ounce) crumbled blue cheese (optional)*

To make the dressing: In a small bowl, combine the tomato juice, vinegar, oil, garlic and Worcestershire sauce; mix well.

To make the salad: Place the chicken breasts in a glass baking dish and pour one-half of the dressing over the chicken, reserving the remaining dressing. Marinate the chicken in the refrigerator for 30 minutes.

Remove the chicken from the marinade; discard any marinade remaining in the dish. Grill or broil the chicken for 5 minutes on each side, or until cooked through. Toss the lettuce and cucumbers with enough dressing to lightly coat the leaves and place on a platter. Sprinkle with the turkey bacon, arrange the tomatoes around the edge and garnish with the avocados and blue cheese. Place the warm chicken breasts in the center of the salad.

Preparation time: 15 minutes plus 30 minutes marinating time
Grilling time: 10 minutes

Chef's note: Avocados are high in fat, but it's unsaturated fat, which is healthier than saturated fat. To lower the total percent of fat in your meal, serve this salad with bread and a light dessert.

Per serving: 200 calories, 10.1 g. fat (44% of calories), 3.4 g. dietary fiber, 44 mg. cholesterol, 135 mg. sodium.

6 SUPER LOW-FAT SALAD DRESSINGS

*I*t's not always what's *in* a salad, but what goes on top that chalks up the calories. Here are six super dressings that are as skinny as the main ingredients.

• **Flavored Vinegars.** Sprinkle cut-up vegetables or mixed greens with flavored vinegars that range from raspberry to rosemary. You can find a variety of these vinegars at your supermarket, deli or gourmet cooking shop. To make your own herb-flavored vinegars, add sprigs of fresh, well-washed herbs such as tarragon, rosemary and thyme to red or white wine vinegars. Cover tightly and let mellow for one week before using.

• **Lemon.** A little squeeze of lemon adds lift to mixed greens or a seafood salad. Top with fresh-ground black or white pepper.

• **Savory Herbed Yogurt Dressing.** For a creamy herbed dressing, add dried or fresh herbs (such as dill, basil, thyme, rosemary and oregano) and cracked fresh pepper to nonfat plain yogurt, then thin to pouring consistency with skim milk or buttermilk.

• **Yogurt Fruit Salad Dressing.** For a fruit dressing, use lemon or other fruit-flavored nonfat yogurt and thin with milk to pouring consistency. Or, add a pinch of ground cinnamon to vanilla nonfat yogurt, then thin.

• **Sour Cream Salsa Dressing.** To top fajitas or taco salads, combine fresh salsa and nonfat sour cream. If necessary, thin slightly with skim milk.

• **Sour Cream Dill Dressing.** To make a dressing perfect for a seafood or potato salad, combine dried or fresh dill with nonfat sour cream and season to taste with salt and pepper. Thin to the desired consistency with skim milk or buttermilk.

TURKEY FRUIT SALAD WITH APRICOT DRESSING

SERVES 4

*S*erve this pretty-as-a-picture salad at a summer luncheon or shower. Although we've suggested cantaloupe, strawberries, blueberries and grapes, take advantage of whatever fruits are at their seasonal best in your region.

Apricot Dressing

½ *cup canned apricots in light syrup, well-drained*
3 *tablespoons defatted chicken stock*
2 *tablespoons orange juice*
1 *tablespoon lemon juice*

Turkey Fruit Salad

4 *cups torn leaf lettuce*
6 *ounces cooked turkey breast, cut into strips (about 1½ cups)*
⅓ *cup sliced scallions*
1½ *cups cantaloupe balls*
1 *cup strawberries, halved*
½ *cup red grapes, halved*
¼ *cup blueberries*
1½ *tablespoons unsalted sunflower seeds*

To make the apricot dressing: In a blender container, combine the apricots, stock, orange juice and lemon juice. Blend on high speed for 20 to 30 seconds, or until smooth.

To make the turkey fruit salad: On a platter or individual plates, place a bed of lettuce. Arrange the turkey on top of the lettuce and sprinkle with the scallions. Place the cantaloupe, strawberries, grapes and blueberries over the salad and sprinkle with the sunflower seeds. Drizzle the apricot dressing over the salad or serve the dressing on the side.

Preparation time: 15 minutes

Per serving: 155 calories, 2.5 g. fat (14% of calories), 3 g. dietary fiber, 35 mg. cholesterol, 57 mg. sodium.

MIXED WINTER GREENS WITH GARLIC CROUTONS

*L*ettuce varieties such as romaine, curly endive and radicchio add texture and interest to this attractive green side-dish salad. For a heartier version, top it with warm sliced potatoes and julienned beets.

Croutons

2	*cups firm whole-wheat bread or French bread, cut into ½″ cubes*
1	*clove garlic, minced*
¼	*teaspoon paprika*

Salad

1	*tablespoon sherry wine vinegar*
1	*tablespoon defatted chicken stock*
2	*teaspoons extra-virgin olive oil*
1	*teaspoon Dijon mustard*
6	*cups torn mixed greens (such as romaine, curly endive, radicchio, mustard greens)*

To make the croutons: Place the bread in a medium bowl. Coat the bread with no-stick spray; toss with the garlic and paprika. Place in a 15″ × 10″ jelly-roll pan and bake at 425° for 5 to 8 minutes, or until lightly browned and crisp.

To make the salad: In a small bowl, combine the vinegar, stock, oil and mustard; mix well. In a large bowl, toss the salad greens with the dressing, sprinkle with the croutons and serve.

Preparation time: 10 minutes
Baking time: 8 minutes
Chef's note: This dressing complements strongly flavored greens such as endive, radicchio and mustard.

Per serving: 68 calories, 3.1 g. fat (38% of calories), 2.3 g. dietary fiber, no cholesterol, 123 mg. sodium.

WILD RICE SHRIMP SALAD

*W*ild rice can take up to an hour to cook fully. You can cook the rice the day before and refrigerate it so that it will be ready when you're assembling the salad.

Salad

3	cups cooked wild rice (see note)
12	ounces peeled and deveined shrimp, cooked
1½	cups halved cherry tomatoes
1	can (8 ounces) sliced water chestnuts, rinsed and drained
½	cup peas
½	cup sliced scallions
½	cup diced red onions
¼	cup chopped fresh dill

Dressing

¼	cup orange juice
1½	tablespoons white wine vinegar
1	tablespoon extra-virgin olive oil
2	teaspoons Dijon mustard
1	clove garlic, minced

To make the salad: In a large bowl, combine the wild rice, shrimp, tomatoes, water chestnuts, peas, scallions, onions and dill; mix well.

To make the dressing: In a small bowl, combine the orange juice, vinegar, oil, mustard and garlic; mix well. Drizzle the dressing over the salad and toss.

Preparation time: 15 minutes

Chef's note: To cook wild rice: Rinse uncooked rice thoroughly until the draining water runs clear. In a heavy saucepan, add 1 cup of the uncooked rice to 4 cups of water and 1 teaspoon salt (optional) and bring to a boil. Reduce the heat and simmer, covered, for 45 to 55 minutes, or until the rice kernels are open and tender but not mushy. One cup of uncooked rice yields 3 to 4 cups cooked.

Per serving: 402 calories, 5.7 g. fat (13% of calories), 7.9 g. dietary fiber, 131 mg. cholesterol, 199 mg. sodium.

NEW YORK WALDORF SALAD

SERVES 4

An apple vinaigrette dressing replaces mayonnaise in an updated version of this crisp, colorful salad.

½	*green apple, thinly sliced*
½	*red apple, thinly sliced*
¼	*cup thinly sliced celery*
1½	*tablespoons apple juice*
1	*tablespoon lemon juice*
1	*teaspoon extra-virgin olive oil*
½	*teaspoon Dijon mustard*
3	*cups torn romaine lettuce*
1	*head Belgian endive, leaves separated*
1	*tablespoon coarsely chopped toasted walnuts*
1½	*tablespoons (½ ounce) crumbled blue cheese (optional)*

In a medium bowl, combine the green apples, red apples and celery. In a small bowl, combine the apple juice, lemon juice, oil and mustard; mix well. Toss the apples with 1½ tablespoons of the dressing.

Place the romaine on a serving platter and arrange the endive leaves spoke fashion on top of the romaine. Drizzle the romaine with the remaining dressing. Place the apple mixture in the center of the platter and top with the walnuts and blue cheese.

Preparation time: 10 minutes

Per serving: 63 calories, 2.6 g. fat (34% of calories), 1.8 g. dietary fiber, no cholesterol, 30 mg. sodium.

ROASTED VEGETABLE SALAD
WITH TARRAGON MUSTARD DRESSING

SERVES 4

*T*arragon, with its subtle licorice flavor, complements the fresh vegetables in this elegant and colorful side dish.

Roasted Vegetables

½ *eggplant, peeled, quartered and cut into ½″ slices*
1 *zucchini, cut into ¼″ slices*
1 *sweet red pepper, cut into 1″ cubes*
1 *onion, cut into ¼″ slices*
2 *cloves garlic, minced*
2 *teaspoons extra-virgin olive oil*

Dressing

3 *tablespoons water*
1 *tablespoon tarragon vinegar*
1½ *teaspoons Dijon mustard*
1 *teaspoon extra-virgin olive oil*
1 *clove garlic, minced*

Salad

4 *cups torn mixed salad greens*
1 *tablespoon minced fresh tarragon*
1 *tablespoon toasted pine nuts*

To make the roasted vegetables: In a large bowl, combine the eggplant, zucchini, peppers, onions and garlic. Toss with the oil. Coat a 15″ × 10″ jelly-roll pan with no-stick spray. Place the vegetables in one layer in the pan. Bake at 425° for 15 minutes, or until the vegetables are crisp-tender. Cool to room temperature.

To make the dressing: In a small bowl, combine the water, vinegar, mustard, oil and garlic. Mix until well-combined.

To make the salad: In a large bowl, toss the salad greens with enough dressing to lightly coat the leaves. Place the greens on a serving platter. Toss the roasted vegetables with the remaining dressing; assemble the vegetables on top of the greens. Sprinkle with the tarragon and pine nuts.

Preparation time: 10 minutes
Baking time: 15 minutes

Per serving: 95 calories, 5 g. fat (44% of calories), 2 g. dietary fiber, no cholesterol, 39 mg. sodium.

RAINBOW VEGETABLE COLESLAW

SERVES 4

Coleslaw without cabbage? This colorful version tosses vegetables such as zucchini, snow peas, onions, sweet red peppers and carrots in a slaw-style dressing.

1½	cups coarsely shredded zucchini
1½	cups thinly sliced snow peas
¾	cup coarsely shredded carrots
¾	cup thinly sliced red onions
½	cup finely diced sweet red peppers
½	cup minced chives
⅓	cup nonfat mayonnaise
1	tablespoon skim milk
2½	teaspoons lemon juice
1	teaspoon Dijon mustard
¼	teaspoon ground black pepper

In a medium bowl, combine the zucchini, peas, carrots, onions, red peppers and chives. In a small bowl, combine the mayonnaise, milk, lemon juice, mustard and black pepper. Pour the dressing over the vegetables and toss.

Preparation time: 10 minutes

Per serving: 74 calories, 0.4 g. fat (5% of calories), 3.7 g. dietary fiber, no cholesterol, 284 mg. sodium.

SEDONA RED TACO SALAD

SERVES 4

*R*ed kidney beans, red salsa, red tomatoes, red onions and red sweet peppers give this taco salad its vibrant color, which is reminiscent of the red rock region of Sedona, Arizona.

6	*tablespoons mild salsa*
1½	*tablespoons lemon juice*
2	*teaspoons olive oil*
¾	*teaspoon ground cumin*
1	*can (15 ounces) red kidney beans, rinsed and drained*
4	*plum tomatoes, diced*
¼	*cup diced red onions*
4	*cups shredded red leaf lettuce*
½	*cup thinly sliced sweet red peppers*
½	*cup shredded low-fat Cheddar cheese*
1	*ounce baked (no-oil) tortilla chips*
2	*tablespoons fresh coriander leaves*

In a medium bowl, combine the salsa, lemon juice, oil and cumin; mix well. Add the beans, tomatoes and onions. Let the mixture marinate for 20 minutes.

To serve, place the lettuce on a serving platter, top with the beans and arrange the peppers and Cheddar on top. Surround with the tortilla chips and garnish with the coriander.

Preparation time: 10 minutes plus 20 minutes marinating time

Chef's note: To make your own low-fat taco chips, cut tortillas into strips or quarters, place on a baking sheet coated with no-stick cooking spray and bake at 350° for 10 minutes or until crisp and golden brown. Or, check your supermarket for chips that are baked with no oil.

Per serving: 224 calories, 6.3 g. fat (24% of calories), 8 g. dietary fiber, 6 mg. cholesterol, 650 mg. sodium.

New Potato Salad with Dill

SERVES 4

*L*eaving the skins on small, sweet new potatoes lends color to this updated version of a popular picnic and backyard barbecue side dish.

1 *pound new potatoes*
3 *hard-cooked eggs, white part only*
⅓ *cup sliced scallions*
¼ *cup thinly sliced radishes*
2 *tablespoons chopped fresh dill*
⅓ *cup nonfat mayonnaise*
¼ *cup nonfat sour cream*
3 *tablespoons skim milk*
1 *teaspoon white wine vinegar*
1 *teaspoon yellow mustard*

Place the potatoes in a large saucepan and cover with water. Bring to a boil over high heat, reduce the heat to medium and boil for 15 to 20 minutes, or until the potatoes are tender. Drain the potatoes, rinse them under cold water and let them cool; do not peel. Cut the potatoes into quarters and slice. In a medium bowl, combine the potatoes, egg whites, scallions, radishes and dill; toss gently.

In a small bowl, combine the mayonnaise, sour cream, milk, vinegar and mustard; mix well. Pour the dressing over the potato mixture and stir gently.

Preparation time: 10 minutes
Cooking time: 20 minutes

Chef's note: The potato skins add fiber as well as color to the salad, but you may peel the potatoes if you prefer.

Per serving: 151 calories, 0.2 g. fat (1% of calories), 0.4 g. dietary fiber, no cholesterol, 346 mg. sodium.

COOLING CUCUMBER COUSCOUS SALAD

---

ouscous is a granular form of pasta popular in Middle Eastern and African dishes. Serve this salad as a side dish with grilled chicken, turkey or lamb.

1½ cups plus 2 tablespoons defatted chicken stock
2 cloves garlic, minced
½ teaspoon salt-free lemon pepper seasoning
1 cup couscous
¼ cup diced carrots
1¼ cups diced cucumbers
¼ cup sliced scallions
1 tablespoon lemon juice
1 tablespoon extra-virgin olive oil

In a 2-quart saucepan, combine 1½ cups of the stock, the garlic and the lemon pepper seasoning. Bring to a boil over high heat, add the couscous and carrots, cover and remove from the heat. Let sit for 5 minutes. Fluff the mixture with a fork and spoon it into a large bowl.

In a blender container, combine ¼ cup of the cucumbers, the scallions, lemon juice, oil and the remaining 2 tablespoons of the stock. Blend on high speed for 15 to 20 seconds, or until smooth. Pour the dressing over the couscous and toss. Stir in the remaining 1 cup of the cucumbers. Refrigerate until cool.

Preparation time: 10 minutes
Cooking time: 5 minutes plus 5 minutes standing time

Chef's note: Hothouse cucumbers—sometimes called European or burpless cucumbers—are a good choice for this salad because they're quite sweet and their seeds are very small. If your cucumbers have many seeds, cut them in half lengthwise and scrape out the seeds before dicing.

Per serving: 148 calories, 2.5 g. fat (15% of calories), 5.2 g. dietary fiber, no cholesterol, 133 mg. sodium.

CHAPTER 5

CHICKEN
AND
TURKEY RULE
THE ROOST

PLAIN AND FANCY POULTRY

The poultry twins—chicken and turkey—have become the mainstay for Americans seeking a low-fat diet, and with good reason. Not only are they low in fat, but they're also incredibly versatile. Chicken and turkey can be baked, roasted, broiled, grilled, stir-fried and stewed. They're wonderfully suited for our melting pot of all-American cooking from meatloaf to pot pie, chili to quesadillas. And if that isn't enough, the poultry twins adapt as well to an elegant after-the-theater dinner party as to an easygoing Saturday night supper.

CHICKEN DIABLO

SERVES 4

eviled dishes were popular in the eighteenth and nineteenth centuries. Mustard is the ingredient that puts the "devil" in dishes such as deviled eggs, deviled crab, deviled ham and deviled ribs. This flavorful chicken dish is deviled with Dijon mustard.

4   *boneless, skinless chicken breast halves (4 ounces each)*
½   *teaspoon ground black pepper*
1   *cup sliced mushrooms*
1   *cup defatted chicken stock*
4   *teaspoons Dijon mustard*
½   *teaspoon dried tarragon*
1   *teaspoon cornstarch mixed with 1 tablespoon cold water*
¼   *cup fresh bread crumbs*

Coat a large no-stick frying pan with no-stick spray. Place the pan over medium heat for 2 minutes. Add the chicken and cook for 4 minutes on each side. Remove the chicken from the pan and season it with the pepper. Transfer to a baking dish large enough to hold the chicken in a single layer.

Preheat the broiler.

Add the mushrooms to the pan and cook until tender, about 3 minutes. Add the stock and bring to a boil. Whisk in the mustard and tarragon. Add the cornstarch mixture to the pan. Cook until the mixture thickens and the sauce looks shiny. Pour over the chicken. Top with the bread crumbs.

Broil 5″ from the heat for 3 to 5 minutes, or until the bread crumbs turn golden brown.

Preparation time: 10 minutes
Cooking time: 20 minutes
Broiling time: 5 minutes
Per serving: 113 calories, 2.5 g. fat (20% of calories), 0.4 g. dietary fiber, 46 mg. cholesterol, 240 mg. sodium.

GRILLED CHICKEN SANDWICH
WITH SUN-DRIED TOMATO MAYONNAISE

SERVES 4

Sun-dried tomatoes add a piquant touch to mayonnaise seasoned with roasted garlic. Sun drying makes tomatoes chewy, deep red and intensely flavorful. You'll find them packed in oil, in bags or available in bulk.

¼ *cup reduced-fat mayonnaise*

4 *cloves garlic, roasted (see note)*

2 *tablespoons minced and drained sun-dried tomatoes in oil*

1 *teaspoon lemon juice*

½ *teaspoon Dijon mustard*

4 *boneless, skinless chicken breast halves (4 ounces each)*

4 *thick slices sourdough bread*

In a medium bowl, combine the mayonnaise with the garlic, tomatoes, lemon juice and mustard. Mix well. Cook the chicken breasts over a charcoal fire for 6 to 8 minutes, or until cooked through, turning once. Coat both sides of the bread with olive oil no-stick spray. Cook each side until grill marks appear, less than 1 minute. Spread 1 tablespoon of the mayonnaise mixture on the bread and top with the chicken breasts.

Preparation time: 10 minutes
Grilling time: 10 minutes

Chef's note: Roasting mellows and sweetens garlic. To roast garlic, place the unpeeled cloves in aluminum foil, spray with no-stick spray and add 1 teaspoon of water. Seal the foil. Place on the grill or in a 400° oven and cook until the garlic softens, about 15 minutes.

Per serving: 251 calories, 8 g. fat (30% of calories), no dietary fiber, 73 mg. cholesterol, 301 mg. sodium.

CHICKEN PARMESAN

SERVES 4

*B*readed cutlets are an American tradition. To trim the fat from this popular recipe, we've used just a smidgen of olive oil and baked the cutlets rather than pan-frying them.

1 tablespoon olive oil

1 tablespoon minced garlic

½ teaspoon ground black pepper

2 teaspoons dried oregano

*4 boneless, skinless chicken breast halves
    (4 ounces each)*

1 cup fresh bread crumbs

2 tablespoons grated Parmesan cheese

1 cup prepared marinara sauce, heated

In a shallow bowl, combine the oil, garlic, pepper and 1 teaspoon of the oregano. Dip the chicken in this mixture. In a flat dish, mix the bread crumbs, Parmesan and the remaining 1 teaspoon oregano. Dredge the chicken in this mixture to coat both sides.

Coat a baking sheet with olive oil no-stick spray. Place the chicken on the prepared sheet. Coat the chicken with no-stick spray. Bake at 400° for 5 minutes. Flip the pieces and bake for 10 minutes, or until the chicken is crisp and golden brown.

Serve topped with the marinara sauce.

Preparation time: 10 minutes
Baking time: 15 minutes

Per serving: 158 calories, 4.6 g. fat (27% of calories), 0.7 g. dietary fiber, 48 mg. cholesterol, 260 mg. sodium.

Oven-Fried Chicken

SERVES 4

*W*hat's more American than fried chicken? We love this finger-lickin' good dish, whether it's Southern-style, Maryland-style or our own home-cooked style. Top this crisp-coated chicken with lemon juice and serve with corn on the cob, sliced tomatoes and whole-wheat biscuits.

½ *cup buttermilk*
1 *cup fresh bread crumbs*
1 *teaspoon paprika*
1 *teaspoon ground black pepper*
½ *teaspoon dried thyme*
½ *teaspoon onion powder*
4 *pieces skinless chicken legs and thighs*

Coat a wire rack with no-stick spray. Place the rack on a foil-lined baking sheet.

Place the buttermilk in a shallow pan. Place the bread crumbs in another shallow pan. Combine the paprika, pepper, thyme and onion powder. Season the bread crumbs with 1 teaspoon of the spice mixture. Add the remaining spices to the buttermilk.

Coat the chicken with the buttermilk. Roll the chicken pieces in the seasoned bread crumbs.

Place the chicken on the prepared rack. Coat the chicken with the no-stick spray.

Bake at 425° for 15 minutes. Turn the chicken, coat it again with the no-stick spray, and bake for 15 minutes more, or until golden brown.

Preparation time: 5 minutes
Baking time: 30 minutes

Per serving: 229 calories, 8.8 g. fat (36% of calories), no dietary fiber, 90 mg. cholesterol, 178 mg. sodium.

GRILLED BREAST OF CHICKEN
WITH TOMATO-BASIL RELISH

SERVES 4

Sweet-and-sour flavors are popular in Pennsylvania Dutch dishes. This recipe, with a sweet-and-sour fresh tomato relish, was inspired by that cooking heritage.

Tomato-Basil Relish

- ½ cup chopped onions
- 1 teaspoon canola oil
- 1 tablespoon cider vinegar
- 2 teaspoons brown sugar
- ½ cup tomato juice
- ½ teaspoon pickling spice
- 1 cup chopped tomatoes
- 1 tablespoon finely chopped fresh basil

Chicken and Marinade

- ½ cup chopped tomatoes
- 1 tablespoon minced garlic
- 2 teaspoons olive oil
- ½ teaspoon dried basil
- 4 boneless, skinless chicken breast halves (4 ounces each)

To make the tomato-basil relish: In a small frying pan over medium heat, sauté the onions in the oil until the onions turn translucent, about 4 minutes. Add the vinegar and brown sugar and cook until the onions turn the color of caramel, about 5 minutes.

In a small saucepan, combine the tomato juice and the pickling spice. Bring to a boil over medium heat and cook for 3 minutes.

In a medium bowl, combine the onions, tomato juice, tomatoes and basil; cool to room temperature.

To make the chicken and marinade: Combine the tomatoes, garlic, oil and basil in a shallow bowl large enough to hold the chicken. Marinate the breasts for 15 minutes. Remove the breasts from the marinade and cook them over a charcoal grill or in a stovetop grill pan for 6 to 8 minutes, or until the chicken is cooked through, turning once. Serve topped with the relish.

Preparation time: 15 minutes plus 15 minutes marinating time
Cooking time: 12 minutes
Grilling time: 8 minutes

Chef's note: Caramelized onions add depth of flavor to the tomato-basil relish.

Per serving: 196 calories, 5.3 g. fat (24% of calories), 1.6 g. dietary fiber, 73 mg. cholesterol, 181 mg. sodium.

FLORIDA CHICKEN

lorida's cuisine melds locally grown citrus fruit with the fire-and-spice seasonings imported from the Caribbean. For a special-occasion luncheon or dinner, serve this chicken—flavored with allspice, ginger, mace and red pepper and topped with a fresh fruit sauce—in a hollowed-out pineapple half.

Chicken and Marinade

- *1 cup chopped tangerine (rind and flesh)*
- *¼ cup pineapple juice*
- *4 allspice berries*
- *⅛ teaspoon ground mace*
- *⅛ teaspoon ground ginger*
- *⅛ teaspoon ground red pepper*
- *4 boneless, skinless chicken breast halves (4 ounces each)*

Fruit Sauce

- *1 cup orange sections*
- *½ cup pineapple cubes (packed in juice)*
- *½ cup sliced strawberries*
- *1 tablespoon chopped mint (optional)*

To make the chicken and marinade: Place the tangerine, pineapple juice, allspice, mace, ginger and pepper in a food processor. Process for 20 seconds. Reserve 1 tablespoon of the marinade and place in a medium bowl. Set aside.

Put the chicken in a shallow bowl and pour the marinade from the processor over it. Cover and marinate for 15 minutes in the refrigerator.

Remove the chicken from the marinade; discard the marinade. Broil or grill the chicken for 4 to 5 minutes per side, or until cooked through.

To make the fruit sauce: In the bowl containing the reserved marinade, combine the oranges, pineapple, strawberries and mint. Mix well and serve with the chicken.

Preparation time: 10 minutes plus 15 minutes marinating time
Broiling time: 10 minutes

Chef's notes: Clementines, minneolas and navel oranges are all suitable replacements for the tangerine.

The chicken shows well on a bed of steamed spinach or kale topped with the fruit sauce and garnished with red and green pepper strips and fresh mint leaves.

Per serving: 155 calories, 2.3 g. fat (13% of calories), 2.5 g. dietary fiber, 46 mg. cholesterol, 41 mg. sodium.

CHICKEN QUESADILLAS

To enhance the color and flavor of these quesadillas, sprinkle an assortment of condiments on top. Chopped red peppers, onions, tomatoes, radishes and avocado are good choices.

¼ *cup lime juice*

2 *tablespoons chopped fresh coriander*

1 *serrano chili pepper, seeded and finely chopped (wear rubber gloves when handling)*

4 *boneless, skinless chicken breast halves (4 ounces each)*

1 *sweet red pepper, seeded and thinly sliced*

1 *green pepper, seeded and thinly sliced*

1 *cup scallions sliced into 1" lengths*

1 *cup thinly sliced mushrooms*

½ *cup jalapeño jelly*

8 *flour tortillas, 8" in diameter*

In a shallow bowl large enough to hold the chicken, combine the lime juice, coriander, chili peppers and chicken. Cover and marinate for 15 minutes. Remove the chicken from the marinade and cook it for 6 to 8 minutes over a charcoal fire or in a stovetop grill pan, turning once, until the chicken is cooked through. Thinly slice the chicken on the diagonal.

Coat a large no-stick frying pan with no-stick spray. Add the red peppers, green peppers, scallions and mushrooms and cook over medium heat until the onions are golden and the vegetables are tender. Add the jalapeño jelly and cook until the jelly melts.

Coat a baking sheet with no-stick spray. Combine the chicken and the vegetables. Divide among the tortillas. Place the tortillas on the prepared baking sheet and bake them at 400° for 5 minutes.

Preparation time: 5 minutes plus 15 minutes marinating time
Cooking time: 15 minutes
Baking time: 5 minutes

Per serving: 401 calories, 5.7 g. fat (13% of calories), 2.9 g. dietary fiber, 46 mg. cholesterol, 52 mg. sodium.

LEMON MUSTARD MEATLOAF

SERVES 4

Comfort food is a term coined to describe homestyle cooking and foods that make us feel cozy. Meatloaf is the "king" of comfort foods, especially when served with mashed potatoes and a salad. This version is lower in fat because it uses lean ground chicken instead of beef and egg whites instead of a whole egg. For quicker cooking, it's baked in a small loaf pan.

12 ounces lean ground chicken
2 medium carrots, peeled and shredded
1 cup fresh bread crumbs
2 egg whites
1 tablespoon Dijon mustard
1 teaspoon grated lemon rind
1 teaspoon dried thyme
¼ teaspoon ground black pepper

Coat a 6″ × 2″ loaf pan with no-stick spray. In a medium bowl, combine the chicken, carrots and bread crumbs. Mix well. In another medium bowl, whisk the egg whites until frothy, about 3 minutes. Add the mustard, lemon rind, thyme and pepper to the whites. Mix well. Combine the egg white mixture with the ground chicken. Place the meatloaf in the prepared pan.

Bake at 350° for 30 minutes, or until a meat thermometer inserted in the center registers 160° and the juices run clear when the meat is pierced with a sharp knife.

Preparation time: 15 minutes
Baking time: 30 minutes
Per serving: 150 calories, 3.1 g. fat (19% of calories), 1.5 g. dietary fiber, 45 mg. cholesterol, 189 mg. sodium.

10 Ways to Use Boneless, Skinless Chicken Cutlets

*B*oneless, skinless chicken cutlets can be the building blocks of a great and easy-to-prepare dinner. Low-fat and versatile, chicken cutlets are ideal for broiling, grilling and stir-frying.

1. Kabobs. Cut the cutlets into 1″ pieces. Marinate in lemon juice, low-sodium soy sauce and ginger. Thread the chicken onto skewers, alternating chicken pieces with mushrooms and chunks of onions, green peppers and tomatoes. Cook on the grill until the chicken is well-done.

2. Herbed. Brush the cutlets lightly with olive oil, then thickly coat with dried herbs such as lemon or cinnamon basil, thyme or an herb combination. Cook on the grill, in a stovetop grill pan or under the broiler. Serve as a main dish or cut into chunks for pasta or wild rice salad.

3. Stir-Fried. Cut the cutlets into ½″ strips. Heat a wok or frying pan, adding a drop or two of sesame oil. Add finely chopped garlic. Stir-fry the garlic until lightly browned. Stir in the chicken strips. Toss lightly until the chicken is white. Add beans sprouts and chunks of green peppers, onions and pineapple. Sprinkle with low-sodium soy sauce; add pineapple juice and stir-fry until the vegetables are heated through and slightly tender. Serve on a bed of rice.

4. Grilled. While grilling the cutlets, brush them with a variety of low-fat condiments such as apricot jam, Dijon mustard, barbecue sauce or a mixture of ground ginger, low-sodium soy sauce and honey. Use these cutlets in sandwiches and salads or serve as a main dish.

5. Fajitas. Cut the cutlets into ½″ strips. Coat a frying pan with no-stick spray and heat. Sprinkle with taco seasoning and add the chicken strips. Cook until the chicken is white. Serve with nonfat refried black beans, chopped onions, salsa, grated low-fat cheese, nonfat sour cream and tortillas.

6. Sandwiches. Grill the cutlets on the grill or in a stovetop grill pan. Tuck into a sourdough bun with lettuce, tomato and reduced-fat mayonnaise, or top with your favorite sandwich ingredients.

7. Salads. Cut cooked cutlets into chunks or strips and toss into Caesar, mixed green, chef or cobb salad.

8. Soups. Adding chunks of chicken to low-sodium and low-fat cream, vegetable or tomato soups transforms them into a light supper when served with crusty bread and fresh fruit.

9. Nuggets. Dredge chunks of chicken cutlets in bread crumbs seasoned with ground red pepper, herbs, Italian seasoning or taco seasoning. Coat a frying pan with no-stick spray and heat. Add the coated chicken nuggets, gently tossing until the bread crumbs are brown and the chicken is fully cooked.

10. Rolls. Lightly pound the chicken cutlets to an even thickness. Sprinkle with pepper, fresh or dried herbs and Parmesan cheese. Roll the cutlets and secure with toothpicks. Place in a microwave-safe dish and sprinkle with herbs. Microwave on high power until the chicken is white and the juices run clear when the meat is pierced with a sharp knife.

CHICKEN AND WHITE BEAN CHILI

SERVES 4

*T*here's nothing bland about this paler version of chili con carne. Jalapeños and roasted chilies give it zing—but you can adjust the "heat index" to your tastes by cutting back on quantities. It's also a great everyday chili—make it ahead on weekends and freeze for a quick supper on those hectic weeknights.

2	*tablespoons canola oil*
1	*cup diced onions*
12	*ounces boneless, skinless chicken thighs, cubed*
½	*cup chopped canned tomatillos or ½ cup green salsa (salsa verde)*
1	*can (4 ounces) roasted and peeled chopped chili peppers, rinsed*
1	*tablespoon minced garlic*
2	*teaspoons chili powder*
1	*teaspoon ground cumin*
	Pinch of ground cinnamon
1¾	*cups canned white beans, rinsed and drained*
1	*cup defatted chicken stock*
½	*cup chopped tomatoes*
2	*teaspoons minced jalapeño peppers (wear rubber gloves when handling)*

In a 2-quart saucepan over medium heat, warm the oil and add the onions. Sauté until translucent, about 3 minutes. Add the chicken and sauté until the chicken loses its raw look. Add the tomatillos or salsa, chili peppers, garlic, chili powder, cumin and cinnamon. Bring to a boil. Add the beans, stock, tomatoes and jalapeño peppers. Simmer for 20 minutes.

Preparation time: 10 minutes
Cooking time: 30 minutes

Per serving: 402 calories, 16.3 g. fat (36% of calories), 1.8 g. dietary fiber, 76 mg. cholesterol, 535 mg. sodium.

Buffalo Drummettes

SERVES 4

*P*opular as appetizers, these spicy-hot mini chicken "legs" are really made from a section of the wing. Cool them down with a tart, blue cheese dipping sauce. This recipe was inspired by Theresa Bellissimo's Buffalo Chicken Wings served at the Anchor Bar in Buffalo, New York.

Chicken Wings

¼	*cup defatted chicken stock*
2	*tablespoons hot-pepper sauce*
16	*skinned chicken wing drummettes*
1⅔	*cups fresh bread crumbs*

Dipping Sauce

½	*cup diced celery*
¼	*cup fat-free cottage cheese*
¼	*cup reduced-fat mayonnaise*
1	*tablespoon crumbled blue cheese*
1	*tablespoon minced onions*
1	*teaspoon red wine vinegar*

To make the chicken wings: Coat a wire rack with no-stick spray. Place the rack on a foil-lined baking sheet. Combine the stock and hot-pepper sauce in a shallow bowl; dip the chicken into this mixture. Place the bread crumbs in a flat dish; dip the chicken into the bread crumbs. Place the chicken on the prepared rack; coat the chicken with no-stick spray. Bake at 450° for 25 minutes, or until crisp and golden brown.

To make the dipping sauce: In a medium bowl, combine the celery, cottage cheese, mayonnaise, blue cheese, onions and vinegar. Cover and refrigerate until the drummettes are cooked. Serve the sauce with the chicken drummettes.

Preparation time: 10 minutes
Baking time: 25 minutes
Per serving: 232 calories, 6.2 g. fat (25% of calories), 0.8 g. dietary fiber, 82 mg. cholesterol, 469 mg. sodium.

CHICKEN POT PIE WITH HERBED LEMON BISCUITS

*P*ot pie may be our first TV dinner! A descendant of the Pennsylvania Dutch bott-boi, a thick stew topped with wide egg noodles, the name "pot pie" appeared in America in 1792. C. A. Swanson made the first frozen chicken pot pie in 1951—just as television began coming into our living rooms.

Chicken Pot Pie

½ *cup pearl onions*

2 *teaspoons canola oil*

12 *ounces chicken, cut into ½" pieces*

1 *cup diced cooked potatoes*

1 *cup snow peas, ends and strings removed*

½ *cup thinly sliced cooked carrots*

½ *cup defatted chicken stock*

¼ *teaspoon dried tarragon*

¼ *teaspoon ground black pepper*

¼ *teaspoon dried dill*

2 *teaspoons cornstarch mixed with 1 tablespoon cold water*

Herbed Lemon Biscuits

½ *cup unbleached flour*

¼ *cup whole-wheat flour*

¼ *cup cake flour*

2 *teaspoons baking powder*

1 *teaspoon dried dill*

¼ *teaspoon salt*

½ *cup buttermilk*

¼ *cup canola oil*

1 *teaspoon grated lemon rind*

To make the chicken pot pie: In a 2-quart saucepan, sauté the onions in the oil until golden brown, about 6 minutes. Add the chicken and cook for 3 minutes. Add the potatoes, peas, carrots, stock, tarragon, pepper and dill. Cook over medium-low heat until the mixture boils. Add the cornstarch mixture to the chicken mixture. Cook until the sauce thickens and becomes shiny, about 2 minutes.

To make the herbed lemon biscuits: Coat a baking sheet with no-stick spray. Preheat the oven to 425°. In a medium bowl, sift the unbleached flour, whole-wheat flour, cake flour, baking powder, dill and salt. In a small bowl, mix the buttermilk, oil and lemon rind. Add to the dry mixture. Mix only to moisten the dry ingredients. Spoon the batter in 6 mounds onto the prepared baking sheet. Bake the biscuits for 15 minutes, or until the tops are golden. Top the pot pie with the biscuits.

Preparation time: 15 minutes
Cooking time: 15 minutes
Baking time: 15 minutes

Per serving: 479 calories, 22.4 g. fat (42% of calories), 3.6 g. dietary fiber, 72 mg. cholesterol, 458 mg. sodium.

SPICED CHICKEN PATTIES
WITH ONIONS AND PEPPERS

SERVES 4

*F*ennel, garlic and Italian seasoning give these grilled patties a flavor reminiscent of what's served at Little Italy street festivals in New York City. Smothered with sautéed red and green peppers, they can be served as a sandwich or as a main dish with pasta and a mixed green salad.

Chicken Patties

12 *ounces lean ground chicken*
2 *teaspoons minced garlic*
2 *teaspoons fennel seeds*
1 *teaspoon dried Italian seasoning*
¼ *teaspoon red-pepper flakes*
⅛ *teaspoon ground black pepper*

Onions and Peppers

2 *cups sliced onions*
1 *sweet red pepper, sliced into thin strips*
1 *green pepper, sliced into thin strips*
2 *teaspoons olive oil*
1 *teaspoon dried Italian seasoning*

To make the chicken patties: Heat a stovetop grill pan for 3 minutes. Combine the chicken, garlic, fennel seeds, Italian seasoning, pepper flakes and black pepper. Mix well. Shape the mixture into 4 patties. Cook the patties in the preheated pan for 6 minutes per side, or until the juices run clear when the meat is pierced with a sharp knife.

To make the onions and peppers: Heat a large no-stick frying pan for 2 minutes. Combine the onions, red peppers, green peppers, oil and Italian seasoning; blend. Sauté over medium heat for 10 minutes, or until the onions are golden and the peppers are tender.

Preparation time: 15 minutes
Cooking time: 25 minutes

Per serving: 210 calories, 6.7 g. fat (29% of calories), 2.5 g. dietary fiber, 59 mg. cholesterol, 60 mg. sodium.

SLOPPY JOSEPHINES

SERVES 4

*S*isters to Sloppy Joes, these sandwiches substitute ground turkey for beef. But even the most dedicated beef lover won't miss the burger. Serve the filling with cornbread or spoon it into onion rolls.

2	*teaspoons canola oil*
1	*cup chopped onions*
1	*cup diced sweet red peppers*
12	*ounces lean ground turkey*
2	*teaspoons all-purpose salt-free seasoning*
1	*cup tomato sauce*
½	*cup reduced-sodium ketchup*
2	*tablespoons chili sauce*
2	*teaspoons red wine vinegar*
1	*teaspoon dark brown sugar*
¼	*teaspoon ground black pepper*

In a 3-quart saucepan, heat the oil. Add the onions and red peppers and cook until the onions are translucent, about 3 minutes. Add the turkey and the salt-free seasoning, and cook until the turkey loses its raw look, about 5 minutes. Add the tomato sauce, ketchup, chili sauce, vinegar, brown sugar and black pepper. Mix well and simmer for 15 minutes.

Preparation time: 15 minutes
Cooking time: 25 minutes

Per serving: 193 calories, 8.8 g. fat (40% of calories), 1.9 g. dietary fiber, 32 mg. cholesterol, 691 mg. sodium.

TURKEY STROGANOFF

aprika is a powder ground from chili peppers grown in Central Europe, especially Hungary. It seasons traditional Hungarian dishes, adding a brick red color and just a bit of bite. Serve this dish with wide-cut noodles topped with toasted caraway seeds, braised cabbage and warm rye bread.

- 2 *cups thinly sliced onions*
- 2 *teaspoons canola oil*
- 2 *cups thinly sliced mushrooms*
- 1 *teaspoon Hungarian paprika*
- ½ *teaspoon ground black pepper*
- ¾ *cup defatted chicken stock*
- 1 *cup nonfat sour cream*
- ½ *teaspoon Dijon mustard*
- 12 *ounces turkey breast tenderloin*

Heat a large no-stick frying pan over medium heat. Add the onions and oil and cook until the onions are translucent, about 3 minutes. Add the mushrooms and cook for 2 minutes. Add the paprika, pepper and stock. Bring to a boil. Add the sour cream and mustard and blend well. Simmer over low heat, about 3 minutes.

Slice the turkey breast, crosswise, into ¼″ cutlets. Coat both sides of each cutlet with no-stick spray. Cook over a charcoal grill, about 2 minutes per side, or until cooked through.

To serve, top the turkey with the stroganoff sauce.

Preparation time: 10 minutes
Cooking time: 10 minutes
Grilling time: 4 minutes

Chef's notes: To cook indoors, broil the turkey 4″ to 6″ from the heat for 3 to 4 minutes per side, or until cooked through.

Some sour creams thicken more than others. You may need to adjust the amount of stock based on the brand you use.

Per serving: 209 calories, 4.4 g. fat (19% of calories), 1.8 g. dietary fiber, 37 mg. cholesterol, 215 mg. sodium.

LEMON TURKEY TENDERS

SERVES 4

*T*urkey tenders are cutlets from the breast. To garnish this Lemon Chicken–like recipe, roll peeled lemon slices in fresh, minced herbs such as thyme or mint. Place a lemon slice on each plate or arrange them on the serving platter.

> 4   *turkey breast cutlets, ¼" thick*
> ¼   *cup whole-wheat flour*
> 4   *teaspoons canola oil*
> ½   *cup defatted chicken stock*
> 1   *teaspoon grated lemon rind*
> 1   *teaspoon fresh thyme*
> 1   *teaspoon cornstarch mixed with*
>   *1 tablespoon cold water*

Dredge the cutlets in the whole-wheat flour. Heat the oil in a large no-stick frying. Add the turkey cutlets and cook for 1 minute per side, or until a light golden brown. Remove the turkey from the pan. Add the stock, lemon rind and thyme to the pan. Bring to a boil. Add the cornstarch mixture to the pan. Cook over medium heat until the mixture thickens and becomes glossy, about 2 minutes. Add the turkey. Heat for 2 minutes and serve.

Preparation time: 10 minutes
Cooking time: 10 minutes

Per serving: 186 calories, 5.3 g. fat (26% of calories), 1 g. dietary fiber, 71 mg. cholesterol, 104 mg. sodium.

BERRY GOOD TURKEY

SERVES 4

*S*piced cranberry sauce adds tang to this open-faced turkey sandwich.

- *4 turkey breast cutlets, ¼" thick*
- *4 slices whole-wheat raisin bread*
- *1 cup cranberries*
- *¼ cup water*
- *2 tablespoons cranberry juice concentrate*
- *½ teaspoon ground ginger*
- *2 cinnamon sticks*
- *2 whole cloves*
- *2 tablespoons maple syrup*

Coat a large no-stick frying pan with no-stick spray. Cook the turkey cutlets over low heat for 2 minutes per side, or until cooked through.

Toast the bread.

In a medium saucepan, cook the cranberries, water and concentrate for 2 minutes. Add the ginger. Place the cinnamon sticks and cloves in a tea ball (or tie in a piece of cheesecloth); add to the saucepan. Simmer until the berries pop or split, about 5 minutes. Stir in the maple syrup. Set aside.

To serve: Remove the tea ball. Place the turkey on the toast and top with the cranberry sauce.

Preparation time: 10 minutes
Cooking time: 15 minutes

Per serving: 242 calories, 1.7 g. fat (6% of calories), 0.6 g. dietary fiber, 71 mg. cholesterol, 141 mg. sodium.

TURKEY STEW

SERVES 4

*C*arrots and cranberries bring a touch of color to this stew. Serve it with crusty whole-wheat bread, poached pears in vanilla sauce and chilled apple cider for a hearty autumn supper.

1	cup small, whole peeled onions
½	cup thinly sliced carrots
2	teaspoons canola oil
12	ounces thinly sliced turkey breast
3	tablespoons whole-wheat flour
1½	cups stock made from a ham hock (see note)
1	cup dried cranberries
2	cups cooked, diced potatoes
½	teaspoon ground black pepper
½	teaspoon dried thyme
½	teaspoon dried marjoram
½	teaspoon dried sage

In a 3-quart saucepan, combine the onions, carrots and oil. Cook for 5 minutes. Add the turkey and cook for 3 minutes, or until the turkey loses its raw look. Add the flour, stir for 1 minute, and cook for 3 minutes more. Add the stock, cranberries, potatoes, pepper, thyme, marjoram and sage. Bring to a boil. Reduce the heat to low and simmer for 15 minutes.

Preparation time: 10 minutes
Cooking time: 30 minutes

Chef's note: To make the ham stock, combine 1 cup defatted chicken broth and ½ cup water. Add an 8-ounce ham hock and simmer for 30 minutes.

Per serving: 273 calories, 3.9 g. fat (13% of calories), 2.6 g. dietary fiber, 71 mg. cholesterol, 75 mg. sodium.

STUFFED PEPPERS

SERVES 4

*R*ed and green sweet peppers are the serving "boats" for the well-seasoned turkey-rice stuffing in this recipe. For variety, try other colors of peppers such as yellow and purple, but remember, purple peppers turn green when cooked.

　1　*large sweet red pepper*
　1　*large green pepper*
　1½　*cups cooked mixed grains or brown rice*
　½　*cup diced onions*
　¼　*cup defatted chicken or vegetable stock*
　1　*teaspoon grated orange rind*
　½　*teaspoon ground black pepper*
　6　*ounces lean ground turkey*
　3　*cloves garlic*
　¼　*cup finely diced dill pickles*
　1　*carrot, shredded*
　1　*egg white, lightly beaten*
　1　*teaspoon yellow mustard*
　¼　*cup nonfat sour cream*
　½　*teaspoon dried dill*

Cut the red pepper and green pepper in half; remove the seeds and ribs. Blanch, drain and set them aside. In a 1-quart saucepan, combine the cooked grains or rice, onions, stock, orange rind and black pepper. Cook over medium heat for 3 minutes. Add the turkey and cook until the turkey loses its raw look; drain.

Add the garlic, pickles, carrots, egg white and mustard. Mix well.

Fill the pepper halves with the turkey mixture. Place in a shallow pan large enough to hold the pepper halves in a single layer. Pour ½ cup of water into the pan and bake at 375° for 15 minutes. Combine the sour cream and dill. Garnish the peppers with the sour cream mixture.

Preparation time: 15 minutes
Cooking time: 5 minutes
Baking time: 15 minutes

Per serving: 190 calories, 4 g. fat (19% of calories), 2.6 g. dietary fiber, 16 mg. cholesterol, 260 mg. sodium.

TURKEY CIOPPINO

SERVES 4

Cioppino originated at San Francisco's Fisherman's Wharf. We've substituted turkey for seafood in this chunky stew. Serve it piping hot with sourdough bread.

  1   *tablespoon olive oil*
  1   *cup diced onions*
  1   *cup diced green peppers*
  1   *cup diced sweet red peppers*
  8   *cloves garlic (size of almonds), sliced thin*
12   *ounces turkey, white and dark meat, cubed*
  1   *cup salt-free tomato sauce*
  1   *cup defatted chicken stock*
  2   *teaspoons dried basil*
  1   *teaspoon red-pepper flakes*
 ½   *teaspoon ground black pepper*
 ¼   *cup fresh Italian parsley*
  2   *teaspoons grated lemon rind*

In a 3-quart saucepan, combine the oil, onions, green peppers, sweet red peppers, garlic and turkey. Cook for 3 to 5 minutes, or until the turkey loses its raw look. Add the tomato sauce, stock, basil, pepper flakes and black pepper. Simmer for 15 minutes. Add the parsley and lemon rind.

Preparation time: 10 minutes
Cooking time: 20 minutes

Per serving: 196 calories, 6.8 g. fat (31% of calories), 2.3 g. dietary fiber, 45 mg. cholesterol, 180 mg. sodium.

HONEY MUSTARD TURKEY THIGHS

*S*weet and tangy, these broiled and breaded turkey thighs can be served as a sandwich or main dish. Round out the meal with new potatoes, broccoli and a fruit salad.

¼	cup lemon juice
2	tablespoons Dijon mustard
2	tablespoons honey
1	teaspoon grated fresh ginger
½	teaspoon dried rosemary
4	boneless, skinless turkey thighs
½	cup fresh bread crumbs

Combine the lemon juice, mustard, honey, ginger and rosemary in a cup or small pitcher. Place the turkey thighs between two sheets of wax paper and pound to equal thickness. Put the turkey in a shallow bowl and pour ½ of the honey-mustard sauce over it. Cover and let marinate for 15 minutes.

Preheat the broiler. Coat a wire rack with no-stick spray and place the rack on a foil-lined baking sheet. Coat the thighs with the bread crumbs. Place the marinated thighs on the prepared rack. Broil 8″ from the heat for 6 to 8 minutes per side, or until the turkey is cooked through and the crumbs are golden brown.

In a small saucepan, warm the reserved sauce over low heat. Serve with the turkey.

Preparation time: 10 minutes plus 15 minutes marinating time
Broiling time: 15 minutes

Chef's note: To keep the bread crumbs from burning before the turkey cooks, place the meat at least 8″ from the broiler.

Per serving: 183 calories, 6.3 g. fat (32% of calories), 0.2 g. dietary fiber, 70 mg. cholesterol, 127 mg. sodium.

Florida Chicken (page 94)

113

Chicken Pot Pie with Herbed Lemon Biscuits (page 102)

Stuffed Peppers (page 110)

115

Cornmeal-Breaded Catfish with Sweet Pepper Relish (page 136)

Grilled Swordfish Kabobs (page 143)

117

Steamed Mussels with Tomatoes and Saffron (page 144)

Chesapeake Bay Crab Cakes with Red Pepper Tartar Sauce (page 150)

Fajitas with Coriander Cream (page 156)

Turkey Kabobs

SERVES 4

*C*ucumber-dill sauce complements these grilled, herbed kabobs. Complete the meal with a mixed-grain pilaf, warm pita bread and sliced cherry tomatoes tossed in olive oil and fresh basil.

Turkey and Marinade

2	*tablespoons lemon juice*
2	*teaspoons canola oil*
2	*teaspoons minced garlic*
2	*teaspoons dried oregano*
12	*ounces boneless, skinless turkey thighs, cut into 1" cubes*
1	*small red onion, quartered and separated*

Sauce

½	*cup finely chopped peeled cucumbers*
½	*cup nonfat sour cream*
2	*tablespoons minced red onions*
½	*teaspoon dried dill*

To make the turkey and marinade: Combine the lemon juice, oil, garlic and oregano in a shallow bowl large enough to hold the turkey. Add the turkey and marinate for 15 minutes. Soak 8 bamboo skewers in water while the turkey marinates. Thread alternating cubes of turkey with sections of the red onion. Cook over a charcoal fire for 3 to 4 minutes per side. Serve with the sauce.

To make the sauce: In a small bowl, combine the cucumbers, sour cream, onions and dill. Mix well. Chill until needed.

Preparation time: 5 minutes plus 15 minutes marinating time
Grilling time: 8 minutes

Per serving: 165 calories, 5.3 g. fat (30% of calories), 0.5 g. dietary fiber, 52 mg. cholesterol, 90 mg. sodium.

TURKEY POSOLE

*P*osole is a stew made with hominy—dried corn with the hull and germ removed. Hominy may be coarsely ground for grits or boiled whole. In this recipe, we've used canned hominy, which is available in both white and yellow corn varieties. Or you may want to substitute fresh corn. Posole thickens when refrigerated, so you may need to add more broth when you reheat the stew.

12 *ounces turkey meat, cubed*
1 *cup diced onions*
2 *teaspoons canola oil*
1 *can (4 ounces) roasted and peeled chopped*
 green chili peppers, rinsed
4 *ounces green salsa (salsa verde)*
8 *ounces defatted chicken stock*
2 *cups white hominy, rinsed and drained*
2 *teaspoons cumin seed*
1 *teaspoon dried oregano*
½ *cup chopped fresh coriander*

In a 3-quart saucepan, cook the turkey with the onions in the oil for 5 minutes, or until brown. Add the peppers, salsa, stock, hominy, cumin and oregano. Cook over medium heat for 15 minutes. Add the coriander.

Preparation time: 5 minutes
Cooking time: 20 minutes

Chef's notes: To serve, garnish with sliced radishes, sliced scallions and diced jícama to add texture to the posole. Jícama is a crunchy, sweet, large white root vegetable also known as a Mexican potato.

Salsa verde is salsa made from green chilies. Its heat index ranges from mild to very hot.

Per serving: 213 calories, 6.4 g. fat (26% of calories), 3.7 g. dietary fiber, 37 mg. cholesterol, 855 mg. sodium.

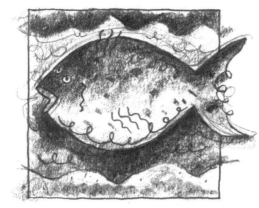

CHAPTER 6

FAMILY
PLEASERS
PLUS
COMPANY
FARE

SEAFOOD FOR ALL OCCASIONS

Littleneck clams, rainbow trout and walleyed pike. Catfish, soft-shelled crabs and shrimp. Lobster, salmon and orange roughy. This list just begins to touch on the incredible variety of finned and shelled creatures that inhabit our lakes, rivers, streams and oceans—and lend versatility and flavor to our diets. Seafood and fish—often called "brain food" and for good reason—are excellent sources of a whole alphabet of vitamins and minerals from vitamin A to calcium to protein. Many fish also are virtually fat-free. As a bonus, fish and seafood can be as casual as crisp-crusted fish sticks or as elegant as Oysters Rockefeller.

HALIBUT WITH SWEET RED PEPPER SAUCE

SERVES 4

*H*alibut season coincides with our May-to-September grilling season. Take advantage of this meaty fish for your barbecues.

Halibut

- 4   1"-thick halibut steaks (6 ounces each)
- 2   teaspoons extra-virgin olive oil
- 2   teaspoons chopped fresh lemon thyme (see note)

Sauce

- 1   jar (7 ounces) roasted red peppers, rinsed and drained
- 1   teaspoon extra-virgin olive oil
- 2   tablespoons minced shallots
- 1   teaspoon unbleached flour
- 3   tablespoons defatted chicken stock

To make the halibut: Coat the halibut with the oil. Sprinkle with the lemon thyme and refrigerate for 20 minutes.

Grill the halibut over hot coals or broil 4″ from the heat for 10 to 15 minutes, or until the fish turns opaque and just begins to flake when gently pressed. While the fish is cooking, make the sauce.

To make the sauce: Dry the peppers on paper towels and place in a food processor. Process until the peppers are pureed; set aside.

In a medium saucepan, heat the oil over medium heat until hot. Add the shallots and cook for 30 to 40 seconds. Whisk in the flour and continue to cook another 30 seconds, stirring constantly. Add the stock and pureed peppers, bring to a boil, reduce the heat to low and simmer for 5 minutes. Serve warm over the halibut.

Preparation time: 5 minutes plus 20 minutes marinating time
Grilling time: 15 minutes
Cooking time: 6 minutes

Chef's note: If lemon thyme is unavailable, substitute 2 teaspoons fresh thyme or ¾ teaspoon dried thyme and 1 teaspoon grated lemon rind.

Per serving: 236 calories, 7.4 g. fat (29% of calories), 0.8 g. dietary fiber, 55 mg. cholesterol, 116 mg. sodium.

NORTHWOODS WALLEYED PIKE

SERVES 4

*A*nglers seek the wily walleye for its firm, tender, sweet meat. This "shore lunch" of crisp, breaded fillets that are baked rather than fried is topped with crunchy onion rings.

¾	cup dry bread crumbs
½	cup grated Parmesan cheese
1½	tablespoons no-salt lemon pepper seasoning
2	teaspoons finely minced garlic
½	cup fat-free egg substitute
4	walleyed pike fillets (5 ounces each)
1	onion

Coat a 15″ × 10″ jelly-roll pan with no-stick spray. In a shallow pan, combine the bread crumbs, Parmesan, lemon pepper seasoning and garlic. Pour the eggs into a second shallow pan. Dip the walleye fillets into the eggs, then place in the bread crumbs, coating well. Place in the prepared pan. Lightly spray the fillets with no-stick spray.

Slice the onion crosswise and separate into rings. Dip the onion rings in the eggs and bread crumbs as directed for the fillets and place on the same baking pan. Bake at 475° for 8 to 12 minutes, or until lightly browned and the fish just begins to flake when gently pressed. To serve, top each fillet with 2 onion rings.

Preparation time: 5 minutes
Baking time: 12 minutes

Per serving: 294 calories, 5.8 g. fat (18% of calories), 1.9 g. dietary fiber, 66 mg. cholesterol, 469 mg. sodium.

FLORIDA SNAPPER WITH GINGERED PINEAPPLE ORANGE SAUCE

SERVES 4

*F*resh ginger adds bite to this sweet-spicy hot sauce. Red snapper is a firm-fleshed, mild-flavored fish that adapts well to many recipes.

Sauce

1   teaspoon olive oil
2   cloves garlic, minced
1   teaspoon grated fresh ginger
1   cup orange juice
2   teaspoons cornstarch mixed with
    1 tablespoon water
⅛   teaspoon red-pepper flakes
    Pinch of ground allspice
¼   cup crushed pineapple (fresh or packed in juice)

Fish

4   red snapper fillets (6 ounces each)
    Ground black pepper
    Fresh chives

To make the sauce: Heat the oil in a medium frying pan over medium heat. Add the garlic and ginger and sauté for 1 minute. Add the orange juice, cornstarch mixture, pepper flakes and allspice. Bring to a boil and cook until thickened, stirring occasionally. Stir in the pineapple, reduce the heat to low and simmer for 5 minutes.

To make the fish: Coat a shallow baking pan with no-stick spray. Lay the fillets in the pan; sprinkle with pepper and lightly coat with no-stick spray. Bake at 450° for 8 to 12 minutes, or until the fish turns opaque and just begins to flake when gently pressed. Serve with the warm sauce and garnish with the chives.

Preparation time: 10 minutes
Cooking time: 8 minutes
Baking time: 12 minutes

Per serving: 220 calories, 3.6 g. fat (15% of calories), 0.6 g. dietary fiber, 62 mg. cholesterol, 76 mg. sodium.

BROILED RAINBOW TROUT WITH PINE NUTS

SERVES 4

*R*ainbow trout is coveted for its sweet flavor and tender, melt-in-your-mouth meat. This elegant, but easy, recipe showcases the trout and makes a perfect special-occasion main dish.

2   *tablespoons lemon juice*
1   *tablespoon minced lemon thyme (see note)*
1   *teaspoon extra-virgin olive oil*
1   *clove garlic, minced*
4   *whole, boneless rainbow trout (5 ounces each)*
2   *tablespoons pine nuts, coarsely chopped*

In a small cup, mix together the lemon juice, thyme, oil and garlic.

Line a 15″ × 10″ jelly-roll pan with foil; coat the foil with no-stick spray. Open the trout and place it, skin side down, in the prepared pan. Sprinkle the trout with the pine nuts and brush with the lemon mixture. Refrigerate for 5 to 10 minutes to allow the flavors to mingle.

Broil 3″ to 4″ from the heat for 2 to 5 minutes, or until the trout turns opaque and just begins to flake when gently pressed.

Preparation time: 5 minutes plus 10 minutes standing time
Broiling time: 5 minutes

Chef's note: If lemon thyme is not available, substitute 1 table-spoon fresh thyme or 1 teaspoon dried thyme and 1 teaspoon grated lemon rind.

Per serving: 209 calories, 8.3 g. fat (37% of calories), 0.2 g. dietary fiber, 81 mg. cholesterol, 42 mg. sodium.

Tuna Steaks with Piquant Relish

A fresh vegetable relish lets you capture the bounty of your garden or a farmers' market without spending hours in a hot kitchen. Not only do relishes provide a colorful sauce for fish, they're also fat-free.

> 4 *tuna steaks (6 ounces each)*
> 2 *teaspoons plus 2 tablespoons rice wine vinegar*
> 1 *teaspoon olive oil*
> ¼ *cup diced onions*
> ⅓ *cup diced green peppers*
> ½ *cup diced zucchini*
> ½ *cup diced tomatoes*
> ¼ *cup frozen corn, thawed*
> 2 *teaspoons capers, rinsed and drained*

Place the tuna steaks in a shallow pan and sprinkle with 2 teaspoons of the vinegar. Refrigerate while preparing the relish.

In a medium frying pan, heat the oil over medium heat until hot. Add the onions and cook for 3 to 4 minutes. Add the peppers and cook for 2 minutes. Add the zucchini, tomatoes and corn. Increase the heat to high and cook for 2 to 3 minutes, stirring, until the vegetables are hot and just beginning to soften.

Place the vegetable mixture in a small bowl, add the remaining 2 tablespoons of vinegar and the capers and stir; cool to room temperature.

Grill the tuna steaks over hot coals or broil 4″ from the heat for 8 to 12 minutes, or until the tuna just begins to flake when gently pressed. Spoon the relish over the steaks or pass the relish separately.

Preparation time: 15 minutes
Cooking time: 10 minutes
Grilling time: 12 minutes
Per serving: 175 calories, 2.6 g. fat (14% of calories), 1.1 g. dietary fiber, 64 mg. cholesterol, 76 mg. sodium.

Orange Roughy with Tomato Orange Sauce

*A*nise seeds give this tangy tomato sauce a hint of licorice flavor. If orange roughy is expensive in your area, choose another mild, white fish such as sole or cod.

1	*teaspoon olive oil*
¼	*cup minced shallots*
8	*plum tomatoes, peeled, seeded and diced (see note)*
1	*tablespoon orange juice*
1¼	*teaspoons grated orange rind*
½	*teaspoon anise seeds*
4	*orange roughy fillets (4 ounces each)*
1	*tablespoon minced fresh parsley*

Coat a 12″ frying pan with no-stick spray. Add the oil and shallots and cook over medium heat for 1 minute. Add the tomatoes, increase the heat to medium-high and cook, stirring, for 2 to 3 minutes, or just until the tomatoes are beginning to soften. Add the orange juice, orange rind and anise seeds; cook for 30 seconds.

Fold the tail portion of the fillets under (see note) and place the fillets in the tomato sauce. Bring the mixture to a boil, cover and cook over medium heat for 5 to 8 minutes, or until the fish turns opaque and just begins to flake when gently pressed. Remove the fish to a serving dish, increase the heat to high and boil the sauce for 1 minute, or until the sauce thickens slightly. Stir in the parsley; spoon the sauce over the fillets and serve.

Preparation time: 15 minutes
Cooking time: 15 minutes

Per serving: 152 calories, 2.8 g. fat (16% of calories), 3.3 g. dietary fiber, 23 mg. cholesterol, 97 mg. sodium.

SALMON AND VEGETABLES IN PAPER

SERVES 4

Cooking fish in parchment paper allows the fish to steam gently. In this recipe—which makes an impressive but easy dish for company—the vegetables are flavored with the juices from the salmon. If you prefer, use foil instead of parchment.

> 2 *teaspoons olive oil*
> 1 *cup thinly sliced carrots*
> 1 *cup thinly sliced zucchini*
> 1 *cup thinly sliced leeks*
>   *Ground black pepper*
> 4 *salmon fillets, skinned (6 ounces each)*
> 2 *teaspoons lemon juice*
> 4 *sprigs fresh tarragon*

Coat a large frying pan with no-stick spray; add the oil and heat over medium heat until the oil is hot. Add the carrots, zucchini and leeks and sauté for 3 to 4 minutes, or until the vegetables begin to wilt. Sprinkle lightly with pepper and set aside to cool.

Cut 4 (12"-long) pieces of parchment paper. Fold each sheet in half and then open the paper up and place a bed of sautéed vegetables in the center toward the fold line of each paper. Place the salmon fillets on top of the vegetables. Sprinkle the salmon with the lemon juice and pepper. Lay a sprig of tarragon on top of each salmon fillet.

Fold the paper over the salmon and seal by folding and creasing the paper in a half circle around the salmon and vegetables, tucking the end piece under the package. Place packages on a 15" × 10" jelly-roll pan.

Bake at 425° for 15 to 20 minutes, or until you can feel the salmon flake when you press gently on the packet. To serve, cut an × in each packet and tear the paper back to reveal the salmon and vegetables.

Preparation time: 15 minutes
Cooking time: 5 minutes
Baking time: 20 minutes

Chef's note: The packets can be made ahead of time and refrigerated until ready to cook.

Per serving: 301 calories, 13.2 g. fat (40% of calories), 1.8 g. dietary fiber, 94 mg. cholesterol, 82 mg. sodium.

ROASTED SALMON WITH PEPPER HERB CRUST

SERVES 4

*T*he seas abound with several especially delectable varieties of salmon: Atlantic salmon from the East, king and chinook from Alaska and the Columbia River region, sockeye from the Pacific Northwest. Yellowish-fleshed dog salmon is almost fat-free.

2   *tablespoons lemon juice*
1   *teaspoon olive oil*
2   *cloves garlic, minced*
3   *tablespoons crushed multicolored peppercorns*
2   *tablespoons minced fresh dill*
2   *tablespoons minced fresh thyme*
4   *salmon fillets (5 ounces each)*

In a small bowl, combine the lemon juice, oil and garlic. In a shallow pan, combine the peppercorns, dill and thyme. Brush the tops of the salmon fillets with the lemon mixture, then press the tops into the peppercorn-herb mixture, pressing lightly to cover.

Line a 15″ × 10″ jelly-roll pan with foil; coat the foil with no-stick spray. Place the fillets, peppercorn side up, in the prepared pan. Bake at 475° for 8 to 12 minutes, or until the fish turns opaque and just begins to flake when gently pressed.

Preparation time: 5 minutes
Baking time: 12 minutes

Per serving: 223 calories, 10 g. fat (42% of calories), 0.4 g. dietary fiber, 78 mg. cholesterol, 64 mg. sodium.

SOLE WITH CUCUMBER CHIVE SAUCE

*T*he cucumber and chive sauce is an unusual and elegant complement for the delicate flavor of sole. Serve with lightly seasoned rice and a medley of summer vegetables.

- *1 teaspoon olive oil*
- *1 tablespoon minced shallots*
- *1 cucumber, peeled, seeded and thinly sliced*
- *2 tablespoons minced chives*
- *½ cup defatted chicken stock*
- *1 tablespoon lemon juice*
- *4 sole fillets (4 ounces each)*
- *½ teaspoon cornstarch mixed with 1 teaspoon water*
- *2 tablespoons nonfat plain yogurt*

Coat a large frying pan with no-stick spray; add the oil and heat over medium-high heat until the oil is hot. Add the shallots and cook for 30 seconds. Add the cucumbers, reduce the heat to medium and sauté for 3 to 4 minutes, or until the cucumbers are tender. Stir in the chives. Place the cucumber mixture in a food processor.

Return the frying pan to the stove; add the stock and lemon juice and bring to a boil over high heat. Add the fillets, cover, reduce the heat to medium and poach the fillets for 3 to 5 minutes, or until the fish turns opaque and just begins to flake when gently pressed. Remove the fillets to a serving dish.

While the fish is cooking, puree the cucumber mixture until almost smooth; set aside.

Add the cornstarch mixture to the fish-poaching liquid and bring to a boil over medium-high heat. Add the cucumber puree and cook until thickened. Remove from the heat and stir in the yogurt. Spoon the sauce over the fillets and serve.

Preparation time: 15 minutes
Baking time: 15 minutes

Per serving: 122 calories, 2.4 g. fat (19% of calories), 0.8 g. dietary fiber, 53 mg. cholesterol, 148 mg. sodium.

Pan-Fried Fillets with Fresh Vegetables

*E*ither ocean or freshwater fish fillets are well-suited for this recipe, so choose any fish that's in season in your area. It's also a colorful and low-fat way to showcase your angler's fresh-caught fish.

2 *teaspoons olive oil*
4 *fish fillets (6 ounces each)*
1 *cup broccoli florets*
1 *carrot, thinly sliced*
½ *cup sliced mushrooms*
⅓ *cup sweet red pepper strips*
¼ *cup diced onions*
¼ *teaspoon ground black pepper*
2 *teaspoons lemon juice*

Coat a large no-stick frying pan with no-stick spray. Add the oil and heat over high heat until the oil is hot. Add the fillets and cook on medium-high to high heat for 3 minutes, or until the bottoms of the fillets are lightly browned.

Turn the fillets; add the broccoli, carrots, mushrooms, red peppers and onions around the fish. Sprinkle with the black pepper and lemon juice. Cover; reduce the heat to medium and cook for 3 minutes. Remove the cover and continue to cook the fish for 2 to 3 minutes, if necessary, until the fish turns opaque and just begins to flake when gently pressed.

Remove the fish to a serving platter and top with the vegetables. The vegetables should be just tender when the fish is done; if they are not, continue to cook them for 1 to 2 minutes after removing the fish.

Preparation time: 10 minutes
Cooking time: 10 minutes
Per serving: 228 calories, 6.3 g. fat (25% of calories), 1.6 g. dietary fiber, 55 mg. cholesterol, 105 mg. sodium.

SOUTHERN FILLETS WITH SPICY SALSA

SERVES 4

*C*atfish is the finny delicacy of the South. Found in rivers of the region, it's also raised on farms. A tangy salsa dotted with black-eyed peas updates a traditional fish-fry favorite. This recipe also works well using any white fish fillets in place of catfish.

Fillets

¼ *cup yellow cornmeal*

2 *tablespoons whole-wheat flour*

½ *teaspoon ground black pepper*

¼ *teaspoon ground red pepper*

4 *catfish fillets (6 ounces each)*

1 *tablespoon olive oil*

Salsa

5 *plum tomatoes, diced*

¾ *cup canned black-eyed peas, rinsed and drained*

⅓ *cup diced green peppers*

¼ *cup diced onions*

¼ *cup tomato juice*

1 *tablespoon lime juice*

1 *tablespoon minced fresh coriander*

1 *serrano chili pepper, seeded and minced*

To make the fillets: In a shallow pan, combine the cornmeal, flour, black pepper and red pepper; mix well. Press one side of each fillet into the cornmeal mixture and coat well.

Line a 15″ × 10″ jelly-roll pan with foil; coat the foil with the no-stick spray.

Place the oil in a large no-stick frying pan and heat until hot. Place the fillets, cornmeal side down, in the frying pan and cook over high heat for 1 to 2 minutes, until lightly browned. Remove from the frying pan and place, cornmeal side up, in the prepared pan. Bake at 450° for 8 to 12 minutes, or until the fish just begins to flake when gently pressed. Serve with the salsa.

To make the salsa: In a medium bowl, combine the tomatoes, peas, green peppers, onions, tomato juice, lime juice, coriander and chili peppers; mix well.

Preparation time: 10 minutes
Cooking time: 5 minutes
Baking time: 12 minutes

Per serving: 349 calories, 11.8 g. fat (30% of calories), 4.7 g. dietary fiber, 98 mg. cholesterol, 330 mg. sodium.

CORNMEAL-BREADED CATFISH
WITH SWEET PEPPER RELISH

*A*vailable throughout the year, catfish is a mild, delicate fish that blends well with the stronger flavors of Southwestern or Mexican dishes. Cool down the Cajun-seasoned cornmeal coating on these catfish fillets with a sweet-and-sour bell pepper relish. (Or spice it up more with the sweet tanginess of jalapeño jelly.) Serve this entrée with fresh green beans and sliced tomatoes.

Catfish

¾ cup cornmeal

1 tablespoon Cajun seafood seasoning

¾ cup buttermilk

4 catfish fillets (5 ounces each)

Sweet Pepper Relish

¾ cup cider vinegar

2 tablespoons apple juice

2 tablespoons honey

½ cup diced sweet red peppers

½ cup diced green peppers

½ cup diced yellow peppers

⅓ cup thinly sliced onions

1 tablespoon chopped fresh mint

To make the catfish: In a shallow pan, combine the cornmeal and Cajun seasoning; mix well. Place the buttermilk in another shallow pan. Dip the fillets in the buttermilk, and then in the cornmeal, coating each fillet thoroughly.

Line a 15″ × 10″ jelly-roll pan with foil; coat the foil with no-stick spray. Place the fillets on the prepared pan. Spray the fillets lightly with no-stick spray and bake at 475° for 10 to 15 minutes, or until lightly browned and the fish just begin to flake when gently pressed. Serve with the relish.

To make the sweet pepper relish: In a small saucepan, combine the vinegar, juice and honey; mix well. Add the red peppers, green peppers, yellow peppers and onions; bring to a boil over medium-high heat and boil for 1 minute, or until the onions are wilted. Stir in the mint and cool to room temperature. Drain and serve.

Preparation time: 15 minutes
Baking time: 15 minutes
Cooking time: 5 minutes

Chef's note: As an alternative to Sweet Pepper Relish, serve this catfish with a spoonful of jalapeño jelly. It also makes a feisty appetizer: Spread low-fat or no-fat cream cheese on low-fat crackers and top with a dollop of the jelly. Jalapeño jelly is available in many supermarkets in the condiment section, or you can make your own. Spoon the contents of a small jar of apple jelly into a microwave-safe bowl. Heat in the microwave until the jelly melts. Finely chop jalapeño peppers (be sure to wear rubber gloves) and add to the melted jelly. Return the mixture to the jar, cover tightly and refrigerate.

Per serving: 316 calories, 7.4 g. fat (21% of calories), 4.2 g. dietary fiber, 83 mg. cholesterol, 148 mg. sodium.

BEYOND TARTAR SAUCE:
10 LOW-FAT SAUCES FOR FISH

When it comes to sauces for fish, tartar sauce has reigned supreme. Until now. Although the sweet-sour tang of tartar sauce complements most varieties of fish, its main ingredient is high-in-fat mayonnaise, whose heaviness can mask, rather than draw out, the delicate flavors of some fish. But the following six simple low-fat sauces take you beyond tartar sauce. Once you've tried them, you'll never use tartar sauce again!

1. Mustard Dill Sauce. This sauce is inspired by the Scandinavians, who serve mustard sauce with marinated salmon fillets. Combine Dijon mustard with nonfat mayonnaise and stir in fresh or dried dill. Thin the sauce with skim milk to pouring consistency.

2. Citrus Herb Splash. Squeeze fresh citrus—lemon, lime, orange or grapefruit—over fish or seafood. Sprinkle it with chopped fresh herbs such as chives, dill, tarragon or basil, which complement delicate fish flavors without overpowering them.

3. Chutney Sour Cream. Chutney is a pungent, East Indian condiment made from fruit, vinegar, sugar and spices. Since it's fat-free, use it to add zip to dishes from curry to chops. For fish, stir chutney into nonfat sour cream. Season to taste with chopped fresh coriander. This sauce is especially good with tuna or swordfish steaks.

4. Tomato Mushroom Sauce. This sauce adds a splash of vibrant color to fish fillets. In a nonstick frying pan, sauté chopped tomatoes, quartered fresh mushrooms and a little minced garlic. Cook until the mushrooms are fork-tender. Squeeze lemon juice over the mixture and season with cracked black pepper.

5. Spicy Pimento Sauce. Spicy red pepper garlic sauce has long been a popular condiment for fish stews. Serve this version with fish fillets as well. In a food processor, combine nonfat mayonnaise with chopped pimentos and minced garlic. Puree the mixture. Stir in red pepper flakes to taste.

6. Yogurt Chive Sauce. Serve this sauce with grilled salmon fillets or as a dressing for crab salad. Stir snipped chives into plain nonfat yogurt. Thin the mixture with skim milk to the desired consistency. For a fresh, green color, puree the mixture in a blender or food processor.

7. Seasonal Salsa. Salsas are showing up in all varieties these days as a great low-fat way to accent and season your food. For a quick fresh-tasting salsa, stir diced colorful peppers, zucchini, onions and fresh coriander into your favorite salsa. This pairs well with many types of fish, especially fish cooked on the barbecue.

8. Gingered Orange Sauce. Fresh ginger adds a zing to seafood, and orange juice brings out the natural sweetness of fish. In a small saucepan, combine orange juice with a small amount of minced fresh ginger. Bring to a boil and add cornstarch mixed with water to thicken slightly. Pour over your favorite fillets and top with finely minced scallions.

9. Fresh Coriander Sauce. Americans have taken to the herb known as coriander, cilantro or Chinese parsley. Its pungent taste shows up in many cuisines. For a quick sauce with lots of flavor, combine nonfat plain yogurt, chopped fresh coriander, lime juice and a little minced garlic. Serve with seafood or fish fillets.

10. Barbecue Sauce. This all-American favorite can also be used to perk up and sauce your fish fillets. Brush on your favorite barbecue sauce as your fish cooks, or combine barbecue sauce with a little nonfat mayonnaise to serve as a condiment on the side. The smoky tomato flavor goes best with full-flavored fish such as tuna, swordfish and halibut.

SUMMER FILLETS

SERVES 4

*S*avor fresh-from-the-garden herbs and vegetables in this simple fish dish.

4 *firm-fleshed fish fillets (halibut, grouper or snapper; 6 ounces each)*
1 *clove garlic, minced*
2 *tablespoons chopped fresh herbs such as basil, thyme, parsley or chives*
8 *thin slices tomato*
8 *thin slices green pepper*
8 *thin slices onion*
1 *teaspoon extra-virgin olive oil*
⅛ *teaspoon ground black pepper*

Coat a 15″ × 10″ jelly-roll pan with no-stick spray. Place the fillets in the prepared pan and sprinkle with the garlic and 1 tablespoon of the herbs. Place the tomatoes, green peppers and onions alternately on the fillets. Sprinkle with the remaining 1 tablespoon of the herbs. Drizzle the oil over the fillets and sprinkle with the black pepper.

Bake at 450° for 8 to 12 minutes, or until the fish turns opaque and just begins to flake when gently pressed.

Preparation time: 5 minutes
Baking time: 12 minutes

Chef's note: If desired, substitute 1 tablespoon Italian seasoning for the fresh herbs and chopped canned tomatoes for the fresh tomatoes.

Per serving: 210 calories, 5.1 g. fat (23% of calories), 0.7 g. dietary fiber, 55 mg. cholesterol, 94 mg. sodium.

Cod Fillets with Fresh Lemon Spinach

*F*resh spinach, laden with vitamins and minerals, makes a deep-green bed for baked fish fillets.

4	*cod fillets (6 ounces each)*
¼	*cup water*
2	*tablespoons lemon juice*
1	*teaspoon olive oil*
1	*large clove garlic, minced*
8	*cups fresh spinach leaves (about 6 ounces)*
1½	*teaspoons lemon juice*
⅛	*teaspoon grated nutmeg*
⅛	*teaspoon no-salt lemon pepper seasoning*

Place the cod fillets in a 13″ × 9″ baking dish. Pour the water and lemon juice around the fillets. Coat a piece of wax paper with no-stick spray and place it, coated side down, over the fish. Bake at 450° for 8 to 12 minutes, or until the fish turns opaque and just begins to flake when gently pressed.

While the fish is cooking, coat a large no-stick frying pan with no-stick spray. Add the oil and heat over medium heat. Add the garlic and sauté for 10 to 15 seconds. Add the spinach, lemon juice, nutmeg and lemon pepper seasoning. Sauté for 30 to 45 seconds, or until the spinach has wilted.

Remove the spinach to a serving dish and top with the cod fillets.

Preparation time: 10 minutes
Baking time: 12 minutes
Cooking time: 3 minutes

Chef's note: At first the spinach leaves will fill the pan to overflowing, but the volume will decrease quickly as they cook down. Keep turning and stirring the spinach as it cooks.

Per serving: 181 calories, 2.7 g. fat (13% of calories), 3 g. dietary fiber, 75 mg. cholesterol, 195 mg. sodium.

SALMON AND FRESH HERB FETTUCCINE

SERVES 4

*P*arsley, dill and chives enhance the distinctive flavor of salmon in this quick pasta main dish.

2	teaspoons olive oil
8	ounces salmon fillet, thinly sliced
3	tablespoons minced shallots
1¼	cups 1% low-fat milk
½	cup defatted chicken stock
2	tablespoons cornstarch mixed with 2 tablespoons water
1	tablespoon lemon juice
1	tablespoon chopped fresh parsley
1	tablespoon chopped fresh dill
1	tablespoon chopped fresh chives
8	ounces fresh or dried fettuccine

Coat a large frying pan with no-stick spray. Add 1 teaspoon of the oil and heat over medium heat until hot. Add the salmon and sauté for 3 to 5 minutes, or until the salmon turns opaque and begins to flake (the pieces will begin to break up as they cook). Remove the salmon to a plate and set aside.

Add the remaining 1 teaspoon of the oil to the pan and heat until hot. Add the shallots and sauté for 1 minute. Add the milk, stock and cornstarch mixture; bring to a boil over high heat. When the mixture thickens, add the lemon juice, parsley, dill and chives. Return the salmon to the sauce and heat for 1 to 2 minutes, until hot.

Cook the fettuccine in a large pot of boiling water for 8 to 10 minutes, or until just tender. Drain the fettuccine and toss with the salmon sauce.

Preparation time: 10 minutes
Cooking time: 20 minutes

Per serving: 352 calories, 8.2 g. fat (21% of calories), 0.1 g. dietary fiber, 83 mg. cholesterol, 133 mg. sodium.

GRILLED SWORDFISH KABOBS

SERVES 4

*T*he meaty texture of swordfish makes it ideal for grilling. Other fish that would work well in this recipe are tuna, halibut and mako shark.

- ¼ cup defatted chicken stock
- 1 tablespoon bottled green peppercorns, drained and crushed
- 1 teaspoon extra-virgin olive oil
- 1 teaspoon lemon juice
- 1¼ pounds swordfish steak
- 1 green pepper
- 1 lemon
- 8 cherry tomatoes

In a medium bowl, combine the stock, peppercorns, oil and lemon juice; mix well. Cut the swordfish into 20 (1½″) cubes. Add the swordfish to the peppercorn marinade and stir to coat. Refrigerate for 20 minutes.

While the fish is marinating, cut the green pepper into 1½″ pieces, and cut the lemon in half lengthwise and slice ½″ thick.

Remove the fish from the marinade, reserving the marinade. Thread the peppers, swordfish, lemon and cherry tomatoes alternately onto 4 (12″) metal skewers, dividing the vegetables and fish evenly among the skewers. Brush each kabob with some of the reserved marinade and grill over hot coals or broil 4″ from the heat for 6 to 10 minutes, turning once.

Preparation time: 10 minutes plus 20 minutes marinating time
Grilling time: 10 minutes

Per serving: 208 calories, 7.1 g. fat (30% of calories), 1.5 g. dietary fiber, 56 mg. cholesterol, 163 mg. sodium.

Steamed Mussels with Tomatoes and Saffron

SERVES 4

*S*affron complements the subtle flavor of mussels. In recent years, saffron has been in short supply, so if you don't see it on the shelf in the seasonings section at your supermarket, ask. Some markets store it in the back.

1 tablespoon olive oil

1½ cups diced onions

4 cloves garlic, minced

2 cans (14½ ounces each) no-salt-added tomatoes, drained and chopped

2 cups defatted chicken stock

½ teaspoon saffron threads, crushed

4 dozen large mussels

Coat a large soup pot with no-stick spray. Add the oil and heat over medium heat until hot. Add the onions and sauté for 4 to 5 minutes, until the onions begin to wilt. Add the garlic and sauté for 30 seconds. Add the tomatoes, stock and saffron. Bring to a boil, reduce the heat to low, partially cover the pot and simmer for 10 to 12 minutes.

While the tomato mixture is cooking, clean the mussels by scrubbing with a brush and cutting away the beard (the threadlike strands that the mussel uses to attach itself to surfaces).

Add the mussels to the tomato mixture; cover and cook over high heat for 6 to 10 minutes, shaking occasionally. As the mussels open, remove them and cook any remaining mussels an extra 1 to 2 minutes. Discard any that have not opened by that time.

Place the mussels in individual shallow bowls and spoon the tomato mixture over the mussels.

Preparation time: 10 minutes
Cooking time: 30 minutes
Per serving: 214 calories, 6.5 g. fat (27% of calories), 2.4 g. dietary fiber, 63 mg. cholesterol, 588 mg. sodium.

SEAFOOD CREOLE

SERVES 4

*N*ew Orleans and the bayou country of Louisiana are the birthplace of Creole. In this recipe, the fiery sauce pairs with fresh shrimp and fish.

1   *teaspoon olive oil*
2   *cups diced onions*
1   *green pepper, diced*
¾   *cup diced celery*
3   *cloves garlic, minced*
2   *cans (14½ ounces each) no-salt-added tomatoes, chopped*
1   *teaspoon dried thyme*
1   *bay leaf*
¼   *teaspoon ground red pepper*
8   *ounces peeled and deveined medium shrimp*
8   *ounces fish fillets (cod, sea bass, orange roughy or catfish), cut into 1" pieces*
2   *cups hot, cooked long-grain white rice*

Coat a large saucepan with no-stick spray. Add the oil and heat over medium-high heat until hot. Add the onions and sauté for 2 minutes. Add the peppers and celery and continue cooking for 2 minutes. Add the garlic and cook for 1 minute. Add the tomatoes, thyme, bay leaf and red pepper. Bring to a boil, reduce the heat to medium-low and simmer for 15 to 20 minutes, or until the vegetables are just tender.

When the vegetables are tender, add the shrimp and fish fillets. Cover and cook over medium heat for 3 to 5 minutes, or until the shrimp turns pink and the fish opaque.

To serve, remove the bay leaf. Place ½ cup of the rice in the center of each plate and surround it with the seafood mixture.

Preparation time: 15 minutes
Cooking time: 30 minutes
Per serving: 314 calories, 3 g. fat (9% of calories), 4.4 g. dietary fiber, 110 mg. cholesterol, 183 mg. sodium.

SCALLOPED OYSTERS

Two popular recipes come together in this oyster dish: scalloped oysters, which are baked simply with cracker crumbs, and the famous Oysters Rockefeller, baked in a bed of spinach.

> 2 teaspoons olive oil
> 6 slices turkey bacon, diced
> ⅓ cup minced shallots
> 2 packages (10 ounces each) frozen chopped spinach, thawed and squeezed dry
> ¼ teaspoon ground black pepper
> ¼ teaspoon grated nutmeg
> 2½ cups coarsely crushed low-sodium saltine crackers
> 3 cups shucked oysters, drained, with 2 tablespoons of the liquid reserved
> ½ teaspoon hot-pepper sauce

Coat a large frying pan with no-stick spray. Add the oil and heat over medium-high heat until hot. Add the turkey bacon and sauté for 3 to 4 minutes until crisp. Add the shallots and cook for 1 minute more.

Add the spinach, pepper and nutmeg to the frying pan. Sauté on medium heat for 1 to 2 minutes; remove from the heat.

Coat a 13″ × 9″ baking pan with no-stick spray. Spread the spinach mixture in the baking pan. Sprinkle 1 cup of the crushed crackers over the spinach and place the oysters in 1 layer on top of the cracker crumbs.

In a small cup, combine the reserved 2 tablespoons of the oyster liquid with the hot-pepper sauce. Spoon the hot-pepper mixture over the oysters. Spread the remaining 1½ cups of the cracker crumbs over the oysters and spray with no-stick spray. Bake at 450° for 8 to 12 minutes, or until the crackers are lightly browned and the oysters are plump and just beginning to curl around the edges.

Preparation time: 10 minutes
Cooking time: 10 minutes
Baking time: 12 minutes

Chef's note: For an elegant appetizer, bake the oysters in scallop shells. Layer the ingredients as described and bake according to the directions.

Per serving: 498 calories, 11 g. fat (19% of calories), 26.3 g. dietary fiber, 116 mg. cholesterol, 595 mg. sodium.

STIR-FRIED SCALLOPS AND VEGETABLES OVER RICE

SERVES 4

*W*hen buying scallops for this colorful stir-fry, look for scallops that have a sweet odor and are free of liquid.

1   *pound sea scallops*
2   *teaspoons olive oil*
3   *cloves garlic, minced*
1   *cup sliced onions*
1   *small sweet red pepper, cut into 1" pieces*
1   *carrot, thinly sliced*
⅓   *cup orange juice*
1   *cup halved pea pods, ends trimmed, strings removed*
1   *cup quartered mushrooms*
⅓   *cup defatted chicken stock mixed with 2 teaspoons cornstarch*
¼   *teaspoon red-pepper flakes (optional)*
4   *cups hot, cooked long-grain white rice*

If the sea scallops are very large, cut them in half horizontally; set aside. Heat a wok or large frying pan over high heat. Add 1 teaspoon of the oil and the garlic and sauté for 30 seconds. Add the scallops and stir-fry for 2 to 4 minutes, or until they are slightly resistant to the touch. Remove the scallops to a plate.

Add the remaining 1 teaspoon of oil and the onions to the pan. Sauté the onions for 1 minute; add the red peppers and carrots and sauté for 1 minute more. Add the orange juice; cover and cook for 2 minutes, or until the vegetables are crisp-tender.

Remove the cover and add the pea pods and the mushrooms. Stir-fry for 1 minute. Return the scallops to the pan; add the stock-cornstarch mixture and the pepper flakes. Bring to a boil and heat until thickened. Serve over the rice.

Preparation time: 15 minutes
Cooking time: 15 minutes
Per serving: 447 calories, 4.4 g. fat (9% of calories), 5 g. dietary fiber, 48 mg. cholesterol, 294 mg. sodium.

Linguine with Red Clam Sauce

*L*ittleneck clams are the smallest clams in the hard-shell family. Tender and sweet, these clams are excellent for chowders and sauces.

1	*teaspoon olive oil*
3	*cloves garlic, minced*
2	*cans (14½ ounces each) no-salt-added tomatoes, drained and diced*
3	*tablespoons chopped fresh basil*
1	*tablespoon chopped fresh oregano*
1	*teaspoon lemon juice*
18	*littleneck clams*
8	*ounces linguine*

Spray a large pot with no-stick spray. Add the oil and garlic and cook on medium heat for 30 seconds. Add the tomatoes, 2 tablespoons of the basil, the oregano and the lemon juice. Bring to a boil and cook for 5 minutes.

While the tomatoes are cooking, clean and scrub the clams free of any sand or dirt. Add the clams to the tomato mixture; cover and cook for 5 to 10 minutes, or until the clams open wide. As the clams open, remove them to a bowl. Discard any clams that do not open.

While the clams are cooking, cook the linguine in a large pot of boiling water for 8 to 10 minutes, or until just tender.

To serve, place the linguine in shallow bowls and top with the tomato sauce, the clams and the remaining 1 tablespoon of basil.

Preparation time: 5 minutes
Cooking time: 25 minutes

Per serving: 282 calories, 3.6 g. fat (11% of calories), 1.5 g. dietary fiber, 63 mg. cholesterol, 60 mg. sodium.

CHESAPEAKE BAY CRAB CAKES
WITH RED PEPPER TARTAR SAUCE

SERVES 4

*M*aryland and the Chesapeake Bay region are renowned for their crab cakes, which are crispy on the outside and flaky and tender on the inside. They're served as an appetizer as well as a main dish.

Crab Cakes

1	*pound crab meat, well-drained*
¼	*cup minced onions*
3	*tablespoons thinly sliced scallions*
2	*egg whites*
1	*tablespoon lemon juice*
¼	*teaspoon dry mustard*
¼	*teaspoon hot-pepper sauce*
¼	*teaspoon Worcestershire sauce*
½	*cup crushed oyster crackers*
¼	*cup low-fat mayonnaise*

Red Pepper Tartar Sauce

¼	*cup bottled roasted red peppers, drained*
½	*cup nonfat yogurt*
2	*tablespoons minced onions*
⅛	*teaspoon ground red pepper*

To make the crab cakes: In a medium bowl, combine the crab meat, onions and scallions. In a small bowl, combine the egg whites, lemon juice, mustard, hot-pepper sauce and Worcestershire sauce; mix until frothy. Add to the crab mixture and stir gently. Stir in the oyster crackers; add the mayonnaise and gently combine.

Line a 15″ × 10″ jelly-roll pan with foil; coat the foil with no-stick spray. Form the crab mixture into 12 patties, ½″ × 2¾″ each. Place the patties on the prepared pan. Broil 3″ from the heat for 5 to

8 minutes, or until lightly browned and cooked through, turning once. Serve with red pepper tartar sauce.

To make the red pepper tartar sauce: Place the red peppers on paper towels to drain; blot gently to dry. Coarsely chop the peppers and place them in a food processor along with the yogurt, onions and ground red pepper. Process the mixture until the ingredients are mixed and it is almost smooth. Refrigerate until ready to serve.

Preparation time: 10 minutes
Broiling time: 8 minutes

Chef's note: To prevent the crab cakes from becoming soggy, it's important to drain the crab meat thoroughly. Place it in a sieve and press the meat gently to force any extra liquid from it.

Per serving: 247 calories, 8.8 g. fat (33% of calories), 0.4 g. dietary fiber, 108 mg. cholesterol, 537 mg. sodium.

CHAPTER 7

BEEF AND
PORK
RECIPES
THAT
CAN'T MISS

MEATY ENTRÉES

The heartland of America raises some of the best beef and pork in the world. But it's far different from the beef and pork our grandparents remember. Producers heard the consumer speak, and the consumer said, "I want less fat in my meat." So today's beef and pork are lean and meaty but just as versatile as ever. There are even new cuts that are especially lean but also tender. Ask your meat cutter for suggestions when preparing a recipe.

ALPINE SWISS STEAK

---

*A*ll-American Swiss steak doesn't hail from Switzerland at all but has its roots in Britain's stewed steak. The secret of Swiss steak is to pound the dry flavoring ingredients into the meat.

> 4 *sun-dried tomatoes*
> ¼ *cup potato flakes*
> ¼ *teaspoon garlic powder*
> ¼ *teaspoon onion powder*
> ¼ *teaspoon ground black pepper*
> 4 *portions top round steak (3 ounces each), trimmed of fat*
> 1 *tablespoon canola oil*
> 1 *cup diced onions*
> 4 *cloves garlic, sliced*
> ½ *cup chopped tomatoes*
> ½ *cup defatted beef stock*

Place the sun-dried tomatoes in a small bowl; cover with hot water. Let them stand for 10 minutes, or until softened. Drain.

In a small bowl, combine the potato flakes, garlic powder, onion powder and pepper. Pound the steaks to ¼″. Firmly press the seasoned flakes onto the steaks on both sides.

In a large no-stick frying pan, heat the oil over medium-high heat. Add the steaks and cook for about 2 minutes per side, or until browned. Remove from the frying pan. Add the onions and garlic to the frying pan and cook over medium-low heat for 8 minutes, or until browned.

Return the steaks to the frying pan, add the chopped tomatoes, stock and sun-dried tomatoes. Cover and simmer for 20 minutes.

Preparation time: 10 minutes
Cooking time: 30 minutes
Per serving: 225 calories, 9.4 g. fat (37% of calories), 1.6 g. dietary fiber, 58 mg. cholesterol, 110 mg. sodium.

SAUERBRATEN STEAK

SERVES 4

*T*rue sauerbraten is a three-to-five-day labor of culinary love. Although this version can be prepared in just minutes, it retains all of the dish's classic sweet-sour flavor. If you have the time, we recommend marinating the meat for a day. Serve sauerbraten with noodles topped with poppy seeds or toasted whole-wheat bread crumbs, peas and broiled tomatoes.

Marinade

1   cup defatted beef stock
½   cup red wine vinegar
2   carrots, thinly sliced
1   onion, chopped
1   stalk celery, chopped
8   whole black peppercorns
6   juniper berries, crushed
4   whole cloves
1   teaspoon coriander seeds, crushed

Meat

4   portions sirloin steak (3 ounces each), trimmed of fat
1   cup sliced onions
1   cup sliced mushrooms
1   tablespoon crushed gingersnaps
1   teaspoon red wine vinegar
½   teaspoon molasses

To make the marinade: In a 1-quart saucepan, combine the stock, vinegar, carrots, onions, celery, peppercorns, juniper berries, cloves and coriander seeds. Boil over high heat for 5 minutes.

To make the meat: Pour the marinade over the steaks and allow them to marinate for 15 minutes. Spray a no-stick frying pan with no-stick spray. Heat over medium heat for 2 minutes. Add the onions and mushrooms and cook for 5 minutes, or until browned. Remove the onions and mushrooms from the frying pan.

Take the steaks from the marinade, dry them and sear on each side for 2 minutes. Remove the steaks from the frying pan and slice them into thin strips.

Return the onions, mushrooms and steak slices to the frying pan. Strain the marinade over the steak. Bring to a boil. Add the gingersnaps, vinegar and molasses. Heat for 2 minutes.

Preparation time: 10 minutes plus 15 minutes marinating time
Cooking time: 15 minutes

Chef's note: If desired, substitute pork for beef in this recipe.

Per serving: 220 calories, 8.3 g. fat (34% of calories), 2.9 g. dietary fiber, 57 mg. cholesterol, 190 mg. sodium.

FAJITAS WITH CORIANDER CREAM

Coriander is one of the herbs that gives southwestern cooking its distinctive flavor. It grows easily in your backyard garden or in patio pots. In this recipe, it seasons both the marinade and the sour cream sauce.

Beef and Marinade

½	cup lime juice
¼	cup chopped fresh coriander
1	tablespoon minced garlic
2	teaspoons cumin seeds, crushed
½	teaspoon ground black pepper
12–16	ounces flank steak

Coriander Cream

1	cup nonfat sour cream
½	cup chopped fresh coriander
½	teaspoon grated lime rind

Vegetables

1	sweet red pepper, halved and seeded
1	green pepper, halved and seeded
1	onion, peeled and quartered
8	flour tortillas, 8" in diameter
1	cup diced avocado
1	cup salsa

To make the beef and marinade: In a large baking dish, mix the lime juice, coriander, garlic, cumin seeds and pepper. Add the steak and turn to coat both sides. Allow the steak to marinate for 15 minutes. Grill the steak for 2 to 3 minutes per side for rare beef. Slice the steak on the diagonal.

To make the coriander cream: In a blender or small food processor, combine the sour cream, coriander and lime rind. Blend until smooth, stopping to scrape down the sides. Serve with the fajitas.

To make the vegetables: Grill the sweet red peppers, green peppers and onions on the grill or under the broiler for 10 to 15 minutes, or until brown. Slice them into thin strips and combine.

Wrap 4 tortillas in a paper towel and microwave on high for 20 seconds, or until hot. Repeat with the remaining 4 tortillas.

Add the avocado to the salsa.

To serve, top the flank steak with the grilled vegetables. Let each diner place this mixture in the tortillas, top it with coriander cream and the avocado salsa, fold the bottom of the tortilla up and roll the sides in.

Preparation time: 15 minutes plus 15 minutes marinating time
Grilling time: 6 minutes
Broiling time: 15 minutes

Chef's notes: To cook indoors, broil the steak for 2 to 3 minutes per side for rare beef.

If you don't have a microwave, wrap all 8 tortillas in foil and warm them at 350° for 3 to 5 minutes.

Per serving: 533 calories, 21 g. fat (34% of calories), 3.1 g. dietary fiber, 46 mg. cholesterol, 370 mg. sodium.

Beef and Black Bean Chili

Serves 4

Braised beef and black bean stew served in a hollowed out brioche at the Trellis Restaurant in Williamsburg, Virginia, was the inspiration for this recipe. It's especially attractive with the red, white and green garnish (see Chef's note).

Chili Puree

2	chipotle peppers (wear rubber gloves when handling; see note)
1	cup defatted beef stock
½	cup diced sweet red peppers
¼	cup diced onions
1	tablespoon chopped garlic
1½	teaspoons dried oregano
1	teaspoon olive oil
1	teaspoon cumin seeds
⅛	teaspoon ground cinnamon

Beef and Black Bean Chili

1	teaspoon olive oil
12	ounces tenderloin of beef, cubed
½	teaspoon cracked black pepper
1	cup diced onions
1	cup diced tomatoes
1	cup defatted beef stock
1	can (15 ounces) black beans, rinsed and drained

To make the chili puree: Cover the chipotle peppers with hot water. Allow them to soften for 10 minutes.

Meanwhile, in a food processor, combine the stock, red peppers, onions, garlic, oregano, oil, cumin seeds and cinnamon. Puree. Scrape down the sides of the processor.

Drain the rehydrated chipotle peppers. Remove the stems and seeds. Add to the stock mixture in the processor. Puree. Set this mixture aside.

To make the beef and black bean chili: In a Dutch oven over medium-high heat, heat the oil for 2 minutes and then add the beef. Cook until no longer raw-looking, about 3 minutes. Season with the pepper and remove the meat from the pan. Add the onions and tomatoes to the pan and cook for 5 minutes. Add the stock, beans and chili puree. Mix well and simmer for 5 minutes. Add the reserved beef and cook for 5 minutes more.

Preparation time: 15 minutes plus 10 minutes rehydrating time
Cooking time: 20 minutes

Chef's notes: A chipotle pepper is the dried, smoked version of the fresh jalapeño pepper. Chipotle peppers can be purchased whole and dried or canned in adobo or adobado sauce, a tomato-based sauce.

To serve, garnish each portion with a swirl of nonfat sour cream, diced sweet red peppers and fresh coriander leaves.

Per serving: 272 calories, 8.9 g. fat (27% of calories), 8.7 g. dietary fiber, 48 mg. cholesterol, 635 mg. sodium.

BEEF AND CARAMELIZED ONIONS

SERVES 4

*B*eef stock and red wine vinegar create a beefy glaze for steak or ground beef patties.

Caramelized Onions

2   *cups sliced onions*
2   *teaspoons canola oil*
½   *cup defatted beef stock*
½   *tablespoon brown sugar*
1   *tablespoon balsamic vinegar*

Steak

4   *portions lean steak (tenderloin, top round steak, sirloin; 3 ounces each), trimmed of fat*
¼   *teaspoon cracked black pepper*
4   *shallots, sliced*
4   *cloves garlic, sliced*
½   *cup defatted beef stock*
1   *teaspoon red wine vinegar*
4   *slices sourdough bread, grilled*

To make the caramelized onions: In a small no-stick frying pan over medium-high heat, cook the onions in the oil for 5 to 7 minutes, or until brown. Add the stock, brown sugar and vinegar. Cook for 10 to 15 minutes, or until all the liquid evaporates.

To make the steak: In a no-stick frying pan over high heat, sear the steaks for 1 to 2 minutes on each side. Season with the pepper, reduce the heat to medium and add the shallots and garlic. Cook for 5 minutes. Add the stock and vinegar. Bring to a boil.

To serve, top each sourdough slice with the steak, the caramelized onions and pan juices.

Preparation time: 15 minutes
Cooking time: 30 minutes

Per serving: 286 calories, 9.4 g. fat (30% of calories), 1.9 g. dietary fiber, 58 mg. cholesterol, 299 mg. sodium.

PHILADELPHIA STEAK SANDWICHES

SERVES 4

*R*ocky Balboa, the boxer-hero of the *Rocky* movies, introduced millions of Americans to Philadelphia's best-loved steak sandwich. This low-fat version features skim-milk mozzarella and plenty of sautéed vegetables. If you're adventuresome, add zing with hot cherry peppers.

1 *sweet red pepper, diced*

1 *green pepper, diced*

1 *medium onion, diced*

8 *mushrooms, thinly sliced*

2 *tablespoons sliced garlic*

12 *ounces beef round tip steak, sliced paper thin (see note)*

¼ *cup reduced-sodium ketchup*

1 *teaspoon dried oregano*

¼ *teaspoon ground black pepper*

1 *cup shredded part-skim mozzarella cheese*

4 *rolls, warmed*

Coat a large frying pan with no-stick spray. Heat over medium-high heat for 2 minutes. Add the sweet red peppers, green peppers, onions and mushrooms and sauté for 6 minutes, or until browned. Add the garlic and steak, and sauté the beef for 1 minute per side. Add the ketchup, oregano, black pepper and mozzarella. Cover and cook over low heat until the cheese melts, about 4 minutes. Divide among the 4 rolls.

Preparation time: 10 minutes
Cooking time: 15 minutes

Chef's note: Freezing the steak slightly will firm it enough to make slicing the steak thinly much easier.

Per serving: 330 calories, 12.6 g. fat (35% of calories), 2.6 g. dietary fiber, 74 mg. cholesterol, 399 mg. sodium.

GRILLED MEATLOAF

*M*eatloaf is an American classic that is synonymous with home cooking. This grilled version is topped with a tomato sauce. Enjoy it hot or cold, for a summertime supper or sliced in sandwiches for a picnic lunch.

Meatloaf

1	*cup diced onions*
½	*cup diced shiitake mushrooms*
2	*teaspoons canola oil*
¼	*teaspoon dried thyme*
12	*ounces extra-lean ground beef*
⅔	*cup fresh bread crumbs*
¼	*cup diced sweet red peppers*
2	*tablespoons reduced-sodium ketchup*
2	*egg whites*
1	*tablespoon snipped fresh chives*
1	*tablespoon minced garlic*

Sauce

1	*cup tomatoes, chopped*
2	*tablespoons reduced-sodium ketchup*
1	*tablespoon chopped dill pickles*
2	*teaspoons olive oil*
1	*teaspoon minced garlic*
½	*teaspoon red wine vinegar*

To make the meatloaf: In a 1-quart saucepan over medium heat, cook the onions and mushrooms in the oil for about 5 minutes, or until soft. Add the thyme. In a large bowl, combine the beef, bread crumbs, peppers, ketchup, egg whites, chives, garlic and the cooked onions and mushrooms. Mix well. Shape into a 1″-thick oval loaf.

For a gas grill, grill at 350°. For a charcoal grill, arrange hot coals in a circle around the perimeter of the grill. Place the meatloaf in the center; cover and grill 20 to 30 minutes, or until brown.

To make the sauce: In a small saucepan over medium heat, combine the tomatoes, ketchup, dill pickles, oil, garlic and vinegar. Bring to a boil and simmer for 5 minutes.

Preparation time: 15 minutes
Grilling time: 30 minutes

Chef's note: This meatloaf can also be oven-baked in a 9″ × 5″ loaf pan at 350° until the meat is brown and pulls away from the sides of a loaf pan, about 30 to 35 minutes.

Per serving: 277 calories, 15.4 g. fat (50% of calories), 1.5 g. dietary fiber, 53 mg. cholesterol, 221 mg. sodium.

BUILDING THE BEST BURGERS

*B*ring out the best in grilled burgers—whether they're extra-lean ground beef or ground turkey—with these six easy-to-make toppings. At your next backyard party, set out several selections and let guests build their own great American burger.

• Season low-fat or nonfat sour cream with chopped chives and a dash of salt and pepper. Use in place of mayonnaise in a California burger or as a topping by itself.

• Just before removing burgers from the grill, crumble 1 teaspoon blue cheese over each patty. Continue cooking until the cheese melts slightly. Or drizzle your burger with low-fat blue cheese dressing.

• Sauté green peppers, onions and mushrooms in a splash of plain or herbed olive oil. Spoon onto each burger.

• Combine ¼ cup brown sugar and ¼ cup low-sodium ketchup for a sweet and tangy topping to brush on burgers at the end of grilling.

• Pile on the veggies! Alfalfa sprouts, thin slices of avocado, tomatoes and onions are especially tasty on ground turkey or seafood burgers, as well as regular beef patties.

• As burgers finish grilling, top with a slice of part-skim mozzarella cheese so that it melts slightly. Spoon on a salsa of finely chopped tomatoes tossed with Italian seasonings or dried or fresh oregano.

BEEF TACOS WITH GRILLED VEGETABLES

SERVES 4

*T*ypically, the only vegetables you'll find in tacos are lettuce and tomatoes. But this version is stuffed with smoky-flavored grilled red and green peppers and onions that take tacos to a new dimension.

1	medium onion, halved
1	sweet red pepper, halved and seeded
½	green pepper, seeded
12	ounces extra-lean ground beef
2	teaspoons canola oil
1½	teaspoons ground cumin
1½	teaspoons dried oregano
¾	teaspoon chili powder
½	teaspoon minced garlic
¼	teaspoon ground black pepper
¼	cup defatted beef stock
8	taco shells
2	cups shredded romaine lettuce
1	cup chopped tomatoes
1	cup shredded fat-free Cheddar cheese
4	lime wedges
	Fresh coriander leaves

Grill the onions, red peppers and green peppers over charcoal, 4″ from the coals, for 15 minutes, or until brown. Peel the peppers, then dice the onions, red peppers and green peppers.

In a large frying pan over medium heat, cook the beef in the oil until the beef loses its raw look, about 5 minutes. Add the cumin, oregano, chili powder, garlic and black pepper. Mix well. Add the stock and the grilled onions, red peppers and green peppers. Cover and simmer for 15 minutes. Heat the taco shells in a 300° oven for 2 to 5 minutes, or until warm.

Place the lettuce, tomatoes, Cheddar, lime and coriander in individual small bowls. Spoon the taco mixture into the shells. Top as desired.

Preparation time: 10 minutes
Grilling time: 15 minutes
Cooking time: 20 minutes
Baking time: 5 minutes

Chef's notes: If desired, substitute ground chicken or turkey for the ground beef.

To broil the vegetables, place on a 15″ × 10″ jelly-roll pan 4″ to 6″ from the heat for 5 to 10 minutes, or until browned.

Per serving: 395 calories, 18 g. fat (40% of calories), 6.2 g. dietary fiber, 53 mg. cholesterol, 527 mg. sodium.

Meatballs Florentine

SERVES 4

Spinach and cheese are what make these versatile and delicious meatballs "florentine." Add them to clear or creamy soups, serve with your favorite tomato sauce and pasta, roll them in fresh bread crumbs and bake or slice them for sandwiches.

8	*cloves garlic*
1	*teaspoon olive oil*
4	*shallots, peeled*
1	*cup fresh spinach leaves*
½	*cup fat-free ricotta cheese*
1	*egg white*
2	*teaspoons dried oregano*
½	*teaspoon ground black pepper*
½	*teaspoon dried dill*
¼	*teaspoon grated nutmeg*
12	*ounces extra-lean ground beef*
⅓	*cup fresh whole-wheat or oatmeal bread crumbs*

Wrap the garlic and oil in foil and bake at 400° for 15 minutes. Remove the outer peel and trim the root end of the roasted garlic. In a food processor, puree the garlic, shallots, spinach, ricotta and egg white. Add the oregano, pepper, dill and nutmeg.

In a large bowl, combine the beef and the bread crumbs. Add the contents of the processor and mix well.

Shape into meatballs using a ¼-cup measure. Line a jelly-roll pan with foil. Place a wire rack on the foil. Spray the rack with no-stick spray. Place the meatballs on the rack and bake at 400° for 20 to 25 minutes, or until brown.

Preparation time: 15 minutes
Baking time: 40 minutes

Per serving: 229 calories, 11.8 g. fat (46% of calories), 0.5 g. dietary fiber, 56 mg. cholesterol, 106 mg. sodium.

SCALLOPS OF PORK WITH PEAR-GINGER SAUCE

*F*or an anniversary, birthday or other special-occasion dinner, try this intriguing and elegant dish. Pears give the sauce its butter-sweet flavor, while fresh ginger adds an unexpected zest.

Pork Scallops

    1 pork tenderloin (12 ounces), cut into 8 slices
    ¼ teaspoon ground black pepper
    ¼ teaspoon dried thyme

Pear-Ginger Sauce

    2 tablespoons pear juice
    1 tablespoon chopped fresh ginger
    4 cups diced pears
    1 tablespoon lemon juice
    1 tablespoon brown sugar
    1 tablespoon minced candied ginger

To make the pork scallops: In a large, no-stick frying pan over medium-high heat, sear the pork on each side, about 1 minute. Reduce the heat and cook until done. Season with the pepper and thyme.

To make the pear-ginger sauce: In a medium saucepan, simmer the pear juice and fresh ginger for 5 minutes over medium heat. Combine the diced pears with the lemon juice and brown sugar. Add the pears to the saucepan and cook for 5 minutes. Place ½ of the sauce in a food processor and puree for about 30 seconds. Combine the puree with the remaining diced pears and add the candied ginger. Serve with the pork.

Preparation time: 20 minutes
Cooking time: 15 minutes

Per serving: 209 calories, 3.2 g. fat (14% of calories), 4.1 g. dietary fiber, 60 mg. cholesterol, 52 mg. sodium.

PULLED PORK BARBECUE

SERVES 4

*P*ull the pork by shredding it with two forks to create this wonderful Southern-style barbecue. Serve the saucy pork on buns along with your favorite slaw, sliced tomatoes, corn on the cob and watermelon.

1   *chipotle pepper (wear rubber gloves when handling; see note)*
1   *pork tenderloin (12 ounces)*
¼   *teaspoon ground black pepper*
⅛   *teaspoon ground red pepper*
⅔   *cup diced onions*
1   *teaspoon canola oil*
1   *tablespoon minced garlic*
½   *cup reduced-sodium barbecue sauce*
¼   *cup reduced-sodium ketchup*
¼   *cup water*
1   *teaspoon maple syrup*
4   *sandwich buns*

Place the chipotle pepper in a small bowl; cover with hot water and let stand for 5 minutes. Drain; remove the stems and seeds. Coarsely chop the chipotle. Set aside.

In a no-stick frying pan over high heat, sear the whole tenderloin on all sides, about 5 minutes. Remove from the heat and season with the black pepper and red pepper.

In a small saucepan over medium heat, combine the onions and the oil and cook for 5 minutes. Add the garlic and cook for 1 minute more. Add the barbecue sauce, ketchup, water, maple syrup and the chipotle. Bring to a boil and simmer for 10 minutes.

Place the tenderloin on a triple layer of aluminum foil and top with one-third of the sauce. Wrap well and bake at 350° for 25 minutes.

Shred the pork using 2 forks. Add the "pulled" pork to the remaining sauce and heat through. Serve on the buns.

Preparation time: 10 minutes
Cooking time: 25 minutes
Baking time: 25 minutes

Chef's note: Chipotle peppers are smoked and dried jalapeños. There is no substitute for the flavor they add, but a fresh serrano or jalapeño can add "heat."

Per serving: 270 calories, 6.4 g. fat (22% of calories), 2.4 g. dietary fiber, 60 mg. cholesterol, 399 mg. sodium.

SUNSHINE PORK

SERVES 4

*R*ed grapefruit puts the sunshine in this grilled main dish. For attractive splashes of color, use a mixture of red, green and yellow sweet peppers. Serve the pork tenderloin with couscous or a blend of wild and white rice.

Pork and Marinade

1   *cup orange juice*

2   *tablespoons fruit vinegar*

1   *tablespoon grated orange rind*

2   *teaspoons minced fresh rosemary*

4   *portions pork tenderloin (4 ounces each)*

Sauce

1   *sweet red pepper, seeded and cut into thin julienne strips*

4   *scallions, cut into ½" slices*

2   *teaspoons canola oil*

¼   *cup apple cider*

2   *oranges, peeled and sectioned*

1   *red grapefruit, peeled and sectioned*

¼   *teaspoon black pepper*

1   *teaspoon cornstarch dissolved in 1 tablespoon cold water*

2   *teaspoons chopped fresh mint*

To make the pork and marinade: In a large glass baking dish, combine the orange juice, vinegar, orange rind and rosemary. Add the pork. Marinate for 15 minutes. Remove the pork from the marinade, dry and grill over charcoal or in a stovetop grill pan for 10 to 15 minutes, or until the pork is no longer pink. Strain and reserve the marinade.

To make the sauce: In a large no-stick frying pan over medium-high heat, combine the red peppers, scallions and oil. Cook for 3 minutes.

In a small saucepan, boil the cider until reduced to 2 tablespoons, about 5 minutes. Add the reduced cider, orange sections. grapefruit sections, black pepper, cornstarch mixture and the reserved marinade to the frying pan. Cook until thick, about 3 to 5 minutes. Pour over the pork; garnish with the mint.

Preparation time: 10 minutes plus 15 minutes marinating time
Grilling time: 15 minutes
Cooking time: 15 minutes

Per serving: 223 calories, 5.8 g. fat (23% of calories), 3.1 g. dietary fiber, 60 mg. cholesterol, 45 mg. sodium.

MAPLE-GLAZED PORK TENDERLOIN

SERVES 4

Serve this lovely dish at a fall dinner party or as a change from Thanksgiving turkey. Complement the sweet-and-sour glazed tenderloin with brussels sprouts, sautéed apples and wild rice pilaf.

4   portions pork tenderloin (3 ounces each)
¼   cup diced shallots
1   tablespoon canola oil
¼   cup sherry wine vinegar
¼   cup maple syrup
¼   cup defatted chicken stock

Heat a large no-stick frying pan on medium-high heat for 2 minutes. Sear the pork tenderloin for about 2 minutes per side. Reduce the heat to medium and add the shallots and oil. Cook until soft, about 3 minutes. Add the vinegar, maple syrup and stock. Bring to a boil and cook until syrupy, about 5 minutes. Spoon the glaze over the tenderloin.

Preparation time: 5 minutes
Cooking time: 15 minutes

Per serving: 198 calories, 6.6 g. fat (30% of calories), no dietary fiber, 60 mg. cholesterol, 76 mg. sodium.

PORK CHOPS WITH APPLE ONION RELISH

SERVES 4

*A*pples and onions are perfect partners for pork. In this recipe, they create a tangy-sweet relish that can be served hot or cold with the chops. Round out the meal with baked sweet potatoes and steamed broccoli.

4 *pork chops (3 ounces each), trimmed of fat*
½ *cup chopped onions*
1 *cinnamon stick (1½″ long)*
¼ *cup apple cider*
2½ *cups diced Granny Smith apples (about 2 large apples)*
1 *teaspoon cider vinegar*
1 *teaspoon honey*

Heat a no-stick frying pan over medium-high heat for 2 minutes. Sear the pork chops on each side until brown, about 2 minutes per side. Reduce the heat to medium and cook until no longer pink.

In a small saucepan, combine the onions, cinnamon stick and cider. Simmer over low heat for 10 minutes. Add the apples and cook for 5 minutes. Remove from the heat and add the vinegar and honey. Remove the cinnamon stick. Serve with the pork chops.

Preparation time: 10 minutes
Cooking time: 25 minutes

Chef's note: You can use any other tart, crisp apple in this recipe. For more color, don't peel the apples and use a mixture of red and green.

Per serving: 178 calories, 7.4 g. fat (37% of calories), 1.8 g. dietary fiber, 44 mg. cholesterol, 36 mg. sodium.

SIMMERED SAUERKRAUT AND PORK

SERVES 4

*B*ring Oktoberfest to your dining room when you serve this authentic German supper to family or guests. Dark rye bread, chunky cinnamon-flavored applesauce and mashed potatoes topped with browned onions complete the meal.

½ *cup dried apple slices*
1 *cup diced onions*
3 *strips turkey bacon, diced*
1 *teaspoon canola oil*
2 *cups sauerkraut, rinsed and drained*
1 *cup defatted chicken stock*
⅛ *teaspoon fennel seeds*
⅛ *teaspoon caraway seeds*
4 *pork chops (3 ounces each), trimmed of fat*

Place the apples in a small bowl; cover with hot water to rehydrate and let stand for 5 minutes. Drain.

In a Dutch oven over medium heat, combine the onions, turkey bacon and oil. Cook for 5 minutes. Add the sauerkraut, stock, rehydrated apples, fennel seeds and caraway seeds. Cover and simmer for 10 minutes.

In a no-stick frying pan, cook the pork chops until browned on each side, about 2 minutes. Place the pork chops in the sauerkraut pot. Deglaze the frying pan that the chops were cooked in with a little water and add the drippings to the sauerkraut. Simmer for 10 minutes, or until the pork chops are cooked through.

Preparation time: 10 minutes plus 5 minutes standing time
Cooking time: 30 minutes

Per serving: 222 calories, 10.4 g. fat (41% of calories), 4.7 g. dietary fiber, 51 mg. cholesterol, 339 mg. sodium.

VEGETARIAN
CASSEROLES,
STIR-FRIES
AND MORE

MEATLESS MEALS

Occasional meatless meals have become popular with many Americans, not only because they're economical but because they're healthful. Meatless dishes bring stimulating variety to our diets through the creative and nontraditional use of vegetables, pasta, dried beans and peas and seasonings. Meatless meals are power-packed with complex carbohydrates, protein, fiber, vitamins and minerals—and can be very low in fat, calories and cholesterol. Many of this chapter's main dishes are meatless variations of American favorites such as Hoppin' John or stuffed green peppers, while others are delectable originals like mushroom turnovers or chick-pea curry.

PASTA WITH FRESH TOMATO ESCAROLE SAUCE

SERVES 4

*E*scarole is another name for endive, a member of the dandelion family with deep-green, narrow, curled leaves. A good source of vitamin A, its sharp, crisp flavor enhances salads and other dishes.

- 2 *cups chopped escarole*
- 3 *ripe tomatoes, chopped and seeded*
- 1 *cup chopped red onions*
- ½ *cup defatted chicken or vegetable stock*
- ¼ *cup chopped fresh basil*
- 3 *tablespoons balsamic vinegar*
- 1 *tablespoon olive oil*
- 1 *teaspoon ground black pepper*
- 2 *cloves garlic, finely minced*
- 8 *ounces angel hair pasta*
- ½ *cup grated Parmesan cheese*

Combine the escarole, tomatoes, onions, stock, basil, vinegar, oil, pepper and garlic in a large bowl.

Cook the pasta in a large pot of boiling water for 4 minutes, or until just tender. Do not overcook. Add the hot cooked pasta to the bowl and toss. Sprinkle on the Parmesan and serve immediately.

Preparation time: 10 minutes
Cooking time: 10 minutes

Per serving: 280 calories, 5.4 g. fat (17% of calories), 2 g. dietary fiber, 49 mg. cholesterol, 85 mg. sodium.

CORIANDER CRÊPES WITH CORN AND BLACK BEAN RELISH

SERVES 4

Build a brunch around these zippy crêpes that creatively blend French and Mexican cooking influences. Serve them with pineapple wedges, mini cornmeal muffins and a key lime sorbet.

Crêpes

1½–2	cups 1% low-fat milk
1	cup instant-blending flour
½	cup fat-free egg substitute
½	cup chopped fresh coriander
¼	cup chopped scallions

Filling

8	ounces nonfat cream cheese
8	ounces nonfat sour cream
¼	cup chopped green chili peppers
½	teaspoon ground cumin

Relish

1	can (14 ounces) black beans, rinsed and drained
1	can (10 ounces) whole kernel corn, drained
1	sweet red pepper, cored and diced
2	tablespoons chopped fresh coriander
2	tablespoons lime juice
2	teaspoons olive oil
1	teaspoon chili powder

To make the crêpes: In a medium bowl, combine the milk, flour, eggs, coriander and scallions. The batter should be the consistency of heavy cream.

Coat an 8″ no-stick pan with no-stick spray; heat over medium heat. When the pan is hot, add about ¼ cup batter and swirl to coat. Cook the crêpe until it easily comes loose from the pan, about

1 minute. Turn and cook on the other side for another 30 seconds.

Repeat until all the batter is gone. Makes 12 to 15 crêpes.

To make the filling: Blend the cream cheese with the sour cream, peppers and cumin in a small bowl.

To make the relish: Combine the beans, corn, peppers, coriander, lime juice, oil and chili powder in a medium bowl.

To assemble: Place a dollop of the cream cheese mixture on each crêpe and roll up. Top each roll with relish.

Preparation time: 15 minutes
Cooking time: 25 minutes

Per serving: 434 calories, 4.7 g. fat (9% of calories), 9.3 g. dietary fiber, 14 mg. cholesterol, 823 mg. sodium.

MINTED BARLEY AND WHITE BEAN CASSEROLE

SERVES 4

Quick-cooking barley adapts this old-fashioned grain to the schedules of today's busy cooks.

1 *can (15 ounces) cannellini beans, rinsed and drained*
1 *can (15 ounces) stewed tomatoes, drained*
1 *cup quick-cooking barley*
2 *tablespoons chopped fresh mint*
1 *tablespoon grated lemon rind*
2 *cups defatted chicken or vegetable stock, heated*

Place the beans, tomatoes, barley, mint and lemon rind in a 4-quart stovetop casserole. Pour the hot stock over the ingredients and stir to blend. Cover and cook over low heat for about 20 minutes, or until the liquid is absorbed and the barley is tender.

Preparation time: 5 minutes
Cooking time: 20 minutes

Per serving: 290 calories, 1.5 g. fat (4% of calories), 15 g. dietary fiber, no cholesterol, 719 mg. sodium.

BLACK BEAN LASAGNA

SERVES 4

*B*ake two pans of this zesty lasagna at a time—one to enjoy now, the other to freeze for later. To easily freeze lasagna, line the baking dish with foil before assembling the lasagna; freeze uncovered. When frozen, remove the lasagna from the baking dish, wrap in foil and return it to the freezer.

1 *can (28 ounces) low-sodium tomatoes, drained and chopped*

1 *can (4 ounces) chopped green chilies, drained*

1 *can (8 ounces) low-sodium tomato sauce*

1 *can (15 ounces) low-sodium black beans, rinsed and drained*

1 *teaspoon ground cumin*

1 *teaspoon chili powder*

6 *no-cook lasagna noodles*

1½ *cups nonfat ricotta cheese*

1½ *cups shredded nonfat mozzarella cheese*

1½ *cups chopped fresh coriander*

In a small bowl, mix the tomatoes and chilies with the tomato sauce.

In a medium bowl, combine the beans, cumin and chili powder. Lightly mash the beans with a fork.

Coat a 9″ × 9″ pan with no-stick spray. Spoon ½ cup of the tomato mixture into the bottom of the pan. Place 2 of the noodles on the sauce. Top the noodles with ⅓ cup of the beans, ½ cup of the ricotta, ½ cup of the mozzarella, ½ cup of the sauce and ½ cup of the coriander. Repeat the layers twice.

Bake at 375° for 30 minutes, or until the lasagna bubbles.

Preparation time: 10 minutes
Baking time: 30 minutes

Per serving: 501 calories, 2.5 g. fat (5% of calories), 8.4 g. dietary fiber, 17 mg. cholesterol, 745 mg. sodium.

WILD MUSHROOM RAGOUT WITH CREAMY GRITS

SERVES 4

*S*hiitake, porcini, trumpet, crimini and morel mushrooms are only a few of the wild varieties now readily available in supermarkets. Although wild mushrooms are more expensive, just a few mixed in with domestic mushrooms add a marvelous woodsy flavor to any dish.

Ragout

¼	*cup chopped shallots*
1	*clove garlic, minced*
4	*cups assorted wild and domestic mushrooms, sliced*
½	*cup defatted chicken or vegetable stock*
¼	*cup chopped sun-dried tomatoes*
1	*teaspoon thyme*

Grits

3	*cups defatted chicken or vegetable stock*
¾	*cup quick-cooking grits*
¼	*cup grated Parmesan cheese*

To make the ragout: Coat a large no-stick frying pan with no-stick spray. Heat the shallots and garlic in the prepared pan over medium heat for about 3 minutes, or until tender. Add the mushrooms, stock, tomatoes and thyme. Sauté until heated through, about 5 minutes. Serve over the grits.

To make the grits: Heat the stock to boiling in a medium saucepan over high heat; add the grits and stir to blend. Reduce the heat to low; cover and cook for 5 to 7 minutes, or until all the liquid is absorbed. Stir in the Parmesan.

Preparation time: 10 minutes
Cooking time: 15 minutes

Per serving: 216 calories, 2.6 g. fat (10% of calories), 4.1 g. dietary fiber, 5 mg. cholesterol, 536 mg. sodium.

BEYOND MACARONI

*O*nce upon a time, spaghetti and macaroni were just about the only pastas to choose from. But now, the pasta section of your supermarket is packed with an eye-popping assortment of shapes, colors and flavors.

Pasta is the generic name applied to noodles made from a dough of durum wheat flour (called semolina) and a liquid, usually water or milk. You can buy it dried or fresh in your supermarket. Or, with a pasta machine, you can make it at home. Pasta is a super addition to a healthful diet because it's an excellent source of the complex carbohydrates that your body needs and loves.

Experiment with these pastas to add interest to your favorite salads, soups, stews, sauces and main dishes.

FLAVORS

Pasta can be subtly flavored and colored with spinach (green), tomatoes (red), beets (red) and squid ink (charcoal grey). For extra pasta pizzazz, try the varieties spiced up with cloves, black or ground red pepper. Basil, oregano, thyme, rosemary and a whole garden full of herbs also perk up plain pasta.

SHAPES

Look for shells—both big and small, wheels, twists, tubes, rings, pockets, beads, rippled strips and even pasta shaped like states, stars, letters, animals or dinosaurs. Although there are hundreds to choose from, below are some of the most common—and most exotic—pastas.

- **Agnolotti:** crescent-shaped dumplings stuffed with meat or pesto

- **Anelli:** little rings

- **Cannelonni:** rectangles stuffed and rolled into tubes, then baked

- **Capellini:** very thin spaghetti, also called angel hair
- **Cavatelli:** pea pod-shaped shells
- **Conchiglie:** shell-shaped pasta available in several sizes
- **Ditalini:** short, ridged tubes, also called thimbles
- **Farfalle:** butterfly- or bow tie-shaped
- **Fettuccine:** a narrow, flat noodle
- **Fusilli:** long or short corkscrew spaghetti
- **Gemelli:** short, thin pasta twists
- **Lasagna:** broad flat noodles with rippled edges; available in several sizes
- **Linguine:** thick spaghetti
- **Mafalda:** very narrow, lasagna-like noodles
- **Manicotti:** large hollow tubes
- **Penne:** (*quills* in Italian); about 2″ long and hollow; also called mostaccioli
- **Orzo:** rice-like pasta; also called *rosamarina*; used in soups, stews
- **Radiatore:** compact, radiator-shaped
- **Ravioli:** two pasta squares filled with meat, cheese or vegetables
- **Rotelli:** short, corkscrew pasta; also called rotini
- **Ruote:** resembles little wagon wheels
- **Tortellini:** round donuts of pasta filled with meat or cheese
- **Vermicelli:** very thin spaghetti
- **Ziti:** long, narrow hollow rods

GRILLED VEGETABLE PASTA
WITH HOT RED-PEPPER SAUCE

SERVES 4

There's nothing shy or subtle about this color-splashed pasta dish. Grilling adds a smoky taste to the vegetables, but they also may be broiled. With a shake of the bottle, you can adjust the fire in the sauce from one-alarm to three-alarm.

8 *ounces rigatoni*
2 *medium zucchini*
2 *medium yellow summer squash*
2 *fennel bulbs, cut into wedges*
1 *red onion, sliced into ¼" rings*
2 *tablespoons chopped fresh rosemary*
1 *jar (7 ounces) roasted red peppers, drained*
½ *cup defatted chicken or vegetable stock*
½ *teaspoon ground red pepper*
¼ *cup grated Parmesan cheese*

Cook the rigatoni in a large pot of boiling water for 10 to 12 minutes, or until just tender. Drain well.

Cut the zucchini and the yellow squash into ¼"-thick diagonal slices. Coat the zucchini, yellow squash, fennel and onions with no-stick spray and sprinkle with the rosemary. Place on a medium-hot grill for about 4 minutes, turning once, until golden.

Place the red peppers, stock and red pepper in a blender and puree. Heat the sauce in a small pan until warmed through.

To serve, toss the pasta with the pepper sauce and top with the grilled vegetables. Sprinkle with the Parmesan.

Preparation time: 10 minutes
Grilling time: 4 minutes
Cooking time: 15 minutes

Per serving: 95 calories, 2.7 g. fat (23% of calories), 3.4 g. dietary fiber, 5 mg. cholesterol, 246 mg. sodium.

SANTA FE SUCCOTASH

SERVES 4

*N*ative Americans of the East Coast introduced succotash—a medley of lima beans and corn—to early settlers. In this southwestern-inspired recipe, use fresh mint and corn from your garden or farmers' market.

4	*scallions, chopped*
1	*teaspoon olive oil*
1	*package (10 ounces) frozen baby lima beans, thawed*
1	*package (10 ounces) frozen corn, thawed*
1	*can (10 ounces) defatted chicken or vegetable stock*
2	*tablespoons chopped fresh mint*
½	*teaspoon black pepper*
1	*large tomato, seeded and coarsely chopped*
¼	*cup nonfat sour cream*
¼	*cup chopped fresh mint*

In a large frying pan over medium heat, sauté the scallions in the oil until just tender. Add the beans, corn, stock, mint and pepper. Simmer the mixture for about 10 minutes, or until the beans are tender. Add the tomatoes and cook for 5 more minutes.

Garnish with sour cream and mint.

Preparation time: 5 minutes
Cooking time: 20 minutes

Per serving: 174 calories, 1.6 g. fat (15% of calories), 5.6 g. dietary fiber, no cholesterol, 285 mg. sodium.

SPICY VEGETABLE POT PIES
WITH JOHNNY CAKE CRUST

SERVES 4

*P*ioneers called the cornmeal bread they made on a griddle *johnny cakes*. In this recipe, cornmeal crusts top individual vegetable casseroles. We've used buttermilk, which is fat-free, and egg substitute to reduce the fat.

Filling

1	cup chopped zucchini
1	cup chopped carrots
1	cup chopped onions
½	cup water
1½	cups prepared salsa

Topping

½	cup cornmeal
½	cup unbleached flour
1	teaspoon baking powder
½	cup buttermilk
¼	cup fat-free egg substitute
1	tablespoon honey

To make the filling: Place the zucchini, carrots and onions in a large no-stick frying pan with the water. Cook over medium heat until the vegetables have softened, about 5 minutes. Add the salsa to the vegetables and continue to cook for about 5 more minutes. Prepare the topping while the vegetables are cooking.

To make the topping: In a medium bowl, mix the cornmeal, flour and baking powder. In a small bowl, combine the buttermilk, eggs and honey. Add the liquid ingredients to the dry ingredients and stir until blended.

To assemble the pies: Divide the vegetable mixture among 4 individual 5″ casseroles or custard dishes. Top each casserole with one-fourth of the cornmeal topping. Bake at 350° for 20 minutes, or until the top is brown and the vegetables are bubbling.

Preparation time: 15 minutes
Cooking time: 10 minutes
Baking time: 20 minutes

Per serving: 210 calories, 3.2 g. fat (13% of calories), 4.8 g. dietary fiber, 1.1 mg. cholesterol, 486 mg. sodium.

CORN, TOMATO AND BASIL TOSTADAS

SERVES 4

*T*ortillas become edible serving plates for this light, layered dish. Using feta cheese and low-fat cream cheese and baking the tortillas keeps fat in this recipe to a minimum.

8	*corn tortillas, 6" in diameter*
½	*cup nonfat cream cheese*
1	*cup cooked corn*
1	*cup chopped, seeded tomatoes*
⅓	*cup chopped black olives*
½	*cup chopped fresh basil*
½	*cup chopped sweet onions*
½	*cup crumbled feta cheese*

Coat the tortillas with no-stick spray. Place the tortillas on a baking sheet and bake at 350° for about 20 minutes, or until crispy. When cool, spread 1 tablespoon of cream cheese on each tortilla.

While the tortillas are crisping, combine the corn, tomatoes, olives, basil, onions and feta in a medium bowl. Top each tortilla with ½ cup of the mixture and serve.

Preparation time: 20 minutes
Baking time: 20 minutes

Per serving: 272 calories, 8.6 g. fat (27% of calories), 5.3 g. dietary fiber, 18 mg. cholesterol, 533 mg. sodium.

BLACK MUSHROOM, PEA POD AND RED PEPPER FRICASSEE

SERVES 4

*F*ricassee is a dish of stewed or fried meat served in a gravy made from its own juices. Dried shiitake mushrooms replace the meat in this vegetarian, stir-fried version.

> 4 *ounces dried shiitake mushrooms*
> 4 *scallions, chopped*
> 1 *tablespoon chopped fresh ginger*
> 1 *clove garlic, minced*
> 2 *red sweet peppers, cored and sliced*
> 4 *ounces pea pods, stemmed*
> 1 *tablespoon cornstarch*
> 1 *cup defatted chicken or vegetable stock*
> 2 *tablespoons hoisin sauce*
> 1 *tablespoon low-sodium soy sauce*
> 4 *cups cooked couscous*

Place the mushrooms in a small bowl and cover with hot water. Let sit 30 minutes, or until soft. Drain; remove stems; chop the mushrooms.

Coat a large no-stick frying pan with no-stick spray. Cook the scallions, ginger and garlic in the prepared pan over medium heat for about 1 minute to release their flavors. Add the peppers, mushrooms and pea pods and cook, stirring, for about 3 minutes, or until the vegetables are cooked but still crispy.

Dissolve the cornstarch in the stock and add the hoisin sauce and soy sauce. Pour the stock mixture over the vegetables and cook until the sauce thickens. Serve over the couscous.

Preparation time: 10 minutes plus 30 minutes standing time
Cooking time: 5 minutes

Chef's note: If shiitake mushrooms are unavailable, 1 ounce dried black mushrooms can be substituted. Dried black mushrooms are available in Asian markets or in the foreign-food aisle of the grocery store.

Per serving: 333 calories, 0.8 g. fat (2% of calories), 9.8 g. dietary fiber, no cholesterol, 339 mg. sodium.

BROCCOLI TIAN

SERVES 4

tian is a type of pan used in France. Although this dish could be called a casserole, *tian* adds a touch of panache to a week-night standby.

1	*medium onion, chopped*
2	*cloves garlic, minced*
3	*cups chopped broccoli*
1½	*cups quick-cooking brown rice*
1½	*cups defatted chicken or vegetable stock, heated*
¼	*cup sunflower seeds*
2	*tablespoons low-sodium soy sauce*
½	*cup shredded nonfat mozzarella cheese*

Coat a medium frying pan with no-stick spray. Sauté the onions and garlic in the prepared pan for about 3 minutes. Transfer the onions and garlic to a large casserole and add the broccoli, rice, stock, sunflower seeds and soy sauce. Sprinkle the mozzarella on top and lightly cover with foil. Bake at 375° for 30 minutes.

Preparation time: 10 minutes
Cooking time: 3 minutes
Baking time: 30 minutes

Per serving: 372 calories, 6.8 g. fat (16% of calories), 7 g. dietary fiber, 3 mg. cholesterol, 620 mg. sodium.

ZUCCHINI BURRITO

SERVES 4

*L*ow-fat Cheddar cheese keeps both fat and calories to a bare minimum in this original variation of the popular burrito. Serve with a mixed melon salad with lime dressing and no-fat refried black beans.

1 small onion, chopped

2 cloves garlic, minced

4 cups shredded zucchini

1 can (8 ounces) sliced water chestnuts, drained

1 tomato, seeded and chopped

½ teaspoon ground red pepper

8 flour tortillas, 8" in diameter

½ cup shredded low-fat Cheddar cheese

Coat a large no-stick frying pan with no-stick spray. Sauté the onions and garlic over medium heat until soft, about 5 minutes. Add the zucchini, water chestnuts, tomatoes and red pepper and continue to cook until just heated through.

While the zucchini mixture is cooking, wrap the tortillas in foil and heat at 325° for about 10 minutes, or until soft.

To serve, place ½ cup of the zucchini mixture in each tortilla, top with 1 tablespoon of the Parmesan and roll up.

Preparation time: 10 minutes
Cooking time: 10 minutes
Baking time: 10 minutes

Per serving: 388 calories, 6.6 g. fat (15% of calories), 8.6 g. dietary fiber, 6 mg. cholesterol, 211 mg. sodium.

BLACK BEAN CAKES

---

*B*lack beans are an excellent source of protein and virtually fat-free. Enjoy them in this supper with a south-of-the-border flair.

1 *can (14 ounces) black beans, rinsed and drained*
2 *tablespoons unbleached flour*
4 *scallions, chopped*
1 *clove garlic, minced*
1 *teaspoon ground cumin*
1 *teaspoon chili powder*
1 *teaspoon ground coriander*
4 *cups cooked rice*
1 *cup salsa*
½ *cup nonfat sour cream*

Place the beans, flour, scallions, garlic, cumin, chili powder and coriander in a food processor and process until blended, but not pureed.

Form the black bean mixture into 4 patties. Heat a large no-stick frying pan over medium heat. Coat the patties with no-stick spray and add them to the hot pan. Cook the patties, turning once, for about 10 minutes, or until they are heated through.

Serve each patty on a bed of rice. Top with the salsa and sour cream.

Preparation time: 5 minutes
Cooking time: 10 minutes

Per serving: 414 calories, 3.1 g. fat (6% of calories), 8.3 g. dietary fiber, no cholesterol, 580 mg. sodium.

LEEK AND SPINACH QUICHE WITH TOMATO SAUCE

SERVES 4

Quiche doesn't require a high-fat crust to be delicious. In this low-fat version, the egg mixture creates its own crust.

2 teaspoons olive oil
1 leek, chopped
1 medium onion, chopped
1 clove garlic, minced
2 cups fat-free egg substitute
1 package (10 ounces) frozen spinach, thawed and squeezed dry
¼ teaspoon black pepper
¼ teaspoon grated nutmeg
1 can (14 ounces) stewed tomatoes
1 cup nonfat yogurt

Heat the oil in a large no-stick frying pan over medium heat and sauté the leeks, onions and garlic until tender, about 5 minutes. Add the eggs, spinach, pepper and nutmeg to the pan and cover. Reduce the heat to low and cook for 10 minutes, or until the egg mixture is set.

Place the pan under a broiler for 1 minute, or until the top is brown.

While the quiche is cooking, heat the tomatoes in a medium frying pan over medium-high heat until thickened, about 3 minutes.

To serve, cut the quiche into wedges and top with the tomato sauce and yogurt.

Preparation time: 10 minutes
Cooking time: 20 minutes
Chef's note: If your frying pan does not have an ovenproof handle, wrap in several layers of aluminum foil before broiling.

Per serving: 181 calories, 2.8 g. fat (13% of calories), 3.5 g. dietary fiber, 1 mg. cholesterol, 529 mg. sodium.

DENVER SPAGHETTI OMELET

SERVES 4

*I*s it an omelet or a spaghetti pie? Is it Italian or is it western? It's all of these and more—colorful, loaded with complex carbohydrates and very low in fat.

> 4 *ounces spaghetti*
> 1 *teaspoon olive oil*
> ½ *cup chopped sweet red peppers*
> ½ *cup chopped green peppers*
> ½ *cup chopped onions*
> 1 *teaspoon dried Italian seasoning*
> 1 *cup fat-free egg substitute*
> 2 *cups low-fat prepared marinara sauce, heated*

Cook the spaghetti in a large pot of boiling water for 8 to 10 minutes, or until just tender. Drain well.

In a large no-stick frying pan coated with the oil, sauté the red peppers, green peppers and onions over medium heat until tender, about 5 minutes. Add the spaghetti to the pan and toss to combine.

Mix the Italian seasoning with the eggs and pour over the spaghetti in the hot pan. Cover and reduce the heat to low. Cook until the omelet has set, about 5 to 8 minutes.

Place the pan under a broiler for about 3 minutes until the top is golden (see Chef's note on page 190).

To serve, cut into wedges and top with the marinara sauce.

Preparation time: 10 minutes
Baking time: 25 minutes
Broiling time: 3 minutes

Per serving: 232 calories, 4.8 g. fat (18% of calories), 0.6 g. dietary fiber, no cholesterol, 657 mg. sodium.

Southern Hoppin' John

SERVES 4

The origins of this dish lie in the South, but the meaning behind the name remains a mystery. It may come from a game played on New Year's Eve. Both the game and the dish—a chunky vegetable stew—were thought to bring good luck.

1 large onion, chopped

2 cloves garlic, minced

1 teaspoon olive oil

1 package (10 ounces) frozen black-eyed peas, thawed

½ cup long-grain rice

2 carrots, diced

2 stalks celery, diced

1 teaspoon dried thyme

½ teaspoon red-pepper flakes

2 cups defatted chicken or vegetable stock

In a large saucepan over medium heat, sauté the onions and garlic in the oil until tender, about 5 minutes. Add the peas, rice, carrots, celery, thyme and pepper flakes to the pan; mix.

Add the stock and bring the mixture to a boil over high heat. Then reduce the heat, cover and simmer for 25 minutes, or until the rice is tender.

Preparation time: 10 minutes
Cooking time: 30 minutes

Per serving: 209 calories, 1.7 g. fat (7% of calories), 7.1 g. dietary fiber, no cholesterol, 271 mg. sodium.

GOLDEN POTATO CURRY WITH PEAS

SERVES 4

*I*nspired by *dam alu*, the potato curry of India, this variation calls for browned, rather than deep-fried, potatoes. Serve the curry with marinated cucumbers, Indian flat bread and a honeydew melon salad.

3 *medium potatoes, washed and cubed*
1 *medium onion, chopped*
1 *clove garlic, chopped*
1 *teaspoon cumin seeds*
1 *teaspoon turmeric*
2 *cups defatted chicken or vegetable stock*
1 *package (10 ounces) frozen peas, thawed*
2 *tablespoons chopped fresh coriander*
1 *tablespoon grated lemon rind*
4 *cups cooked basmati rice (see note)*
¼ *cup chopped peanuts*

Coat a large no-stick frying pan with no-stick spray. Sauté the potatoes, onions, garlic, cumin seeds and turmeric over medium heat. Stir the mixture frequently to keep it from sticking, and cook until the potatoes are browned, about 3 minutes.

Add the stock, peas, coriander and lemon rind to the pan and continue cooking for 15 minutes, or until the potatoes are tender.

Serve over the rice and sprinkle with the peanuts.

Preparation time: 10 minutes
Cooking time: 20 minutes

Chef's note: Basmati rice is a fragrant rice native to India; you may substitute converted rice.

Per serving: 487 calories, 5.4 g. fat (10% of calories), 7 g. dietary fiber, no cholesterol, 378 mg. sodium.

EGGPLANT STRATA

SERVES 4

*S*trata means layers, and in this layered dish, ricotta cheese and roasted red peppers are sandwiched between slices of eggplant. Serve it with herbed rolls and a mixed green salad tossed with a raspberry vinaigrette dressing.

1	*1-pound eggplant, thinly sliced*
1½	*cups nonfat ricotta cheese*
2	*tablespoons Dijon mustard*
1	*jar (7 ounces) roasted red peppers, drained*
½	*cup chopped black olives*
1	*cup shredded low-fat mozzarella cheese*

Coat the eggplant slices with no-stick spray and cook them in a no-stick pan over medium heat until softened, about 5 minutes.

While the eggplant is cooking, mix the ricotta cheese and Dijon mustard in a medium bowl.

Coat a 9″ × 9″ baking pan with no-stick spray.

Line the bottom of the prepared pan with half of the eggplant slices. Place the red peppers over the eggplant, then spread the ricotta mixture on top. Sprinkle the black olives evenly over the ricotta.

Add another layer of the remaining eggplant, and top the dish with the mozzarella.

Bake at 375° for 20 minutes.

Preparation time: 10 minutes
Cooking time: 20 minutes

Per serving: 223 calories, 9.5 g. fat (34% of calories), 1.4 g. dietary fiber, 9 mg. cholesterol, 428 mg. sodium.

CHICK-PEA CURRY

SERVES 4

*A*lso known as garbanzo beans, nutlike chick-peas have a firm but creamy texture. They supply the protein for this tomato-based curry.

2   *teaspoons olive oil*
1   *large onion, chopped*
1   *green pepper, chopped*
4   *stalks celery, chopped*
3   *cloves garlic, minced*
3   *cups defatted chicken or vegetable stock*
1   *can (15 ounces) chick-peas, rinsed and drained*
1   *can (14 ounces) reduced-sodium tomatoes, drained and chopped*
6   *small new potatoes, quartered*
3   *tablespoons tomato paste*
1   *tablespoon curry powder*

Heat the oil in a large saucepan over medium heat. Add the onions, peppers, celery and garlic and sauté until the vegetables are tender, about 10 minutes.

Stir in the stock, chick-peas, tomatoes, potatoes, tomato paste and curry powder. Cover and simmer over medium heat for 30 minutes, or until the potatoes are tender.

Preparation time: 15 minutes
Cooking time: 40 minutes

Per serving: 376 calories, 5.2 g. fat (12% of calories), 11 g. dietary fiber, no cholesterol, 951 mg. sodium.

SPAGHETTI SQUASH WITH SPINACH PESTO

SERVES 4

*S*quash is the "spaghetti" in this pastalike dish. When cooked and shredded, it forms spaghetti-like strands.

- 1 *spaghetti squash, halved*
- 2 *tablespoons pine nuts*
- 1 *clove garlic, minced*
- 4 *ounces fresh spinach*
- ½ *cup crumbled feta cheese*
- 1 *tablespoon lemon juice*
- 1 *tablespoon grated lemon rind*
- ½ *cup nonfat yogurt*

Cover both halves of the squash with a large sheet of plastic wrap and microwave for about 10 minutes, or until tender. Remove the seeds from the squash and shred the squash with a fork to form spaghetti-like strands.

While the squash is cooking, prepare the pesto. Add the pine nuts and the garlic to a food processor fitted with a steel blade; pulse to chop. Add the spinach and pulse to chop. Then add the cheese, lemon juice and lemon rind; pulse to blend.

To serve, toss the squash with the pesto and top each serving with 2 tablespoons of the yogurt.

Preparation time: 10 minutes
Microwaving time: 10 minutes

Chef's note: Spaghetti squash can also be baked in the oven at 350° for 45 minutes.

Per serving: 100 calories, 5.7 g. fat (48% of calories), 0.9 g. dietary fiber, 13 mg. cholesterol, 206 mg. sodium.

MUSHROOM AND ASPARAGUS STROGANOFF

*N*o-yolk egg noodles help reduce the fat and cholesterol in this vegetarian adaptation of a classic dish.

- *1 sweet red pepper, cored and sliced*
- *4 ounces mushrooms, sliced*
- *1 small onion, sliced*
- *6 stalks asparagus, chopped*
- *1 cup defatted chicken or vegetable stock*
- *1 teaspoon paprika*
- *¼ teaspoon grated nutmeg*
- *8 ounces wide no-yolk noodles*
- *½ cup nonfat sour cream*
- *½ cup grated Parmesan cheese*

Coat a large no-stick pan with no-stick spray. Sauté the red peppers, mushrooms, onions and asparagus over medium heat about 5 minutes, or until soft. Add the stock, paprika and nutmeg, and continue to cook for 10 minutes.

While the vegetables are cooking, cook the noodles in a large pot of boiling water for 8 to 10 minutes, or until just tender. Drain well.

Just before serving, stir the sour cream into the warm vegetables. Serve the stroganoff over the cooked noodles; sprinkle with the Parmesan.

Preparation time: 10 minutes
Cooking time: 25 minutes

Per serving: 316 calories, 4.9 g. fat (14% of calories), 1.4 g. dietary fiber, 10 mg. cholesterol, 403 mg. sodium.

Lentil Potato Cakes

SERVES 4

*S*weet-tart mango chutney is a tangy accompaniment to these no-fat potato cakes. For easier handling, use mashed potatoes that are fairly dry.

½ *cup lentils*
1 *medium onion, chopped*
1 *clove garlic, minced*
1 *teaspoon ground coriander*
1 *teaspoon curry powder*
½ *teaspoon turmeric*
½ *teaspoon ground cumin*
2 *cups prepared mashed potatoes*
½ *cup mango chutney*
½ *cup nonfat yogurt*

Bring 4 cups of water to a boil over high heat in a large saucepan. Add the lentils; reduce the heat and simmer for 15 minutes, or until barely tender. Drain the lentils.

While the lentils are cooking, coat a medium frying pan with no-stick spray. Sauté the onions and garlic in the prepared pan over medium heat until soft, about 3 minutes. Add the coriander, curry powder, turmeric and cumin to the pan; continue to sauté for 1 more minute.

In a large bowl, combine the onion mixture, lentils and mashed potatoes until blended. Form into small patties about 3″ in diameter and ¼″ thick. Heat a large no-stick pan until hot. Coat the patties with no-stick spray and add them to the pan. Cook the patties until browned, about 2 minutes on each side.

Serve the patties with the chutney and yogurt.

Preparation time: 10 minutes
Cooking time: 25 minutes
Per serving: 287 calories, 1.2 g. fat (4% of calories), 1.3 g. dietary fiber, 3 mg. cholesterol, 551 mg. sodium.

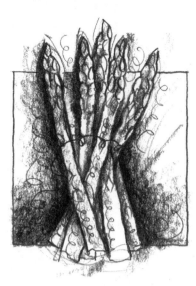

CHAPTER 9

ALL-TIME
FAVORITE
SIDE DISHES

CLASSIC ACCOMPANIMENTS

hink of a meal's main dish as the star and the side dishes as the supporting cast. They make the star look (and in this case, taste) great, but they can also earn some applause on their own. Side dishes enhance the entrée by providing contrasting or complementary flavors, colors and textures. They also bolster the healthful benefit of a meal by adding nutrients the main dish lacks. But dreaming up creative side dishes can be trying at best. So here are 34 classic accompaniments that will complement your meal's star—whether it's meatloaf or grilled salmon steaks.

GRILLED VEGETABLES

rilling vegetables helps keep you out of the kitchen on sultry summer evenings. It's quick and easy to do and adds a light smoky flavor without adding a lot of fat.

½	small eggplant, sliced ½″ thick
1	yellow summer squash, halved lengthwise
1	zucchini, halved lengthwise
1	sweet red pepper, cut lengthwise into 2″ wedges
1	small onion, sliced ½″ thick
1	tablespoon extra-virgin olive oil
1	clove garlic, minced
¼	cup chopped fresh basil
2	teaspoons lemon juice
⅛	teaspoon ground black pepper

In a large bowl, combine the eggplant, summer squash, zucchini, red peppers, onions, oil and garlic. Toss well. Place the vegetables in a single layer directly on a grill rack, 4″ to 6″ from the heat. Grill for 6 to 8 minutes, turning once.

In a large bowl, toss the grilled vegetables with the basil, lemon juice and black pepper.

Preparation time: 10 minutes
Grilling time: 8 minutes

Chef's note: To cook the vegetables indoors, toss them with oil and garlic and place in a single layer on a 15″ × 10″ jelly-roll pan. Broil 4″ from the heat for 8 to 12 minutes, turning occasionally, until lightly browned.

Per serving: 71 calories, 3.7 g. fat (43% of calories), 1.8 g. dietary fiber, no cholesterol, 4 mg. sodium.

Beef and Caramelized Onions (page 160)

Pulled Pork Barbecue (page 168)

Sunshine Pork (page 170)

Coriander Crêpes with Corn and Black Bean Relish (page 176)

Grilled Vegetable Pasta with Hot Red-Pepper Sauce (page 182)

Black Mushroom, Pea Pod and Red Pepper Fricassee (page 186)

Garlicky Green Beans (page 223)

Molasses Baked Beans (page 229)

SUMMER LAYERED VEGETABLES

here's more than one variety of thyme, so experiment with different kinds such as lemon or broadleaf in this baked dish that takes advantage of luscious, fresh-from-the-garden summer vegetables.

> 4 *plum tomatoes, sliced ¼" thick*
> 1 *tablespoon extra-virgin olive oil*
> 1 *tablespoon chopped fresh thyme*
> *Ground black pepper*
> 1 *small onion, thinly sliced and separated into rings*
> 1 *small zucchini, sliced ⅛" thick*
> 1 *small yellow summer squash, sliced ⅛" thick*

Spray an 11" × 7" oval gratin dish with no-stick spray. Layer one-half of the tomatoes in the bottom of the dish. Lightly brush with ½ teaspoon oil and sprinkle with ½ teaspoon thyme and some pepper. Place one-third of the onions over the tomatoes. Layer the zucchini over the onions and top with 1 teaspoon oil, 1 teaspoon thyme and a sprinkle of pepper. Finish with another third of the onions.

Repeat, using the yellow squash, brushing with oil and sprinkling with thyme and pepper. Lay the remaining onions over the yellow squash and top with the remaining tomatoes. Brush the tomatoes with the remaining ½ teaspoon oil and sprinkle with the remaining ½ teaspoon thyme and pepper. Cover with foil and bake at 425° for 20 to 30 minutes, or until the vegetables are crisp-tender.

Preparation time: 10 minutes
Baking time: 30 minutes

Per serving: 73 calories, 4 g. fat (44% of calories), 2.7 g. dietary fiber, no cholesterol, 13 mg. sodium.

Souffléed Broccoli and Corn

*A*lthough the recipe calls for frozen vegetables, this puffed casserole is also an attractive way to use fresh garden produce. It should be served immediately because it will gradually begin to sink as it cools.

1½	*tablespoons cornstarch*
¾	*cup skim milk*
½	*cup fat-free egg substitute*
1	*cup frozen chopped broccoli, thawed*
1	*cup frozen corn, thawed*
½	*cup shredded reduced-fat Cheddar cheese*
¼	*cup snipped chives*
¼	*teaspoon grated nutmeg*
	Pinch of ground black pepper
1	*egg white, beaten to stiff peaks*

Place the cornstarch in a medium saucepan and slowly whisk in the milk, stirring until the cornstarch is dissolved. Bring to a boil over medium-high heat and boil for 1 minute, stirring constantly.

Remove from the heat and slowly whisk in the eggs. Add the broccoli, corn, ¼ cup of the Cheddar, chives, nutmeg and pepper; stir until combined. Fold in the egg white.

Coat an 11″ × 17″ oval gratin dish with no-stick spray. Pour the mixture into the prepared dish and sprinkle with the remaining ¼ cup of Cheddar. Bake at 425° for 15 to 20 minutes, or until puffed and lightly browned.

Preparation time: 10 minutes
Cooking time: 25 minutes

Per serving: 129 calories, 2.3 g. fat (15% of calories), 2.8 g. dietary fiber, 7 mg. cholesterol, 294 mg. sodium.

LEMON PEPPER CAULIFLOWER

*L*ook for the unusual green or purple cauliflower for a change of pace. All varieties are high in vitamin C and very low in calories—about 15 per ½-cup serving.

4 cups cauliflower florets
¼ cup defatted chicken stock
2 teaspoons lemon juice
2 teaspoons grated lemon rind
½ teaspoon no-salt lemon pepper seasoning
1 teaspoon cornstarch mixed with 1 tablespoon water

In a large saucepan, bring 1″ of water to a boil. Arrange the cauliflower in a steamer basket and place over the boiling water. Cover and steam for 3 to 5 minutes, or until the cauliflower is crisp-tender.

Meanwhile, in a small saucepan, combine the stock, lemon juice, lemon rind and lemon pepper. Bring to a boil over medium heat and stir in the cornstarch mixture. Cook for 30 to 60 seconds, or until the mixture is bubbly and slightly thickened.

Place the steamed cauliflower in a serving bowl and toss with the lemon pepper mixture.

Preparation time: 5 minutes
Cooking time: 5 minutes

Per serving: 29 calories, 0.2 g. fat (5% of calories), 2.4 g. dietary fiber, no cholesterol, 45 mg. sodium.

SPINACH AND RICE CASSEROLE

SERVES 6

*S*erve this triple-layered, green-and-white dish with baked salmon steaks or shish kabob.

> 1 *cup long-grain white rice*
> ½ *cup diced onions*
> 2 *tablespoons sliced scallions*
> 1 *tablespoon chopped fresh dill*
> 1 *tablespoon chopped fresh parsley*
> 2 *teaspoons canola oil*
> 1 *teaspoon grated lemon rind*
> ⅛ *teaspoon ground black pepper*
> 4 *cups lightly packed chopped fresh spinach*
> 2 *cups defatted chicken stock*

In a medium bowl, combine the rice, onions, scallions, dill, parsley, oil, lemon rind and pepper; mix well.

Coat an 8-cup casserole with no-stick spray. Place one-third of the spinach on the bottom; spoon half of the rice mixture over the spinach. Repeat, using the remaining spinach and rice (ending with spinach).

In a medium saucepan, bring the stock to a boil over high heat. Pour the boiling stock over the casserole mixture, cover and bake at 350° for 30 to 35 minutes, or until the rice is tender and the liquid has been absorbed.

Preparation time: 10 minutes
Cooking time: 40 minutes

Per serving: 146 calories, 1.9 g. fat (12% of calories), 1.6 g. dietary fiber, no cholesterol, 189 mg. sodium.

FRIED GREEN TOMATOES AND ONIONS

*P*opularized by the movie of the same name, old-time cornmeal-coated fried green tomatoes are the perfect accompaniment to barbecued chicken or beef. Try sweet onions such as Vidalia in this recipe.

½ *cup yellow cornmeal*

¼ *cup dry Italian bread crumbs*

1 *tablespoon dried basil*

⅛ *teaspoon ground black pepper*

½ *cup fat-free egg substitute*

2 *green tomatoes, sliced ¼" thick*

1 *onion, sliced ¼" thick*

In a shallow bowl, combine the cornmeal, bread crumbs, basil and pepper. Pour the eggs into a second shallow bowl.

Dip the tomato slices and onion slices into the eggs, and then into the cornmeal mixture, coating well.

Cover a 15″ × 10″ jelly-roll pan with foil; spray foil with no-stick spray. Place the tomato slices and onions slices on the prepared pan. Spray the tomatoes and onions lightly with no-stick spray.

Broil 4″ from the heat for 3 minutes on each side, or until lightly browned.

Preparation time: 10 minutes
Broiling time: 6 minutes

Per serving: 120 calories, 1.2 g. fat (8% of calories), 3.9 g. dietary fiber, no cholesterol, 99 mg. sodium.

Low-Fat Pizzazz for Plain Vegetables

America's backyard gardens, farmers' markets and supermarket produce departments abound with a cornucopia of fresh vegetables. If salt, pepper and a pat of butter are your traditional toppings, try one of these six low-fat but flavor-filled tricks for putting pizzazz in plain veggies from squash to beets to brussels sprouts.

• **Flavored vinegars.** You'll find flavored vinegars in your supermarket's condiment or gourmet section. Use them to marinate vegetables or sliced fresh tomatoes, or as a dressing for a tossed salad of mixed greens and vegetables.

• **Low-fat or nonfat sour cream.** Crown baked potatoes or beets with a dollop of sour cream. Top with a dusting of fresh or dried herbs such as basil, thyme, oregano, mint, chives or dill.

• **Parmesan cheese.** Just a teaspoon or two will add zest to squash, mashed potatoes, broccoli, cauliflower and Brussels sprouts. For maximum flavor, buy a chunk of fresh Parmesan and grate it yourself. Although Parmesan cheese is high in fat, a little goes a long way when sprinkled over vegetables.

• **Herbed olive oil.** Olive oil, a monounsaturated fat that may help lower cholesterol, easily absorbs the flavors of fresh herbs. Use herbed olive oil in salad dressings, drizzle it over hot vegetables or brush it onto vegetables during grilling.

To make your own herbed olive oil, choose a single herb or an herb combination. Wash and pat dry the herbs, discarding any damaged or brown leaves. Large-leafed herbs such as basil or sage should be cut or torn into pieces. Choose a small glass jar with a tight-fitting lid. Firmly pack it with the herb. Fill the jar with extra-virgin olive oil until it completely covers the herb, and seal. Refrigerate for at least 1 week.

Remove the jar from the refrigerator and allow it to come to room temperature (the olive oil will have solidified). When the oil is liquid, pour the herb/oil mixture through a wire strainer to remove any pieces of herb. Refill the jar with the herbed olive oil and refrigerate. Keep refrigerated after use to prevent bacterial growth, such as botulism.

• **Seasoned salts.** In the spices and seasonings section of your supermarket, you'll find a wide range of seasoned salts and peppers that dress up vegetables with just a dash. Or try one of these make-your-own combinations:

Mix 1 tablespoon *each* of dried thyme, ground bay leaves, dried basil and dried rosemary; 1½ teaspoons *each* of paprika and dry mustard; ½ teaspoon *each* of dried dill and ground black pepper; 1 teaspoon garlic powder and 2 tablespoons salt. Crush in a mortar or in a blender at lowest speed until mixture is finely ground. Store in a glass container with a tight-fitting lid.

Combine 2 tablespoons *each* of dried parsley, paprika and salt; 1 tablespoon of chives; ½ teaspoon *each* of ground black pepper, ground red pepper, marjoram and garlic powder; and ½ cup sesame seeds. Store in a glass container with a tight-fitting lid.

• **Fresh and dried herbs.** With salt and pepper or a smidgen of olive oil, fresh and dried herbs make plain veggies something special. Basil, dill, rosemary, thyme and oregano are versatile herbs to keep on hand, either dried or in a kitchen window herb garden. For a simple, flavorful side dish, cut red potatoes into ½"-thick slices. Place the slices in a shallow pan and brush with olive oil. Sprinkle with crushed dried rosemary, salt and pepper. Place the pan on the top rack of the oven. Roast at 400° until the potatoes are fork-tender.

SPICY VEGETABLE SAUTÉ

*C*omplement simple grilled chicken, pork or fish with this zippy stir-fry of colorful vegetables.

   2   *teaspoons olive oil*
   1   *medium onion, sliced*
   2   *cloves garlic, minced*
   1   *medium carrot, thinly sliced on the diagonal*
   2   *tablespoons water*
   1   *green pepper, cut into 1" pieces*
   2   *plum tomatoes, diced*
  ¼   *cup defatted chicken stock*
   1   *teaspoon cornstarch mixed with 1 tablespoon water*
   1   *teaspoon low-sodium soy sauce*
  ¼   *teaspoon red-pepper flakes, or to taste*

Coat a large no-stick frying pan with no-stick spray. Over medium heat, heat the oil until hot. Add the onions and garlic and sauté for 1 minute. Add the carrots and water; cover and cook for 2 minutes.

Remove the cover, increase the heat to high, add the green pepper and sauté for 1 minute. Add the tomatoes and cook for 1 to 2 minutes.

In a small bowl mix together the stock, cornstarch mixture, soy sauce and pepper flakes. Add to the vegetable mixture, bring to a boil and cook until the liquid has thickened.

Preparation time: 10 minutes
Cooking time: 10 minutes

Per serving: 64 calories, 2.6 g. fat (34% of calories), 2.2 g. dietary fiber, no cholesterol, 87 mg. sodium.

SPICED BEETS

*S*erve these sweet-spicy beets with grilled or roasted meats or your favorite deli sandwich. They'll keep in the refrigerator for up to a week.

2 *tablespoons raspberry vinegar*
2 *tablespoons orange juice*
1 *tablespoon all-fruit apricot spread*
1 *teaspoon grated orange rind*
½ *teaspoon whole fennel seeds*
½ *teaspoon whole cloves*
½ *cinnamon stick*
1 *can (16 ounces) sliced beets, drained, with 2 tablespoons juice reserved*

In a small saucepan, combine the vinegar, orange juice, apricot spread, orange rind, fennel seeds, cloves and cinnamon stick. Bring to a boil over medium heat and stir until the apricot spread is dissolved.

In a medium bowl, combine the beets with the reserved beet juice. Pour the hot vinegar mixture over the beets and cool for 20 minutes, or until room temperature.

Preparation time: 5 minutes plus 20 minutes cooling time
Cooking time: 2 minutes

Chef's note: To substitute fresh beets for canned, cut the tops from the beets, leaving a 1″ stem. Wash the beets and steam them until tender, or place them in a pan and half cover them with water. Cover the pan and cook for ½ to 1 hour, or until tender. You may need to add water during the cooking period. When the beets are done, let them cool slightly, then slip the skins off of them.

Per serving: 55 calories, 0.2 g. fat (3% of calories), 2 g. dietary fiber, no cholesterol, 312 mg. sodium.

EGGPLANT AND TOMATOES WITH GARLIC

SERVES 4

estern eggplant is the most common variety in this country, but you might want to try sweet, mild white or Japanese eggplant in this recipe, which is reminiscent of ratatouille.

½ medium eggplant, peeled and cut into ¾" cubes
1 can (14½ ounces) tomatoes, chopped
1 tablespoon minced shallots
1 tablespoon chopped fresh basil
1 tablespoon chopped fresh oregano
1 tablespoon chopped fresh Italian parsley
2 cloves garlic, minced
¼ teaspoon cracked black pepper

In a large saucepan, bring 1" of water to a boil. Arrange the eggplant in a steamer basket; place over the boiling water. Cover and steam for 5 to 8 minutes, or until the eggplant is tender.

In a large frying pan, combine the eggplant, tomatoes, shallots, basil, oregano, parsley, garlic and pepper. Bring to a boil over high heat, reduce the heat to low and simmer for 10 to 12 minutes, or until the vegetables are tender and slightly thickened.

Preparation time: 10 minutes
Cooking time: 20 minutes

Per serving: 39 calories, 0.4 g. fat (8% of calories), 0.9 g. dietary fiber, no cholesterol, 170 mg. sodium.

FRESH BASIL-STUFFED TOMATOES

SERVES 6

*L*emon, cinnamon or Greek basil will add an intriguing flavor twist to this tomato-lover's dish.

½   *cup fresh whole-wheat bread crumbs*
¼   *cup grated Parmesan cheese*
¼   *cup lightly packed chopped fresh basil*
⅛   *teaspoon ground black pepper*
2   *teaspoons extra-virgin olive oil*
3   *medium tomatoes*

In a small bowl, combine the bread crumbs, Parmesan, basil and pepper; mix well. Add the oil and stir until well-combined.

Slice the tomatoes in half crosswise and squeeze gently to remove the seeds. Place 2 tablespoons of the bread crumb stuffing into each tomato, mounding slightly. Place on a broiling pan or a small baking sheet. Broil 4″ from the heat for 1 to 2 minutes, or until lightly browned.

Preparation time: 10 minutes
Broiling time: 2 minutes

Chef's note: To make fresh bread crumbs, cut bread into cubes and place them in your food processor. Pulse the processor on and off until crumbs form. Or use a fork to pull the bread apart, repeating until you produce the desired crumb size.

Per serving: 56 calories, 3.1 g. fat (48% of calories), 0.9 g. dietary fiber, 3.3 mg. cholesterol, 102 mg. sodium.

ASPARAGUS WITH SESAME AND ORANGE

SERVES 4

*S*pring is the season for asparagus. Celebrate the first delectable crop with this elegant side dish.

1   teaspoon canola oil
1   clove garlic, minced
1   pound asparagus, trimmed and cut diagonally
     into 1" pieces
¼   cup orange juice
½   teaspoon honey
1   teaspoon cornstarch mixed with 1 tablespoon water
1   tablespoon toasted sesame seeds
1   teaspoon grated orange rind
⅛   teaspoon ground black pepper

In a large frying pan over medium heat, heat the oil until hot. Add the garlic and sauté for 30 seconds. Stir in the asparagus, orange juice and honey. Cover and cook for 3 to 5 minutes, or until the asparagus is crisp-tender.

Remove the cover and continue cooking over medium heat while slowly stirring in the cornstarch mixture. Use only enough of the cornstarch mixture to lightly thicken the sauce; you may not need all of it. Once the sauce has thickened, stir in the sesame seeds, orange rind and pepper.

Preparation time: 10 minutes
Cooking time: 8 minutes

Chef's note: To toast the sesame seeds, place them in a dry, no-stick skillet. Do not add any oil to the pan. Cook the seeds over medium heat for 1 to 2 minutes, shaking the pan occasionally until the seeds turn golden brown. Once the sesame seeds begin to brown, watch them carefully because they can get too dark very quickly.

Per serving: 62 calories, 2.6 g. fat (34% of calories), 0.1 g. dietary fiber, no cholesterol, 5 mg. sodium.

ASPARAGUS WITH RASPBERRY SAUCE

hen shopping for asparagus, choose firm, bright green stalks with tight tips. For an unusual variation of this sophisticated recipe, try it with white asparagus.

1   *pound asparagus, trimmed*
¼   *cup all-fruit raspberry spread*
2   *tablespoons raspberry vinegar*
1   *tablespoon chopped fresh mint*
⅛   *teaspoon ground black pepper*

In a large saucepan, bring 1″ of water to a boil. Arrange the asparagus in a steamer basket and place over the boiling water. Cover and steam the asparagus for 3 to 5 minutes, or until crisp-tender.

Meanwhile, in a small saucepan, combine the raspberry spread and vinegar. Cook over medium heat, stirring constantly, for 1 minute, or until the raspberry spread has melted. Stir in the mint and pepper.

Place the asparagus in a serving bowl and toss with the raspberry sauce.

Preparation time: 5 minutes
Cooking time: 5 minutes

Per serving: 83 calories, 0.3 g. fat (3% of calories), 0.2 g. dietary fiber, no cholesterol, 6 mg. sodium.

Green and White Bean Medley

SERVES 4

*N*avy beans really are served in the Navy! They've been a staple in a Navy cook's galley since the mid-1800s. In this recipe, they provide color contrast and a wealth of nutrients from protein to iron to fiber.

8 *ounces fresh green beans, trimmed and cut in half crosswise*

1 *teaspoon olive oil*

2 *cloves garlic, minced*

2 *plum tomatoes*

½ *cup canned navy beans, rinsed and drained*

⅛ *teaspoon freshly ground black pepper*

In a large saucepan, bring 1″ of water to a boil. Arrange the green beans in a steamer basket and place over the boiling water. Cover and steam the green beans for 3 to 4 minutes, or until crisp-tender. Then cool the green beans under cold running water to stop the cooking.

Coat a large frying pan with no-stick spray. Over medium heat, heat the oil until hot. Add the garlic and sauté for 15 to 20 seconds. Increase the heat to high, add the tomatoes and cook for 1 minute, or until the tomatoes soften slightly. Add the navy beans and green beans and cook for 1 to 2 minutes, or until hot.

Preparation time: 5 minutes
Cooking time: 10 minutes

Chef's note: To save time, cook the green beans ahead of time and refrigerate them until you're ready to use them.

Per serving: 82 calories, 1.6 g. fat (16% of calories), 0.8 g. dietary fiber, no cholesterol, 154 mg. sodium.

GARLICKY GREEN BEANS

*G*arlic lovers—take note! This recipe uses 6 cloves of garlic. But boiling mellows and sweetens the flavor, so even garlic likers will enjoy this dish.

6 *cloves garlic, peeled*
1 *pound fresh green beans, trimmed*
2 *tablespoons lemon juice*
1 *teaspoon extra-virgin olive oil*
⅛ *teaspoon ground black pepper*

In a large saucepan filled with water, bring the garlic cloves to a boil. Boil over medium-high heat for 5 to 7 minutes, or until the garlic is just tender when pierced with the tip of a knife.

Increase the heat to high and add the green beans. Boil for 3 to 5 minutes, or until the beans are crisp-tender. Drain; return the beans to the saucepan. Remove the garlic cloves from the saucepan and mash them with a fork. In a small cup, combine the garlic, lemon juice, oil and pepper. Add the garlic mixture to the green beans and toss.

Preparation time: 5 minutes
Cooking time: 15 minutes

Chef's note: To remove the skin from a clove of garlic, cut the root end off and firmly press the flat of a knife on the clove. The skin will loosen and the clove will easily slip out. This same technique can be used to ease mincing once the clove is peeled.

Per serving: 58 calories, 1.5 g. fat (20% of calories), no dietary fiber, no cholesterol, 4 mg. sodium.

ORANGE MARMALADE GINGERED CARROTS

*A*ll-fruit orange marmalade forms a glossy glaze on these zesty carrots. Along with wild rice pilaf and a spinach salad, they round out a dinner of sliced turkey breast or grilled tuna steaks.

- 1½ *cups baby carrots, quartered lengthwise*
- ¼ *cup defatted chicken stock*
- 2 *tablespoons all-fruit orange marmalade spread*
- 1 *teaspoon finely chopped crystallized ginger*

In a medium no-stick frying pan, combine the carrots and stock. Cover, bring to a boil over medium-high heat and cook for 3 to 5 minutes, or until the carrots are crisp-tender.

Remove the cover; stir in the marmalade and ginger. Continue to cook for 1 to 2 minutes, or until the marmalade melts and a light glaze forms.

Preparation time: 5 minutes
Cooking time: 10 minutes

Per serving: 47 calories, 0.1 g. fat (2% of calories), 1.3 g. dietary fiber, no cholesterol, 44 mg. sodium.

CORN PUDDING

*T*his old-fashioned soufflé has its roots in New England and is a classic accompaniment for roasts, wild game, lobster or clams.

- 1 *package (10 ounces) frozen corn, thawed*
- 1 *cup fat-free egg substitute*
- ¼ *cup unbleached flour*
- 3 *tablespoons maple syrup*

In a blender container, combine the corn, eggs, flour and maple syrup. Blend on high speed for 20 to 25 seconds, or until the corn is well chopped and the mixture is combined.

Coat a 4-cup casserole dish with no-stick spray. Pour the mixture into the prepared dish. Bake at 425° for 25 to 30 minutes, or until slightly puffed and a knife inserted into the center comes out clean.

Preparation time: 5 minutes
Cooking time: 30 minutes

Per serving: 149 calories, 0.1 g. fat (1% of calories), 1.7 g. dietary fiber, no cholesterol, 88 mg. sodium.

MAPLE PECAN SQUASH

SERVES 4

Maple syrup is a low-calorie, nonfat way to add a rich touch of flavor to squash. Any winter squash such as hubbard or turban would work well in this recipe.

    1   *medium butternut squash, peeled and shredded*
    6   *tablespoons maple syrup*
   ⅛   *teaspoon ground black pepper*
   ¼   *cup fresh whole-wheat bread crumbs*
    2   *tablespoons chopped pecans*

In a medium bowl, combine the squash, maple syrup and pepper; stir with a fork to mix well.

Coat a 6-cup casserole with no-stick spray. Place the squash mixture in the prepared casserole. Sprinkle the bread crumbs and pecans over the top. Bake at 425° for 20 to 25 minutes, or until the squash is tender and lightly browned.

Preparation time: 10 minutes
Baking time: 25 minutes

Per serving: 136 calories, 2.5 g. fat (15% of calories), 1.6 g. dietary fiber, no cholesterol, 21 mg. sodium.

RED LENTILS WITH THYME

SERVES 4

*R*ed or Egyptian lentils are similar to common brown lentils, but they're smaller, rounder and don't have the grayish-brown seed coat. Look for them in your supermarket or a Middle Eastern or Indian market. Serve as an accompaniment to grilled meats or shish kabobs.

> 1 teaspoon olive oil
> 1 clove garlic, minced
> 2 cups defatted chicken stock
> 1 cup red lentils
> 1½ teaspoons chopped fresh thyme
> ⅛ teaspoon ground black pepper

Coat a medium saucepan with no-stick spray. Over medium heat, heat the oil until hot. Add the garlic and sauté for 30 seconds. Add the stock, lentils, thyme and pepper. Cover, bring to a boil, reduce the heat to low and cook for 15 to 18 minutes, or until the lentils are tender.

Preparation time: 5 minutes
Cooking time: 20 minutes

Chef's note: For a creamier consistency, stir in 3 tablespoons of nonfat plain yogurt before serving.

Per serving: 71 calories, 1.4 g. fat (15% of calories), no dietary fiber, no cholesterol, 240 mg. sodium.

VEGETABLE FRITTERS

ritters are often deep-fried, which leads to their high-fat reputation. But this variation uses nonfat Great Northern beans and egg whites to make the coating, then the fritters are quickly pan-fried without oil. Serve them as a snack or appetizer or with a hearty soup.

> 1 *cup canned Great Northern beans, rinsed and drained*
>
> 2 *egg whites, beaten to stiff peaks*
>
> 1 *cup cooked chopped broccoli*
>
> 1 *cup cooked shredded carrots*
>
> ⅓ *cup diced onions*
>
> ⅓ *cup grated Parmesan cheese*
>
> ⅛ *teaspoon ground black pepper*

Puree the beans in a food processor or mash by hand until smooth. In a large bowl, combine the beans and the egg whites, whisking until smooth. Stir in the broccoli, carrots, onions, Parmesan and pepper.

Coat a large frying pan with no-stick spray. Heat the pan over medium heat until hot. Drop the fritters by rounded tablespoons into the frying pan, pressing lightly to flatten to ½″ thick.

Cook for 3 minutes per side, or until cooked through and lightly browned. Repeat with the remaining mixture.

Preparation time: 10 minutes
Cooking time: 15 minutes

Per serving: 149 calories, 3 g. fat (17% of calories), 2.1 g. dietary fiber, 7 mg. cholesterol, 205 mg. sodium.

RED BEANS AND RICE

SERVES 4

The classic Southern and Caribbean main dish was the inspiration for this lower-fat version. Turkey bacon provides the only added fat but plenty of smoky flavor.

- 3 slices turkey bacon, diced
- ⅓ cup diced onions
- ⅓ cup diced green peppers
- 1 cup water
- ½ cup long-grain white rice
- ½ cup canned kidney beans, rinsed and drained
- ¼ teaspoon hot-pepper sauce
- ⅛ teaspoon ground black pepper

Coat a medium saucepan with no-stick spray. Heat the pan over medium heat until hot. Add the bacon and sauté for 3 minutes. Add the onions and green peppers and sauté for 2 minutes.

Add the water, rice, beans, hot-pepper sauce and black pepper. Bring to a boil; cover, reduce the heat to low and cook for 15 to 20 minutes, or until all the water has been absorbed.

Preparation time: 5 minutes
Cooking time: 25 minutes

Per serving: 146 calories, 2.2 g. fat (14% of calories), 2.1 g. dietary fiber, 7 mg. cholesterol, 109 mg. sodium.

MOLASSES BAKED BEANS

SERVES 4

*B*aked beans are an all-American dish. To create a lighter variation, we've used reduced-fat turkey sausage rather than bacon. Although they're cooked on top of the stove to save time, they retain their baked-all-day flavor.

⅓ *cup reduced-fat turkey sausage*
¾ *cup diced onions*
1 *can (14½ ounces) pinto beans, rinsed and drained*
¼ *cup molasses*
3 *tablespoons chili sauce*
2 *teaspoons Worcestershire sauce*

In a medium saucepan, break up and cook the turkey sausage over medium heat for 2 to 3 minutes, or until the sausage is almost cooked through. Add the onions and continue cooking for 3 to 4 minutes, or until the onions are translucent.

Add the beans, molasses, chili sauce and Worcestershire sauce, stirring well. Bring to a boil, reduce the heat to medium-low and cook for 10 to 15 minutes, or until the sauce has thickened.

Preparation time: 5 minutes
Cooking time: 25 minutes

Per serving: 164 calories, 1 g. fat (6% of calories), 0.5 g. dietary fiber, 6 mg. cholesterol, 701 mg. sodium.

SOUTHERN GRITS

SERVES 4

*G*rits, which are made from coarsely ground corn, are a main-stay of Southern meals. Serve this variation as a side dish for your morning eggs or with baked chicken for dinner.

1 teaspoon canola oil
½ cup diced onions
2½ cups defatted chicken stock
⅓ cup diced green peppers
⅛ teaspoon ground black pepper
¾ cup quick-cooking grits
½ cup shredded reduced-fat Cheddar cheese

Coat a medium saucepan with no-stick spray. Heat the oil over medium heat until hot. Add the onions and sauté for 2 minutes.

Add the stock, green peppers and black pepper. Bring to a boil and slowly stir in the grits. Cover, reduce the heat to medium-low and cook for 5 to 7 minutes, or until the mixture is thick and creamy. Stir in the Cheddar.

Preparation time: 5 minutes
Cooking time: 10 minutes

Per serving: 174 calories, 3.6 g. fat (19% of calories), 3.9 g. dietary fiber, 6 mg. cholesterol, 496 mg. sodium.

Buckwheat with Two Mushrooms

*I*f you've experienced buckwheat only in pancakes, give this side dish a try. Buckwheat comes to us from Russia, where it's most commonly used as flour. It gives this dish a hearty, nutty flavor and texture.

⅓ *cup dried shiitake mushrooms*
¾ *cup hot water*
¾ *cup buckwheat groats*
3 *tablespoons fat-free egg substitute*
2 *teaspoons olive oil*
½ *cup diced onions*
¾ *cup sliced mushrooms*
¾ *cup defatted chicken stock*

In a small bowl, combine the shiitake mushrooms with the water. Let stand for 5 minutes. Strain, reserving the liquid. Coarsely chop the mushrooms, discarding the stems.

Meanwhile, in a small bowl, combine the buckwheat with the eggs, mixing well. Heat a medium no-stick frying pan over medium-high heat until hot. Add the buckwheat and cook, stirring constantly, for 2 to 3 minutes, or until the buckwheat kernels are dry and separated. Set aside.

Coat a medium saucepan with no-stick spray. Heat the oil over medium heat until hot. Add the onions and sauté for 1 minute. Add the sliced mushrooms and the shiitakes and sauté for 1 minute.

Pour in the stock and reserved mushroom liquid and bring to a boil. Add the buckwheat; cover, reduce the heat to low and cook for 7 to 10 minutes, or until the liquid has been absorbed.

Preparation time: 10 minutes plus 5 minutes standing time
Cooking time: 15 minutes

Per serving: 152 calories, 3.4 g. fat (19% of calories), 3.9 g. dietary fiber, no cholesterol, 105 mg. sodium.

SETTLER SUCCOTASH

SERVES 4

*T*hree different varieties of beans lend color and texture to this original Native American dish. A favorite in the South, it's especially good with barbecued meats.

> 2   *teaspoons olive oil*
> ½   *cup sliced onions*
> 1   *clove garlic, minced*
> ¾   *cup cooked green beans, cut into 1" pieces*
> ½   *cup frozen baby lima beans, thawed*
> ½   *cup canned navy beans, rinsed and drained*
> ½   *cup frozen corn, thawed*
> 2   *teaspoons chopped fresh dill*
> ⅛   *teaspoon ground black pepper*

Coat a large no-stick skillet with no-stick spray. Add the oil; heat over medium heat until hot. Add the onions and sauté for 1 minute, then add the garlic and sauté for 30 seconds.

Stir in the green beans, lima beans, navy beans and corn. Sauté over medium heat for 3 minutes, or until the vegetables are cooked and the mixture is hot. Stir in the dill and pepper.

Preparation time: 10 minutes
Cooking time: 5 minutes

Per serving: 112 calories, 2.6 g. fat (20% of calories), 2.2 g. dietary fiber, no cholesterol, 161 mg. sodium.

BARLEY CHESTNUT PILAF

SERVES 4

*Q*uick-cooking barley lets you make this nutlike pilaf in just minutes. Serve it with roasted turkey or pork.

2 teaspoons canola oil
½ cup diced onions
½ cup diced carrots
2 cups defatted chicken stock
1 cup quick-cooking barley
¾ cup diced canned chestnuts
¼ cup sliced scallions

Coat a medium saucepan with no-stick spray. Heat the oil over medium heat until hot. Add the onions and sauté for 1 minute, then add the carrots and sauté for 1 minute.

Pour in the stock and bring to a boil. Stir in the barley and chestnuts; cover, reduce the heat to low and cook for 10 to 12 minutes, or until the barley is tender and the water has been absorbed. Stir in the scallions.

Preparation time: 10 minutes
Cooking time: 15 minutes

Per serving: 277 calories, 3.7 g. fat (12% of calories), 10.1 g. dietary fiber, no cholesterol, 247 mg. sodium.

BULGUR PILAF

SERVES 4

*B*ulgur is wheat kernels that have been steamed, dried and crushed. It has a tender, chewy texture and is a staple of Middle Eastern cooking. Serve this colorful pilaf with chicken or lamb.

2   *teaspoons olive oil*
½   *cup diced onions*
¼   *cup diced celery*
1   *cup bulgur*
2   *cups defatted chicken stock*
½   *cup diced sweet potatoes or yams*
⅓   *cup diced sweet red peppers*
⅛   *teaspoon ground black pepper*
2   *tablespoons chopped fresh parsley*

Coat a medium saucepan with no-stick spray. Heat the oil over medium heat until hot. Add the onions and celery and sauté for 2 minutes. Stir in the bulgur, mixing well. Add the stock, sweet potatoes or yams, red peppers and black pepper.

Bring to a boil; cover, reduce the heat to medium-low and cook for 15 minutes, or until the vegetables are tender and the liquid has been absorbed. Stir in the parsley.

Preparation time: 10 minutes
Cooking time: 20 minutes

Per serving: 185 calories, 2.8 g. fat (13% of calories), 9.4 g. dietary fiber, no cholesterol, 251 mg. sodium.

CONFETTI COUSCOUS

SERVES 4

*C*ouscous, which hails from North Africa, is a pastalike product made from semolina flour. Its fine, pearly texture is well-suited to salads and pilafs. Serve this color-flecked dish with grilled chicken or beef.

1	cup defatted chicken stock
¼	cup diced carrots
¼	cup frozen corn, thawed
1	clove garlic, minced
⅛	teaspoon ground black pepper
⅔	cup couscous
2	tablespoons diced sweet red peppers
⅓	cup sliced scallions

In a medium saucepan, combine the stock, carrots, corn, garlic and black pepper. Bring to a boil over high heat; add the couscous and red peppers. Cover and remove from the heat. Let stand for 5 minutes.

Fluff with a fork and stir in the scallions.

Preparation time: 5 minutes
Cooking time: 2 minutes plus 5 minutes standing time

Per serving: 134 calories, 0.2 g. fat (2% of calories), 5.4 g. dietary fiber, no cholesterol, 124 mg. sodium.

PEPPERED BROWN RICE
WITH CARAMELIZED ONIONS

*F*or more snappy pepper flavor, increase the amount of cracked black pepper to ½ teaspoon. To decrease cooking time, this recipe uses quick-cooking brown rice, which has been partially cooked then dried.

2	*teaspoons olive oil*
1	*medium onion, sliced crosswise and separated into rings*
1	*teaspoon brown sugar*
1¼	*cups defatted chicken stock*
1	*cup quick-cooking brown rice*
¼	*teaspoon cracked black pepper*

In a medium saucepan, heat the oil on medium until hot. Add the onions and stir. Cover and cook over medium heat for 3 minutes. Remove the cover, add the brown sugar and mix well. Increase the heat to medium-high and cook for 7 to 10 minutes, or until the onions are browned.

Add the stock; cover and bring to a boil over high heat. Stir in the rice and pepper and cook, covered, for 10 minutes, or until all the water has been absorbed.

Preparation time: 5 minutes
Cooking time: 25 minutes

Per serving: 212 calories, 3.7 g. fat (15% of calories), 3.2 g. dietary fiber, no cholesterol, 151 mg. sodium.

CRANBERRY RICE

*C*elebrate autumn with this delightful nutty, tangy side dish. It colorfully complements game hens, pork roast or roast turkey.

1	*teaspoon canola oil*
¼	*cup diced onions*
1¼	*cups water*
1	*cup quick-cooking brown rice*
½	*cup dried cranberries*
¼	*teaspoon grated nutmeg*
1	*tablespoon chopped fresh parsley*

In a medium saucepan, heat the oil on medium until hot. Add the onions and sauté for 3 minutes.

Add the water and bring to a boil over high heat. Add the rice, cranberries and nutmeg; reduce the heat to low, cover and cook for 10 minutes, or until all the water has been absorbed. Stir in the parsley.

Preparation time: 5 minutes
Cooking time: 15 minutes

Per serving: 200 calories, 2.6 g. fat (12% of calories), 2.9 g. dietary fiber, no cholesterol, 4 mg. sodium.

WILD RICE PANCAKES

SERVES 4

*W*ild rice is harvested from rivers, streams and lakes as well as from commercial paddies. Lake wild rice has a longer grain and is well-suited to pilafs and soups. Use commercial or quick-cooking wild rice in this recipe to bring a taste of the northwoods home. Garnish with a dollop of nonfat sour cream and a snippet of chives.

¼ cup fat-free egg substitute
1 tablespoon whole-wheat flour
1 tablespoon skim milk
¼ teaspoon baking powder
⅛ teaspoon dried thyme
⅛ teaspoon ground black pepper
1 cup cooked wild rice
3 tablespoons minced onions
2 tablespoons chopped fresh parsley

In a medium bowl, whisk together the eggs, flour, milk, baking powder, thyme and pepper. Add the wild rice, onions and parsley; stir well.

Coat a medium no-stick frying pan with no-stick spray. Heat the pan over medium heat until hot. Drop tablespoons of the mixture onto the frying pan, pressing down to flatten. (The pancakes should be about ¼" thick and 2" in diameter.)

Cook over medium heat for 1 to 2 minutes per side, or until firm and lightly browned. Repeat with the remaining mixture.

Preparation time: 10 minutes
Cooking time: 15 minutes

Per serving: 60 calories, 0.2 g. fat (3% of calories), 1.1 g. dietary fiber, no cholesterol, 46 mg. sodium.

CLASSIC ACCOMPANIMENTS

GARLIC MASHED POTATOES

*T*here's virtually no fat in these wonderfully creamy potatoes with more than a hint of garlic. We've eliminated the fat by using nonfat sour cream and skim milk.

4   *medium potatoes, peeled and cut into 1" cubes*
6   *cloves garlic, peeled*
⅓   *cup skim milk*
¼   *cup nonfat sour cream*

In a medium saucepan, combine the potatoes and garlic. Cover with water and bring to a boil over medium-high heat. Boil for 6 to 10 minutes, or until the potatoes are tender; drain well.

Place the potatoes and garlic in a medium bowl; mash the potatoes and garlic with a potato masher until smooth.

In a small saucepan, heat the milk over medium heat for 1 to 2 minutes until hot. Add the milk and sour cream to the potatoes and mix well.

Preparation time: 10 minutes
Cooking time: 15 minutes

Per serving: 145 calories, 0.2 g. fat (1% of calories), 1.5 g. dietary fiber, no cholesterol, 38 mg. sodium.

Twice-Baked New Potatoes

*L*ow- and nonfat dairy products are the secrets behind this slimmed-down adaptation of a family favorite.

4   *medium new potatoes*
2   *tablespoons minced onions*
3   *tablespoons nonfat sour cream*
1   *tablespoon finely diced sweet red peppers*
1   *tablespoon snipped chives*
     Pinch of ground black pepper
1   *tablespoon finely shredded reduced-fat sharp Cheddar cheese*

Pierce the potatoes in several places with a fork and microwave on high for 7 to 10 minutes, turning once, or until the potatoes are tender.

Meanwhile, coat a small no-stick frying pan with no-stick spray. Heat the pan over medium heat until hot. Add the onions and sauté for 3 to 4 minutes, or until lightly browned.

Remove the potatoes from the microwave and let stand for 5 minutes, or until cool enough to handle.

Slice ¼″ off the top of each potato and scoop out the centers with a spoon, leaving ¼″-thick shells. Place the centers in a medium bowl and mash with a potato masher or fork. Add the onions, sour cream, red peppers, chives and black pepper; stir well.

Spoon the filling into the potato shells and top with the Cheddar.

Place the potatoes in an 8″ pie plate and bake at 475° for 3 to 5 minutes, or until the filling is hot and the Cheddar has melted.

Preparation time: 10 minutes
Microwaving time: 10 minutes
Cooking time: 10 minutes
Baking time: 5 minutes

Chef's note: In place of microwaving, the potatoes also may be baked at 475° for 20 to 25 minutes, or until tender.

Per serving: 134 calories, 0.4 g. fat (3% of calories), 1.6 g. dietary fiber, no cholesterol, 47 mg. sodium.

MINTED NEW POTATOES

SERVES 4

Sweet-flavored new potatoes usher in spring. Serve these herbed potatoes, which can be either grilled or broiled, with lamb cutlets.

> 6 *new potatoes, unpeeled and quartered*
> 1 *tablespoon olive oil*
> 1 *tablespoon chopped fresh mint*
> 1 *tablespoon chopped fresh chives*
> ⅛ *teaspoon ground black pepper*

Place the potatoes in a large saucepan and cover with water. Bring to a boil over medium-high heat and boil for 5 minutes, or until the potatoes are almost tender; drain well.

Place the potatoes in a large bowl and toss with the oil. Set this bowl aside without rinsing while the potatoes are being grilled.

To grill, place the potatoes directly on the grill rack, 4″ to 6″ above the hot coals. Grill for 5 to 8 minutes, turning occasionally, until all sides are golden brown.

Return the potatoes to the bowl and toss with the mint, chives and pepper.

Preparation time: 5 minutes
Cooking time: 15 minutes

Chef's note: To broil the potatoes, coat a 15″ × 10″ jelly-roll pan with no-stick spray. Place the potatoes, skin side down, in a single layer on the prepared pan. Broil the potatoes about 4″ from the heat for 5 to 8 minutes, or until they are golden brown.

Per serving: 207 calories, 3.6 g. fat (15% of calories), 3.1 g. dietary fiber, no cholesterol, 8 mg. sodium.

SONORAN POTATO FRIES

SERVES 4

*P*erk up Saturday night burgers with these south-of-the-border potato wedges. They're baked rather than fried to keep fat at a minimum.

- *1 teaspoon ground cumin*
- *1 teaspoon chili powder*
- *1 teaspoon paprika*
- *1 teaspoon dried oregano*
- *¼ teaspoon ground red pepper*
- *3 large baking potatoes*
- *1 tablespoon olive oil*

In a small bowl, combine the cumin, chili powder, paprika, oregano and red pepper; set aside.

Cut each potato lengthwise into 8 wedges and place in a large bowl. Toss the potatoes with the oil until coated, then toss the potatoes with the seasoning mixture.

Coat a 15″ × 10″ jelly-roll pan with no-stick spray. Place the potatoes in a single layer on the prepared pan. Bake at 475° for 15 to 20 minutes, or until the potatoes are lightly browned and tender.

Preparation time: 10 minutes
Baking time: 20 minutes

Per serving: 125 calories, 3.8 g. fat (26% of calories), 1.8 g. dietary fiber, no cholesterol, 12 mg. sodium.

CHAPTER 10

FRESH
FROM
THE
OVEN OR
GRIDDLE

BAKED GOODIES

Wake up to a breakfast of crisp waffles, dress up a main dish with a round soda bread piping hot from the oven or make an open-faced sandwich on a slice of home-baked bread. You can enjoy these goodies, even as you pare fat from your diet. Ingredients such as skim milk and buttermilk, nonfat sour cream and yogurt and fat-free egg substitute greatly reduce the fat without reducing the flavor of these baked treats. We've adapted a whole bakery full of tempting American favorites such as brown bread, spoon bread, popovers and muffins to fit your lower-fat lifestyle.

DRIED CHERRY WHOLE-WHEAT LOAF

*S*our Montmorency is the most popular cherry for drying. Drying deepens its bright-red color and concentrates the tart flavor. Dried cherries add texture and lovely color to this quick-to-fix filled bread.

Flour

- 1   *loaf frozen whole-wheat dough, defrosted according to manufacturer's directions*
- ¼   *cup all-fruit cherry spread*
- ½   *cup dried cherries*
- 2   *teaspoons almond extract*
- 2   *tablespoons skim milk*

Lightly flour the counter; roll the dough into an 11″ × 7″ rectangle. Place the cherry spread over the surface of the dough, stopping 1″ from all the edges.

In a small bowl, combine the dried cherries with the almond extract. Sprinkle this mixture over the fruit spread. Starting at one 7″ side, roll the dough into a cylinder. Firmly press the edges of the loaf together. (Water pressed on the seam helps keep the seal.)

Coat a 9″ × 5″ loaf pan with no-stick spray. Place the loaf in the prepared pan, seam down. Brush with the milk. Cover with plastic wrap and let rise for 30 minutes. Bake at 375° for 30 to 35 minutes, or until the loaf is golden brown and a toothpick inserted in the center comes out clean.

Preparation time: 5 minutes plus 30 minutes rising time
Baking time: 35 minutes

Chef's notes: For other variations of this bread, substitute any dried fruit and its matching all-fruit spread for the dried cherries and cherry spread.

For a round loaf, shape the bread into a 12″- to 14″-long cylinder. Bake it in a tube or angel food cake pan coated with no-stick spray.

Per slice: 81 calories, 1.8 g. fat (19% of calories), no dietary fiber, no cholesterol, 153 mg. sodium.

Dried Blueberry Lemon Loaf

MAKES 1 LOAF; 18 SLICES

*D*rying greatly concentrates the color and sweetness of blueberries. They add raisinlike bits of fruit to this zesty lemon bread that's perfect for breakfast or as an afternoon snack with milk or tea.

> 1 *cup unbleached flour*
> ½ *cup whole-wheat pastry flour*
> ½ *cup dried blueberries*
> 1 *tablespoon finely grated lemon rind*
> 1½ *teaspoons baking powder*
> ½ *teaspoon baking soda*
> ½ *cup buttermilk*
> ½ *cup nonfat lemon yogurt*
> ¼ *cup all-fruit blueberry spread*

In a large bowl, whisk the unbleached flour, whole-wheat flour, blueberries, lemon rind, baking powder and baking soda.

In a small bowl, combine the buttermilk, yogurt and blueberry spread. Mix well.

Pour the wet ingredients over the dry ingredients. Stir only enough to moisten the dry ingredients.

Coat a 9″ × 5″ loaf pan with no-stick spray. Pour the batter into the prepared pan. Bake at 350° for 40 minutes, or until a toothpick inserted in the center comes out clean. Cool.

Preparation time: 10 minutes
Baking time: 40 minutes

Per slice: 61 calories, 0.2 g. fat (3% of calories), 0.8 g. dietary fiber, no cholesterol, 62 mg. sodium.

PINEAPPLE UPSIDE-DOWN MUFFINS

MAKES 12

Brighten your morning with these sunny, fruity muffins. There's a pineapple surprise on the bottom of each one!

> 1 *can (8 ounces) crushed pineapple, packed in its own juice*
> *Skim milk*
> ¼ *cup canola oil*
> 2 *egg whites*
> 2 *teaspoons rum extract*
> 1 *cup unbleached flour*
> ½ *cup whole-wheat flour*
> ¼ *cup whole-wheat pastry flour*
> 2½ *teaspoons baking powder*
> 2 *teaspoons baking soda*
> ½ *cup all-fruit pineapple spread*

Coat 12 muffin cups with no-stick spray.

Drain the crushed pineapple over a measuring cup. Put the pineapple into a medium bowl; add to the pineapple juice enough milk to bring the volume to ½ cup. Pour this liquid into the bowl with the pineapple and add the oil, egg whites and rum extract. Mix well.

In a large bowl, whisk together the unbleached flour, whole-wheat flour, whole-wheat pastry flour, baking powder and baking soda. Pour the pineapple mixture over the dry ingredients and, using a spatula, mix only enough to moisten the dry ingredients.

Heat the pineapple spread in a small saucepan over low-medium heat for 1 to 2 minutes, or until melted. Place 2 teaspoons of the melted spread in each of the muffin cups. Spoon the batter into the prepared muffin cups, filling them two-thirds full. Bake at 375° for 20 to 25 minutes, or until a toothpick inserted in the center comes out clean and the muffins are golden brown. Cool in cups; invert to serve.

Preparation time: 10 minutes
Baking time: 25 minutes

Per muffin: 160 calories, 4.8 g. fat (27% of calories), 1.5 g. dietary fiber, no cholesterol, 220 mg. sodium.

ORANGE POPPYSEED LOAF

MAKES 1 LOAF; 18 SLICES

Orange extract and low-fat orange yogurt put a new twist on a popular poppyseed brunch or breakfast bread.

2	*cups unbleached flour*
1⅓	*cups whole-wheat flour*
3	*tablespoons poppyseeds*
4	*teaspoons baking soda*
1	*cup nonfat orange yogurt*
¼	*cup canola oil*
¼	*cup honey*
1	*tablespoon orange extract*

In a large bowl, combine the unbleached flour, whole-wheat flour, poppyseeds and baking soda.

In a medium bowl, combine the yogurt, oil, honey and orange extract. Mix well. Pour the liquids over the dry ingredients and mix until the dough forms a shaggy mass. (Dough will appear rough.) Place on the counter and knead until the dough comes together. Using your hands, roll the dough into a log shape (dough will be sticky).

Coat a 9″ × 5″ loaf pan with no-stick spray. Press the dough into the pan, being sure to press the dough firmly into the corners. Bake at 350° for 30 to 35 minutes, or until a toothpick inserted in the center comes out clean. Cool.

Preparation time: 10 minutes
Baking time: 35 minutes

Chef's note: Use a liquid measuring cup to measure the yogurt.

Per slice: 142 calories, 4 g. fat (25% of calories), 1.5 g. dietary fiber, 0.3 mg. cholesterol, 191 mg. sodium.

MINI BOSTON BROWN BREADS WITH DRIED APRICOTS

MAKES 8

This dark, sweet, steamed bread is a traditional favorite at New England clambakes or paired with Boston baked beans. It's also a yummy breakfast bread when spread with nonfat cream cheese.

½ *cup cornmeal*
½ *cup rye flour*
½ *cup whole-wheat flour*
½ *cup chopped dried apricots*
1 *teaspoon baking soda*
¾ *cup buttermilk*
⅓ *cup dark molasses*
1 *teaspoon almond extract*
Boiling water

In a large bowl, combine the cornmeal, rye flour, whole-wheat flour, apricots and baking soda.

In a medium bowl, combine the buttermilk, molasses and almond extract. Pour the buttermilk mixture over the dry ingredients. Mix well.

Coat 8 muffin cups with no-stick spray. Spoon the batter into the prepared muffin cups. Smooth the tops of the muffins. Coat a piece of foil with no-stick spray. Cover the muffins with the foil, sprayed side down. Place the muffin cups in a baking pan a little larger than the muffin pan. Place the pan in the oven. Add enough boiling water to the pan to reach two-thirds up the sides of the muffin cups.

Bake at 375° for 35 minutes. Remove the foil and allow the mini breads to rest in a turned-off oven for 5 minutes. Cool.

Preparation time: 10 minutes
Baking time: 35 minutes plus 5 minutes resting time

Per bread: 135 calories, 0.6 g. fat (4% of calories), 2.8 g. dietary fiber, no cholesterol, 143 mg. sodium.

ROSEMARY SODA BREAD

MAKES 1 LOAF; 8 WEDGES

*I*rish soda bread was the inspiration for this herbed, biscuitlike round bread. Serve it with soups, stews or grilled seafood.

1¾	*cups whole-wheat flour*
1½	*cups unbleached flour*
2	*tablespoons packed brown sugar*
2	*teaspoons dried rosemary*
2	*teaspoons baking powder*
1	*teaspoon baking soda*
1	*teaspoon cracked black pepper*
1¼	*cups buttermilk*
1	*tablespoon canola oil*

In a food processor fitted with the steel blade, mix the whole-wheat flour, unbleached flour, brown sugar, rosemary, baking powder, baking soda and pepper. Add the buttermilk and oil. Pulse to form a wet dough. (The dough could require up to ¼ cup more buttermilk if the flours are dry.)

Place the dough on a floured counter. Knead 10 times to form a round loaf. Cover lightly with flour.

Coat a 9″ round cake pan with no-stick spray. Press the dough into the pan. Cut an × into the center of the dough. Bake at 400° for 30 to 35 minutes, or until the bread is dark brown and shrinks from the sides of the pan. Cool.

Preparation time: 10 minutes
Baking time: 35 minutes

Per wedge: 218 calories, 2.5 g. fat (10% of calories), 4 g. dietary fiber, no cholesterol, 228 mg. sodium.

Sun-Dried Tomato Semolina Bread

*S*emolina is a coarsely ground flour made from durum wheat. It gives this bread—flecked with bits of sun-dried tomatoes—a chewy, hearty texture.

1	cup semolina flour
½–¾	cup unbleached flour
½	cup cornmeal
2	teaspoons baking powder
2	teaspoons oregano
½	teaspoon baking soda
8	sun-dried tomato halves
1	cup boiling water
1	cup tomato juice
2	tablespoons olive oil
1	tablespoon cornmeal

In a food processor fitted with the steel blade, combine the semolina flour, ½ cup of the unbleached flour, cornmeal, baking powder, oregano and baking soda. Pulse for 20 seconds to combine.

Rehydrate the tomatoes in the boiling water until the tomatoes soften, about 5 minutes. Drain the tomatoes and add them to the processor along with the tomato juice and oil. Pulse a few seconds to form the dough, adding enough of the remaining unbleached flour to form a soft, moist dough.

Coat a 9″ round baking pan with no-stick spray. Dust the pan with the cornmeal to cover the interior evenly. With lightly floured hands, press the dough in the pan. Bake at 400° for 30 to 35 minutes, or until a toothpick inserted in the center comes out clean.

Preparation time: 10 minutes
Baking time: 35 minutes

Per wedge: 185 calories, 4.1 g. fat (19% of calories), 2.2 g. dietary fiber, no cholesterol, 253 mg. sodium.

WHOLE-WHEAT PEPPERCORN POPOVERS

*F*at-free egg substitute and skim milk help trim the fat from this classic American quick bread. Serve these popovers piping hot from the oven with soups, salads, grilled meats or seafood.

¾	*cup unbleached flour*
¼	*cup whole-wheat flour*
1	*cup skim milk*
½	*cup fat-free egg substitute*
1	*tablespoon canola oil*
½	*teaspoon cracked black pepper*

Heat 6 popover pans in the oven at 450° for 5 minutes. In a food processor fitted with the steel blade, combine the unbleached flour with the whole-wheat flour. Pulse for 20 seconds.

Add the milk, eggs, oil and pepper. Process for 30 seconds.

Remove the popover pans from the oven; coat them with no-stick spray and fill the pans with the batter. Bake at 450° for 20 minutes. Reduce the temperature to 375° and bake for 15 minutes more, or until the popovers are inflated and golden brown.

Preparation time: 5 minutes
Baking time: 35 minutes plus 5 minutes preheating time

Chef's notes: Ovenproof 6- or 8-ounce glass baking cups also work well.

For a drier popover, at the end of the baking time, pierce the popovers with the tip of a paring knife. Turn off the oven, and let the popovers dry out for 5 minutes.

Substitute 1 teaspoon dried herbs for the cracked black pepper, if desired.

Per popover: 117 calories, 2.6 g. fat (20% of calories), 1.1 g. dietary fiber, no cholesterol, 49 mg. sodium.

AMERICAN HARVEST LOAF

MAKES 1 LOAF; 12 WEDGES

You'll be glad you spent the time baking this wonderfully flavorful and versatile bread. It freezes well and makes great toast. Cut slices into cubes and dry them for crunchy croutons to sprinkle on soups or salads.

½ cup cracked wheat
1 cup boiling water
1 cup whole-wheat flour
2 cups unbleached flour
¼ cup oat bran
¼ cup sunflower seeds
1 package quick-rise yeast (about 2¼ teaspoons)
¼ teaspoon salt
2 tablespoons honey
¾ cup hot water (125°–135°)
   Whole-wheat flour

In a small bowl, combine the cracked wheat and boiling water; stir. Set aside.

In a large bowl, combine the whole-wheat flour, 1 cup of the unbleached flour, the oat bran, sunflower seeds, yeast and salt. Use a whisk to mix well.

Combine the honey with the water.

Pour the cracked wheat into the large bowl with the flours. Pour in the honey mixture and mix until the dough forms a shaggy mass. Use a sturdy wooden spoon to mix well.

Place the dough on a counter and knead in the remaining 1 cup of the unbleached flour. (The dough needs to remain moist and sticky, so add only enough of the flour to keep the surface tacky.) Knead the dough for 5 minutes.

Coat a large bowl with no-stick spray. Place the dough in the prepared bowl. Cover with plastic wrap and allow to rise for 10 minutes. Press the dough down to eliminate any air bubbles. Shape the dough into 1 (12") round.

Coat a baking sheet with no-stick spray. Place the loaf on the sheet. Sprinkle with whole-wheat flour. Cover with plastic wrap. Let rise until double in volume (about 30 minutes, or until the impression of your fingers stays in the dough). Bake at 350° for 35 minutes, or until a toothpick inserted in the center comes out clean.

Preparation time: 15 minutes, plus 40 minutes rising time
Baking time: 35 minutes

Chef's notes: To make 2 (1-pound) loaves, divide the dough into 2 (6") rounds. Allow the dough to rise as stated in the directions. Bake the bread at 350° for 25 to 35 minutes, or until a toothpick inserted in the center comes out clean.

For another variation, substitute other seeds for the sunflower seeds in this recipe.

Per wedge: 58 calories, 0.7 g. fat (11% of calories), 0.9 g. dietary fiber, no cholesterol, 15 mg. sodium.

CARAMELIZED APPLE PANCAKES

SERVES 4

*B*its of caramelized apples dot these kid-pleasing pancakes. Serve them for a harvest-time brunch or freeze them for a super after-school snack.

    1   *large Granny Smith apple, peeled,*
         cored and diced
    ¼   *cup apple cider*
    1   *cup unbleached flour*
    ½   *cup skim milk*
    ¼   *cup fat-free egg substitute*
    3   *tablespoons canola oil*
    2   *teaspoons maple syrup*
    1½   *teaspoons vanilla*
    1½   *teaspoons baking soda*
    ½   *teaspoon ground cinnamon*

In a medium no-stick frying pan over medium heat, cook the apples in the cider until all the cider evaporates and the apples brown, about 15 minutes.

In a large bowl, combine the flour, milk, eggs, oil, maple syrup, vanilla, baking soda and cinnamon. Whisk to blend. (Mixture will be lumpy.) Add the apples and use a spatula to fold them into the batter.

Heat a large no-stick frying pan or griddle over medium-high heat until a bead of water skips on its surface. Coat the frying pan with no-stick spray. Pour ¼ cup of the batter on the prepared pan. Cook until bubbles appear on the surface of the pancake and the surface appears dry. Turn and cook about 2 minutes. Repeat until all the batter is used.

Preparation time: 20 minutes
Cooking time: 35 to 40 minutes

Chef's notes: For best results, it's important to use a tart, firm-textured, crispy apple variety such as Granny Smith in this recipe.

Using ¼ cup of batter per pancake, this recipe makes about 8 pancakes. For smaller pancakes, use 2 tablespoons of batter per pancake.

Serve the pancakes plain or top with warm maple syrup, apple-sauce, all-fruit apricot spread or a dollop of nonfat sour cream.

Per serving: 262 calories, 10.7 g. fat (37% of calories), 1.6 g. dietary fiber, no cholesterol, 345 mg. sodium.

LEMON RICOTTA PANCAKES

SERVES 4

Light, fluffy and *delicious* best describe these sour cream and ricotta cheese pancakes. Spoon fresh raspberries or blueberries or all-fruit spread over them. Or for a feather-light dessert, surround them with a pool of fresh fruit puree.

> *15 ounces fat-free ricotta cheese*
> *½ cup fat-free sour cream*
> *½ cup unbleached flour*
> *¼ cup fat-free egg substitute*
> *½ tablespoon finely grated lemon rind*
> *2 teaspoons orange extract*

In a food processor fitted with the steel blade, combine the ricotta, sour cream, flour, eggs, lemon rind and the orange extract. Pulse until smooth, about 1 minute.

Heat a large no-stick frying pan over medium-high heat for 1 minute. Coat with no-stick spray.

Spoon the batter by heaping tablespoons onto the pan. Cook for 2 minutes per side, or until brown.

Preparation time: 10 minutes
Cooking time: 10 minutes

Per serving: 178 calories, 0.2 g. fat (1% of calories), 0.4 g. dietary fiber, 12 mg. cholesterol, 119 mg. sodium.

OVEN-PUFFED PANCAKE

---

he Dutch call them *pannekoeken*. You'll just call them fabulous. For the most dramatic "puff," cook the pancake in a wide pan.

½   cup unbleached flour
¾   cup fat-free egg substitute
½   cup skim milk
2   tablespoons canola oil
2   teaspoons vanilla
1   teaspoon grated nutmeg
2   tablespoons packed brown sugar
2   tablespoons lemon juice

Sift the flour into a large bowl. In a medium bowl, combine the eggs, milk, oil, vanilla and nutmeg. Slowly pour the liquid ingredients into the flour, using a whisk to form a smooth batter.

Coat a large no-stick ovenproof frying pan or cast-iron skillet with no-stick spray. Place over medium heat and add the batter. Cook for 2 minutes to set the batter. Bake at 450° for 15 minutes. Reduce the oven temperature to 350° and bake for 5 minutes more. The pancake should be puffed and golden brown.

Sprinkle the brown sugar over the top of the cooked pancake. Pour the lemon juice over the pancake.

Preparation time: 5 minutes
Cooking time: 2 minutes
Baking time: 20 minutes

Chef's note: For variations of this recipe, substitute other spices and extracts for the nutmeg and vanilla. Bake the pancake with cinnamon and serve with apple butter, or add orange rind and top with fresh strawberries, or stir in lemon rind and sprinkle with fresh blueberries.

Per serving: 185 calories, 7.2 g. fat (36% of calories), 0.4 g. dietary fiber, no cholesterol, 80 mg. sodium.

Wild Rice Pancakes (page 238)

Sun-Dried Tomato Semolina Bread (page 250)

Oven-Puffed Pancake (page 256)

Strawberry Waffles with Strawberry-Rhubarb Sauce (page 268)

Mango Sorbet (page 280)

Praline Cookie Cups (page 285)

Sweetheart Cherry Pie (page 288)

New York Cheesecake (page 291)

ON-THE-GO BREAKFASTS

*M*om always said, "Eat your breakfast." That's great advice, since breakfast lays your body's nutritional foundation for the day, puts all your systems on "go" and gets your day off to a wide-awake start. But finding time for breakfast is a trick, especially when you're trying to get yourself or your kids out the door and on with the day's activities. Here is more than a week's worth of tips for easy, tasty, on-the-go breakfasts.

1. Toast a slice of your favorite bread and top it with nonfat cream cheese and bits of dried fruit.

2. Take a few minutes (about 30 in all) over the weekend to make a batch of muffins. Put the muffins in individual freezer bags; freeze. Then, on busy weekdays, wrap each muffin you'd like that morning in a damp paper towel and microwave on high for 20 to 30 seconds.

3. Cut an onion bagel in half, top it with slices of tomato and reduced-fat Cheddar cheese, sprinkle with cracked black pepper or dried herbs and pop in the microwave until the cheese melts.

4. Stir low-fat granola or other crunchy cereal into 1 cup of plain or vanilla nonfat yogurt. Top with bananas, berries, peaches or other fresh fruit in season. If you're really in a hurry, put it in a plastic container with a tight-fitting lid so you can eat it on the bus or at your desk.

5. Spoon nonfat cottage cheese into a cantaloupe half. Drizzle with nonfat French dressing or a nonfat fruit salad-type dressing.

6. If you make waffles on the weekend, make a few more, freeze them and then reheat them in the toaster or microwave. The Coconut Waffles (page 266) or Strawberry Waffles with Rhubarb Sauce (page 268) would work great.

7. Make an omelet or scrambled eggs with nonfat egg substitute, reduced-fat cheese and cut-up vegetables. Precut veggies from the produce department make this breakfast even easier.

8. This is a bonus tip. Breakfast can be any food that you like. But a well-rounded breakfast should provide protein, carbohydrates and at least one serving of fruits or vegetables.

COCONUT WAFFLES WITH AMBROSIA

SERVES 4

*W*hat could be lovelier for a spring brunch than these coconut-flavored waffles topped with a creamy fruit sauce? We've kept fat to a minimum by using fat-free buttermilk, egg substitute, yogurt and coconut extract rather than high-fat flaked or shredded coconut.

Waffles

1	*cup unbleached flour*
¼	*cup cornmeal*
1½	*teaspoons baking powder*
¼	*teaspoon baking soda*
1	*cup buttermilk*
¼	*cup fat-free egg substitute*
2	*tablespoons canola oil*
2	*tablespoons coconut extract*
2	*egg whites, whipped to soft peaks*

Ambrosia

1	*cup diced pineapple*
1	*cup chopped orange sections*
½	*cup nonfat vanilla yogurt*
2	*tablespoons unsweetened raw coconut chips*

To make the waffles: In a large bowl, combine the flour, cornmeal, baking powder and baking soda. In a small bowl, mix the buttermilk, eggs, oil and coconut extract.

Pour the buttermilk mixture over the dry ingredients. Use a whisk to blend. Use a spatula to fold the egg whites into the batter.

Heat the waffle iron. Brush the grids of the waffle iron with additional oil. Pour ½ cup of the batter on the Belgian waffle grids. Cook for 3 minutes per waffle. Keep waffles warm in a 250° oven while the remainder of the batter is being used. Serve with the ambrosia.

To make the ambrosia: In a medium bowl, combine the pineapple, oranges, yogurt and coconut. Mix well. Set aside until the waffles are cooked.

Preparation time: 10 minutes
Cooking time: 9 minutes

Chef's notes: It's important to preheat the waffle iron and use it according to the manufacturer's instructions.

A Belgian waffle iron requires ½ cup of batter per grid. The amount of batter may differ if you use a different type or shape of waffle iron.

Avoid overbeating the waffle batter—a few lumps are fine. The batter should be thick but pourable.

To keep cooked waffles warm until you're ready to serve them, place the waffles in a single layer on a wire cooling rack. Set the wire rack on a baking sheet and place it in a 250° oven.

Look for coconut chips in the bulk or health-food section of your supermarket.

Per serving: 272 calories, 1.7 g. fat (6% of calories), 3.6 g. dietary fiber, no cholesterol, 309 mg. sodium.

STRAWBERRY WAFFLES
WITH STRAWBERRY-RHUBARB SAUCE

SERVES 4

*T*he Dutch are given credit for introducing waffles in 1796. Among the most popular today are Belgian waffles.

Strawberry Waffles

1¼	*cups unbleached flour*
1	*teaspoon baking soda*
1	*cup buttermilk*
¼	*cup all-fruit strawberry spread*
2	*tablespoons fat-free egg substitute*
2	*tablespoons canola oil*
1	*egg white, whipped to soft peaks*

Strawberry-Rhubarb Sauce

1	*package (10-ounces) frozen strawberries, thawed*
1	*cup sliced rhubarb*
2	*tablespoons honey*
1	*tablespoon grated orange rind*

To make the strawberry waffles: In a medium bowl, combine the flour and baking soda. In a small bowl, mix the buttermilk, fruit spread, eggs and oil.

Pour the buttermilk mixture over the flour and blend well. Fold in the egg white. Heat the waffle iron. Brush the grids of the waffle iron with canola oil. Pour ½ cup of the batter on Belgian waffle grids. Cook for 2 minutes per waffle.

To keep cooked waffles warm, see Chef's notes on page 267.

To make the strawberry-rhubarb sauce: In a small saucepan, combine the strawberries, rhubarb and honey. Bring to a boil over medium heat and cook for 3 to 5 minutes, stirring occasionally, until the rhubarb is tender. Stir in the orange rind. Serve warm or at room temperature.

Preparation time: 15 minutes
Cooking time: 10 minutes

Per serving: 323 calories, 7.4 g. fat (20% of calories), 2.9 g. dietary fiber, no cholesterol, 176 mg. sodium.

CRACKED PEPPER CORNSTICKS

MAKES 20

Whole kernels of corn add texture and color to these cornbread sticks. For a colorful variation, try using blue cornmeal, which can be found in the gourmet section of your supermarket.

> 1   *cup cornmeal*
> ¾   *cup unbleached flour*
> 1   *tablespoon baking powder*
> ½   *teaspoon cracked black pepper*
> ¾   *cup skim milk*
> ¾   *cup corn*
> ¼   *cup fat-free egg substitute*
> 1½   *tablespoons olive oil*

In a medium bowl, combine the cornmeal, flour, baking powder and pepper; mix well. In a separate medium bowl, combine the milk, corn, eggs and oil. Add to the flour mixture and stir until combined.

Preheat a 10-cornstick pan in a 425° oven for 10 to 15 minutes. Remove the pan from the oven and coat it with no-stick spray. Spoon the batter into the molds, filling halfway. Bake for 8 to 10 minutes, or until lightly browned and a toothpick inserted in the center comes out clean.

Remove the cornsticks from the pan immediately and place them on a wire cooling rack. Spray the pan with no-stick spray, spoon the remaining batter into the molds and bake as directed above. Serve warm.

Preparation time: 5 minutes plus 15 minutes preheating time
Baking time: 20 minutes

Per cornstick: 58 calories, 1.3 g. fat (20% of calories), 1.2 g. dietary fiber, no cholesterol, 61 mg. sodium.

MUSHROOM SPOONBREAD

---

*S*oft, puddinglike spoonbread gets its name because it can be served and eaten with a spoon. Serve this old-fashioned side dish with baked chicken, seafood gumbo or roasted meats.

¾	*cup cornmeal*
1½	*cups water*
1	*cup diced onions*
1	*tablespoon canola oil*
1	*large shallot*
8	*ounces mushrooms, quartered*
½	*teaspoon low-sodium chicken bouillon dissolved in ¼ cup water*
¼	*teaspoon ground black pepper*
⅛	*teaspoon dried thyme*
½	*cup skim milk*
½	*cup fat-free egg substitute*
2	*egg whites, whipped to soft peaks*
4	*scallions, sliced*

In a small saucepan, combine the cornmeal and water. Over medium-high heat, bring to a boil; reduce the heat to low and cook, stirring occasionally, until the cornmeal is stiff.

In a small no-stick frying pan over medium heat, cook the onions in the oil until brown, about 5 minutes.

While the onions are browning, finely chop the shallot and mushrooms in a food processor fitted with the steel blade. Add the mushroom-shallot mixture to the onions, along with the bouillon, pepper and thyme. Cook over medium heat until the liquid evaporates, about 5 to 10 minutes.

Meanwhile, place a 9″ × 9″ pan in a 400° oven for 5 minutes.

In a large bowl, combine the milk, eggs, egg whites and scallions. Add the cornmeal and mushrooms to the milk mixture.

Remove the hot pan from the oven; coat it with no-stick spray. Pour the batter into the pan. Bake for 30 to 35 minutes, or until a toothpick inserted in the center comes out clean.

Preparation time: 15 minutes
Cooking time: 15 minutes
Baking time: 35 minutes

Per square: 80 calories, 2 g. fat (22% of calories), 2.2 g. dietary fiber, no cholesterol, 56 mg. sodium.

D E L E C T A B L E
D E S S E R T S
T H A T   A R E
L O W   I N
F A T ,   T O O

SWEET TEMPTATIONS

Like the rest of American cooking, our desserts have been inspired by and borrowed from the diverse cultures that make up this country. Custardy flan originated in Spain, featherlight soufflés and cream-filled Napoleons were brought from France, and bread puddings were an English import. But we've also created our own all-American sweet traditions—brownies, cherry pie, pandowdy, shortcake and chocolate sundaes. Now if you're thinking that these desserts are off your eating list because they're high in fat, think again! We've reduced the fat in nearly two dozen delectable desserts that you can enjoy for special—and everyday—occasions.

Easy Apricot Soufflé with Raspberry Sauce

SERVES 4

*I*n French, *soufflé* means a puff or breath. This airy dessert is as light as a puff of air, and we've lightened the calories and fat by using only egg whites rather than whole eggs.

> 4   *egg whites*
> ¼   *cup honey*
> ¼   *cup all-fruit apricot spread*
> 1   *package (10 ounces) frozen raspberries, thawed*

In a large bowl, beat the egg whites with an electric mixer until they form soft peaks, about 2 minutes.

In a small saucepan, heat the honey and apricot spread over low heat until warm, about 1 minute. Fold the warm honey mixture into the egg whites until just blended.

Coat 4 (8-ounce) custard cups with no-stick spray. Spoon the soufflé mixture into the prepared cups. Place the cups on a baking sheet and bake at 400° for 10 minutes, or until puffed and golden brown.

Meanwhile, place the berries with their juice in a sieve over a small bowl. Push the berries through the sieve with the back of a spoon. Discard the seeds. Stir the raspberry pulp and juice together to combine. Pour the raspberry sauce into a pitcher.

Serve the soufflés right from the oven; pass the raspberry sauce.

Preparation time: 10 minutes
Baking time: 10 minutes

Chef's note: A soufflé is very sensitive to temperature changes, so avoid checking on it during baking. Also, a soufflé will begin to deflate as soon as you remove it from the oven, so serve it immediately.

Per serving: 210 calories, no fat, 3.4 g. dietary fiber, no cholesterol, 59 mg. sodium.

GINGERSNAP PEAR TART

SERVES 12

*M*ake this gingery tart year-round with canned pears or use fresh pears in season such as Bartletts in late summer, Boscs from October to April and Anjous and Comices from fall to mid-winter.

Crust

2 *cups gingersnap cookie crumbs*

1 *egg white, lightly beaten*

Filling

8 *ounces light cream cheese, room temperature*

1 *tablespoon honey*

2 *tablespoons chopped crystallized ginger*

1 *can (16 ounces) pears in light syrup, drained and sliced*

2 *tablespoons all-fruit apricot spread, melted*

To make the crust: Combine the crumbs and egg white in a medium bowl and blend. Press the mixture into a 10″ tart pan. Bake the crust at 350° for 15 minutes, or until set. Place on a rack to cool.

To make the filling: In a medium bowl, combine the cream cheese, honey and ginger. Beat with an electric mixer for 1 to 2 minutes, or until fluffy.

To assemble the tart, spread the cream cheese mixture over the tart shell and top with the sliced pears. Spoon the apricot spread over the pears.

Preparation time: 15 minutes
Baking time: 15 minutes

Chef's note: Pears actually improve in texture, flavor and aroma after they've been picked. To ripen pears at home, place them in a brown paper bag and close it lightly. Check the pears every day by pressing gently near the stem. When a pear gives slightly, it's ripe.

Per serving: 169 calories, 7.2 g. fat (37% of calories), 0.7 g. dietary fiber, 7 mg. cholesterol, 163 mg. sodium.

Pumpkin Flan with Apple Walnut Syrup

*F*lan, a baked custard topped with a caramelized sauce, is a popular Spanish dessert. This low-fat version, made with skim milk and fat-free egg substitute, celebrates the rich flavors of autumn—pumpkin, walnut and apple.

Pumpkin Flan

    1   *can (16 ounces) pumpkin*
    1   *cup evaporated skim milk*
    1   *cup fat-free egg substitute*
    ½   *cup maple syrup*

Apple Walnut Syrup

    2   *medium apples, peeled, cored and chopped*
    ½   *cup maple syrup*
    2   *tablespoons chopped toasted walnuts*

To make the pumpkin flan: In a large bowl, combine the pumpkin, milk, eggs and maple syrup; mix until blended. Coat a 9″ round microwave-safe cake pan with no-stick spray. Pour the mixture into the prepared pan. Microwave on high for 20 minutes, turning every 5 minutes, until set.

To make the apple walnut syrup: Place the apples, maple syrup and walnuts in a medium microwave-safe bowl. Microwave on high for 10 minutes.

To serve, slice the flan into wedges and top with the warm apple walnut syrup.

Preparation time: 10 minutes
Microwaving time: 30 minutes

Chef's note: If you don't have a microwave, bake the flan at 350° for 40 minutes, or until the center is set. To make the sauce, combine the apples, maple syrup and walnuts in a medium sauce-pan. Cook the mixture over medium heat for 20 minutes, or until the apples are soft.

Per serving: 187 calories, 1.4 g. fat (7% of calories), 1.9 g. dietary fiber, 1 mg. cholesterol, 85 mg. sodium.

DOUBLE BLUEBERRY TARTS

SERVES 4

*F*resh blueberries folded into a blueberry sauce fill paper-thin and crisp phyllo tarts. The finished tarts have a decorative, ragged edge.

> 2   *sheets phyllo dough*
> 1   *tablespoon cornstarch*
> ½   *cup frozen apple juice concentrate, thawed*
> 2   *cups blueberries*
> 2   *tablespoons lemon juice*
> 1   *tablespoon honey*
> ¼   *teaspoon ground cinnamon*

Lay 1 sheet of phyllo on a work surface, keeping the other sheet covered with a damp cloth. Spray the phyllo with no-stick spray and cut it into 6 (4″) squares. Layer 3 squares on top of each other, each at a different angle, and press them gently into a muffin cup. Repeat with the remaining 3 squares to make the second tart shell. Repeat the entire process with the remaining sheet of phyllo dough for a total of 4 tart shells. Bake at 375° for 10 minutes, or until golden brown.

Meanwhile, in a medium saucepan, combine the cornstarch and juice concentrate, stirring until the cornstarch is dissolved. Add 1 cup of blueberries, the lemon juice, honey and cinnamon. Cook the mixture over medium heat, stirring, until the mixture thickens, about 5 minutes. Let cool for 15 minutes, or until room temperature; stir in the remaining 1 cup of the blueberries.

To assemble the tarts, place ¼ cup of the blueberry filling in each tart shell and serve immediately.

Preparation time: 10 minutes
Baking time: 10 minutes
Cooking time: 5 minutes plus 15 minutes cooling time

Per serving: 127 calories, 0.4 g. fat (3% of calories), 1.7 g. dietary fiber, no cholesterol, 14 mg. sodium.

APPLE APRICOT PANDOWDY

SERVES 4

A biscuit crust tops this deep-dish fruit-and-molasses dessert. When served, the crust is *dowdied*—broken up and stirred into the filling with a spoon or knife.

2 medium Golden Delicious apples, peeled, cored and sliced

½ cup water

¼ cup chopped dried apricots

¼ cup frozen apple juice concentrate, thawed

1 tablespoon molasses

¾ cup reduced-fat baking mix

⅓ cup skim milk

¼ teaspoon ground cinnamon

In a large saucepan, combine the apples, water, apricots, juice concentrate and molasses. Cook over medium heat until the apples are soft, about 5 minutes.

Meanwhile, in a medium bowl, combine the baking mix, milk and cinnamon. Mix with a fork until just blended.

Drop 4 biscuit mounds on top of the apple mixture. Cover and continue to cook over medium heat until the dumplings are cooked through, about 10 minutes. Serve warm.

Preparation time: 10 minutes
Cooking time: 15 minutes

Per serving: 308 calories, 2.6 g. fat (8% of calories), 5.1 g. dietary fiber, no cholesterol, 944 mg. sodium.

Winter Fruit Crisp

SERVES 6

*F*at-free fruit cookies make a crispy-sweet, crunchy crust for this classic American dessert.

Fruit Filling

1	package (8 ounces) mixed dried fruit, coarsely chopped
2	cups water
¼	cup honey
1	tablespoon lemon juice
½	teaspoon grated nutmeg

Topping

4	fat-free chewy fruit cookies
¼	cup unbleached flour
¼	cup rolled oats
1	tablespoon honey

To make the fruit filling: In a large glass bowl, combine the dried fruit and water. Microwave on high for 10 minutes. Drain off the water; toss the fruit with the honey, lemon juice and nutmeg. Place the fruit mixture in an 8″ round cake pan or casserole.

To make the topping: Place the cookies in a food processor fitted with the steel blade. Process until ground, about 20 seconds. Add the flour, oats and honey and pulse until blended, about 10 seconds.

To assemble, sprinkle the topping over the fruit filling and coat with no-stick spray. Bake at 375° for 20 minutes, or until golden brown. Serve warm.

Preparation time: 10 minutes
Microwaving time: 10 minutes
Baking time: 20 minutes

Per serving: 198 calories, 0.5 g. fat (2% of calories), 4.3 g. dietary fiber, no cholesterol, 29 mg. sodium.

CHOCOLATE CRÊPES WITH BERRIES

SERVES 4

*A*long the streets of Paris, you'll find walk-up crêpe stands where Parisians buy crêpes-to-go filled with sugar, liqueurs, chocolate, jam, cheese or ham. Serve this elegant, fruit-filled version at a brunch, shower or summertime tea.

½ *cup instant-blending or finely milled flour*
2 *tablespoons unsweetened cocoa powder*
½ *cup skim milk*
2 *eggs, lightly beaten*
2 *tablespoons honey*
2 *cups nonfat frozen vanilla yogurt*
2 *cups fresh berries*

In a medium bowl, combine the flour and cocoa. Add the milk, eggs and honey. Stir until combined, about 1 minute. The mixture should be the consistency of heavy cream. If the mixture is too thick, add more milk, 1 tablespoon at a time.

Coat an 8″ no-stick frying pan with no-stick spray and heat over medium heat until hot. Pour 3 tablespoons of batter into the pan and swirl to coat. Cook the crêpe until it releases easily from the pan, about 1 minute. Turn the crêpe and cook on the other side for about 30 seconds. Continue until all the batter is gone. The batter makes about 8 crêpes.

To serve, place ¼ cup frozen yogurt on each crêpe and roll. Top with ¼ cup berries.

Preparation time: 5 minutes
Cooking time: 15 minutes

Chef's note: If you use unbleached or all-purpose flour, let the batter stand for 30 minutes before making the crêpes.

Per serving: 266 calories, 3.2 g. fat (10% of calories), 2 g. dietary fiber, 109 mg. cholesterol, 124 mg. sodium.

MANGO SORBET

SERVES 4

*T*o the French, it's sorbet. To the Italians, it's sorbetto, and to Americans, it's sherbet. But true sorbet contains no milk, making it completely fat-free. Mangoes give this icy-smooth dessert its brilliant orange color and sweet-tangy flavor.

- *1 can (15 ounces) mangoes, drained and pureed*
- *½ cup carbonated water*
- *⅓ cup honey*
- *1 tablespoon lime juice*

In a medium bowl, combine the mango puree, water, honey and lime juice; mix until well-blended.

Transfer the mixture to an ice cream maker and freeze according to the manufacturer's directions.

To serve, scoop into dessert bowls.

Preparation time: 5 minutes plus chilling time

Per serving: 185 calories, 0.4 g. fat (2% of calories), 3.5 g. dietary fiber, no cholesterol, 4 mg. sodium.

Banana Nut Quesadilla

*C*rown a south-of-the-border brunch or dinner with this unusual but deliciously sweet dessert. Light cream cheese and nonfat caramel sauce are the secret ingredients for keeping fat to a minimum.

> *4   flour tortillas, 8" in diameter*
> *½   cup light cream cheese*
> *2   bananas, sliced*
> *2   tablespoons chopped honey-coated nuts*
> *¼   cup nonfat caramel sauce*

Lay out the tortillas and spread 2 tablespoons of the cream cheese over the entire surface of each tortilla. Top half of each tortilla with banana slices and sprinkle with ½ tablespoon of the nuts. Fold the tortillas in half.

Heat a large no-stick frying pan over medium heat until hot. Place 2 of the tortillas in the pan and cook until golden brown, about 2 minutes per side. Repeat for the remaining tortillas.

Cut each tortilla into 3 wedges and drizzle with 1 tablespoon of the caramel sauce.

Preparation time: 5 minutes
Cooking time: 8 minutes

Per serving: 311 calories, 10.5 g. fat (30% of calories), 2.3 g. dietary fiber, 10 mg. cholesterol, 240 mg. sodium.

CHOCOLATE RASPBERRY SUNDAES

SERVES 4

*C*hocolate and raspberry is a flavor marriage made in heaven! This dessert features a fruity, cocoa-flavored sauce over frozen raspberry yogurt.

¼   *cup light corn syrup*
¼   *cup water*
3   *tablespoons all-fruit raspberry spread*
2   *tablespoons unsweetened cocoa powder*
2   *teaspoons cornstarch*
½   *teaspoon vanilla*
1   *pint nonfat frozen raspberry yogurt*

In a small saucepan, combine the corn syrup, water and raspberry spread.

In a small bowl, stir together the cocoa and cornstarch.

Add the cocoa mixture to the saucepan and mix well. Cook over medium-low heat until thickened, about 2 minutes. Remove from the heat and stir in the vanilla.

Serve warm or cold over the frozen yogurt.

Preparation time: 5 minutes
Cooking time: 2 minutes

Per serving: 203 calories, 0.3 g. fat (1% of calories), 0.2 g. dietary fiber, 2 mg. cholesterol, 88 mg. sodium.

TROPICAL FRUIT NAPOLEONS

SERVES 4

*W*onton skins and nonfat frozen yogurt replace the high-fat pastry layers and cream filling of this traditional dessert. For another variation, use whatever fresh berries are in season.

8   *wonton skins*
½   *teaspoon ground cinnamon*
1   *pint nonfat frozen vanilla yogurt*
1   *kiwi, peeled and sliced*
1   *banana, sliced*
½   *cup pineapple chunks*
2   *tablespoons shredded coconut*

Coat each side of the wonton skins with no-stick spray and place on a 10″×15″ jelly-roll pan. Sprinkle with the cinnamon and bake at 375° for 5 minutes, or until golden brown.

To serve, lay out 4 wontons. Top with half of the frozen yogurt, then with half of the kiwis, bananas and pineapple. Repeat the layers. Sprinkle the coconut on top of the Napoleons and serve them immediately.

Preparation time: 5 minutes
Baking time: 5 minutes

Per serving: 193 calories, 1.2 g. fat (5% of calories), 1.6 g. dietary fiber, 2 mg. cholesterol, 110 mg. sodium.

PEACH MELBA

SERVES 4

*N*ellie Melba, the famous 19th century Australian opera star, inspired many chefs to create dishes for her. This peach sundae is one of the most famous.

2   *ripe peaches, peeled and halved*
1   *cup water*
¼   *cup honey*
1   *package (10 ounces) frozen raspberries, thawed*
1   *tablespoon cornstarch*
1   *pint nonfat frozen vanilla yogurt*

In a medium saucepan, combine the peaches, water and honey. Cook over medium heat until the peaches are soft, about 5 minutes. Remove the peaches with a slotted spoon and set aside to cool.

Meanwhile, in a medium saucepan, combine the raspberries and cornstarch, stirring until the cornstarch is dissolved. Cook over medium heat until the mixture thickens, about 3 minutes. Remove from the heat and let cool for 10 minutes.

To serve, place a peach half in a dessert dish and top with a scoop of frozen yogurt and the warm raspberry sauce.

Preparation time: 10 minutes
Cooking time: 10 minutes plus 10 minutes cooling time

Chef's note: To peel peaches, put them into a pot of boiling water for 10 to 20 seconds, or until the skin begins to loosen. Drain and place in ice water to cool. The skin should easily slip off when gently pulled.

Per serving: 254 calories, 0.2 g. fat (1% of calories), 3.9 g. dietary fiber, 2 mg. cholesterol, 72 mg. sodium.

PRALINE COOKIE CUPS

*F*ill these thin, buttery, nutty cups with fresh berries or low-fat frozen yogurt.

¼ *cup unbleached flour*
¼ *cup packed brown sugar*
2 *tablespoons unsalted butter, softened*
2 *tablespoons light corn syrup*
2 *tablespoons chopped toasted hazelnuts*

In a medium bowl, combine the flour, brown sugar, butter, corn syrup and nuts. Mix until well-blended. Divide the dough into 8 pieces and form into balls.

Cover a large baking sheet with parchment paper or coat with no-stick spray. Place the dough 3″ apart on the prepared baking sheet and press lightly to flatten. Bake at 375° for 5 to 7 minutes, or until lightly browned. The cookies will spread and be very thin.

Cool on the baking sheet for 2 minutes. Loosen gently from the pan and drape the cookies, while still warm, over the bottom of 8 (4-ounce) custard cups. The cookies will cool quickly and set in a bowl shape.

Preparation time: 5 minutes
Baking time: 7 minutes plus 2 minutes cooling time

Per cookie cup: 93 calories, 4.2 g. fat (40% of calories), 0.3 g. dietary fiber, 8 mg. cholesterol, 6 mg. sodium.

BLUEBERRY PEACH HONEY SHORTCAKES

SERVES 6

*T*hese honey shortcakes have a hint of nutmeg that enhances the flavor of fresh fruit. To keep the shortcakes light and fluffy, avoid overmixing the dough.

1¼	cups unbleached flour
2	tablespoons rolled oats
1	tablespoon baking powder
½	teaspoon baking soda
¼	teaspoon grated nutmeg
3	tablespoons margarine
1¾	cups nonfat vanilla yogurt
¼	cup skim milk
¼	cup honey
⅓	cup all-fruit peach spread
2	cups sliced peaches
2	cups blueberries

In a medium bowl, combine the flour, 1 tablespoon of the oats, baking powder, baking soda and nutmeg; mix well. Add the margarine. Using a pastry blender or 2 knives, cut the margarine into the flour mixture until the margarine is the size of peas.

In a small bowl, combine ¼ cup of the yogurt, the milk and honey. Add to the flour mixture and stir until combined. Coat a large baking sheet with no-stick spray. Drop the batter by tablespoons onto the prepared sheet, making 6 shortcakes. Sprinkle with the remaining 1 tablespoon of the oats. Bake at 425° for 8 to 10 minutes, or until lightly browned and a toothpick inserted in the center comes out clean. Cool on a wire rack.

In a small bowl, combine the remaining 1½ cups of the yogurt with the peach spread; stir gently. To serve, split the shortcakes in half horizontally and fill with the yogurt filling, peaches and blueberries.

Preparation time: 10 minutes
Baking time: 10 minutes

Per serving: 240 calories, 4.3 g. fat (16% of calories), 2.3 g. dietary fiber, 1.3 mg. cholesterol, 234 mg. sodium.

RHUBARB CHERRY SAUCE

SERVES 4

*T*art, tangy and a lovely shade of red, this chunky sauce can be served alone or as a topping for frozen yogurt, angel food cake or shortcake.

4	*cups sliced rhubarb*
½	*cup all-fruit cherry spread*
¼	*cup honey*
¼	*cup dried cherries*
½	*cup water*
1	*cup nonfat vanilla yogurt*

In a large microwave-safe bowl, combine the rhubarb, cherry spread, honey, cherries and water; mix well. Microwave on high for 15 minutes, stirring once, or until the rhubarb is tender.

Serve warm or chilled with a dollop of the yogurt.

Preparation time: 5 minutes
Cooking time: 15 minutes

Chef's notes: If you don't have a microwave, place the sauce ingredients in a large saucepan and cook over medium heat for 40 minutes, or until the rhubarb is tender.

Hothouse rhubarb can be found year-round, while field-grown rhubarb appears in the markets in late spring or early summer. Choose slender young stalks that are tender and firm. Store rhubarb tightly wrapped in the refrigerator to retain its crispness.

Per serving: 256 calories, 0.3 g. fat (1% of calories), 0.5 g. dietary fiber, 1 mg. cholesterol, 46 mg. sodium.

SWEETHEART CHERRY PIE

SERVES 4

*A*mericans love cherry pie! This pretty, low-fat version is decorated with cutout pastry hearts.

Cherry Filling

4 *cups fresh tart cherries, pitted*
½ *cup maple syrup*
3 *tablespoons quick-cooking tapioca*
1 *teaspoon ground cinnamon*

Pastry

1 *cup cake flour*
¼ *cup margarine, cut into 8 pieces*
1 *egg white, lightly beaten*

To make the cherry filling: In a large saucepan, combine the cherries, maple syrup, tapioca and cinnamon. Let the mixture stand for 5 minutes; place over medium heat and cook for 10 minutes, stirring occasionally. While the cherries are cooking, prepare the pastry.

To make the pastry: In a small bowl, combine the flour and margarine. Using a pastry blender, blend the margarine into the flour until the mixture resembles coarse meal. Add the egg white and stir until a dough forms. Knead the dough on a lightly floured board until smooth, about 30 seconds.

Reserve ¼ cup of the dough; place the remaining dough between 2 sheets of wax paper that have been lightly floured. Roll the dough into a 9″ circle. Remove 1 sheet of wax paper, invert the pastry onto an 8″ pie pan and carefully remove the other sheet of wax paper. Fold over the excess pastry and crimp the edges. Prick the bottom of the pastry with a fork and bake at 400° for 10 minutes.

Meanwhile, roll the reserved dough to ⅛″ thickness. Using a 2″ heart-shaped cookie cutter, cut out 7 hearts.

To assemble: Pour the cherry filling into the prebaked pie shell and place the pastry hearts in a circle, tips pointing toward the center. Bake at 350° for 30 minutes.

Preparation time: 15 minutes plus 5 minutes standing time
Cooking time: 10 minutes
Baking time: 40 minutes

Chef's note: You can substitute frozen tart cherries that have been thawed for the fresh cherries.

Per serving: 203 calories, 6 g. fat (26% of calories), 0.3 g. dietary fiber, no cholesterol, 78 mg. sodium.

5 HEAVENLY
ANGEL FOOD CAKE DESSERTS

*S*infully versatile, light and delicious, angel food cake is a smart addition to your low-fat meal plan. Smart because it's made with egg whites—not the fat-filled yolks—and no oil, shortening or butter, so it's virtually fat-free. And smart because it lets you eat your cake and enjoy every bite of it, too.

Here are 5 quick ways to dress up plain angel food cake for a snack or special occasion:

1. Top each slice with fresh or frozen strawberries, blueberries, raspberries or peaches, and then add a dollop of fat-free whipped topping.

2. Spoon a scoop of your favorite nonfat frozen yogurt flavor onto each slice. Dust with cocoa, sprinkle with coconut or drizzle with maple syrup.

3. Cut an angel food cake in half horizontally. Spread the bottom half with all-fruit spread such as raspberry or apricot. Top with the remaining cake half. Frost the top of the cake with the spread.

4. Top cake slices with warm rhubarb sauce such as Rhubarb Cherry Sauce on page 287, or with Mango Sorbet, page 280.

5. Poke holes in the top of an angel food cake with a skewer or other long, slender tool. Drizzle a thin glaze of powdered sugar, lemon juice and grated lemon rind over the cake. Serve cake slices garnished with thin slices of lemon and sprigs of mint.

ALL-AMERICAN RASPBERRY BROWNIES

MAKES 16

*A*ll-fruit raspberry spread is the filling for these scrumptious brownies. We've used egg whites and cocoa to trim the fat in this version.

1   *cup unbleached flour*
⅓   *cup unsweetened cocoa powder*
1   *teaspoon baking soda*
⅔   *cup dark corn syrup*
3   *egg whites*
1   *teaspoon vanilla*
¼   *cup all-fruit raspberry spread*

In a medium bowl, combine the flour, cocoa and baking soda; set aside. In a small bowl, combine the corn syrup, egg whites and vanilla. Beat the mixture with a fork for 30 seconds, or just until well-mixed. Add the liquid mixture to the dry mixture and stir until the dry ingredients are moistened.

Coat an 8″ × 8″ baking pan with no-stick spray. Pour the batter into the prepared pan. Bake at 350° for 20 to 25 minutes, or until a toothpick inserted in the middle of the brownies comes out clean.

Cool the brownies on a rack for 10 minutes; then invert the pan to remove the brownies. With a serrated knife, cut the brownies in half horizontally to create 2 layers. Cover the bottom layer with the raspberry spread and replace the top layer. To serve, cut into 16 (2″) squares.

Preparation time: 10 minutes
Cooking time: 25 minutes

Chef's note: For another variation, just before baking drop spoonfuls of the spread onto the batter. Use a knife to swirl the spread through the batter. Bake as indicated in the directions.

Per brownie: 90 calories, 0.2 g. fat (2% of calories), 0.3 g. dietary fiber, no cholesterol, 73 mg. sodium.

New York Cheesecake

A cheesecake that's low in fat? You bet! Low-fat cream cheese, low-fat ricotta cheese and a skinny cookie crust reduce the fat without reducing a forkful of flavor.

- *8 ounces light cream cheese*
- *1 cup low-fat ricotta cheese*
- *2 eggs, separated*
- *¼ cup honey*
- *¼ cup golden raisins*
- *3 tablespoons cornstarch*
- *1 tablespoon grated orange rind*
- *⅓ cup amaretti cookie crumbs*

In a large bowl, combine the cream cheese and ricotta until smooth. Stir in the egg yolks, honey, raisins, cornstarch and orange rind, mixing until thoroughly combined.

In a medium bowl, whip the egg whites with clean beaters for about 2 minutes, or until they form soft peaks. Fold the whites into the cheese mixture.

Coat a 9″ pie plate with no-stick spray and cover with the amaretti crumbs. Pour the cheese mixture into the pie plate. Bake at 400° for 30 minutes, or until golden and set.

Preparation time: 10 minutes
Baking time: 30 minutes

Chef's note: You can substitute graham cracker crumbs for the amaretti crumbs.

Per serving: 121 calories, 5.2 g. fat (37% of calories), no dietary fiber, 47 mg. cholesterol, 126 mg. sodium.

MIXED BERRY SUMMER PUDDING

SERVES 4

*D*esserts don't get much simpler than this three-ingredient, no-bake delight. Garnish each pudding with fresh berries and a dollop of nonfat vanilla yogurt.

> 3   *cup mixed berries (blueberries, raspberries, strawberries or blackberries)*
> ⅓   *cup honey*
> 8   *slices homemade-style bread, crusts removed*

In a medium saucepan, combine the berries and honey, pressing the berries to release the juices. Cook over medium heat for 3 minutes, or until the berries are warmed through. Remove from the heat and strain the berries in a large sieve over a bowl, reserving the juice. Set the berries and reserved juice aside.

Line 4 (8-ounce) custard cups with plastic wrap. Cut each slice of bread diagonally into 4 triangles. Dip the triangles into the reserved berry juice. Line the bottom and sides of each custard cup with 6 bread triangles, overlapping slightly.

Fill each cup with one-fourth of the berry mixture and top with the remaining 2 triangles of bread. Pour any remaining berry juice over the cups. Cover with plastic and wrap and chill for 30 minutes. Unmold to serve.

Preparation time: 10 minutes
Cooking time: 3 minutes
Chilling time: 30 minutes

Per serving: 266 calories, 3.7 g. fat (12% of calories), 9 g. dietary fiber, no cholesterol, 182 mg. sodium.

Native American Pudding

SERVES 6

*M*olasses or maple syrup often was the sweetener of choice for Native Americans and early settlers alike because white sugar was expensive and difficult to come by.

3	cups skim milk
½	cup cornmeal
⅓	cup molasses
1	teaspoon ground ginger
1	teaspoon vanilla
1½	cups nonfat vanilla yogurt

In a large microwave-safe bowl, combine the milk, cornmeal, molasses, ginger and vanilla. Microwave on high for 20 minutes, or until thickened, stirring after 10 minutes. Lumps that form during cooking should be broken up while stirring.

Serve warm with a dollop of yogurt.

Preparation time: 5 minutes
Cooking time: 20 minutes

Chef's note: If you don't have a microwave, bake the pudding at 375° for 1 hour, or until it has thickened.

Per serving: 168 calories, 0.6 g. fat (3% of calories), 1.6 g. dietary fiber, 3.2 mg. cholesterol, 118 mg. sodium.

CHAPTER 12

ALL-AMERICAN MENUS

Whether you're serving a meal to celebrate an anniversary, a first home run by your resident Little Leaguer or the Fourth of July, or whether you're just looking for new ideas for a weeknight supper, here are 21 complete menus to help you with your planning. You'll find menus influenced by regional specialties, special holidays from Mardi Gras to Thanksgiving and seasonal ingredients like summer-fresh fruits and vegetables. But mostly you'll find 21 low-fat, great-tasting meals that your family or guests will applaud.

CHILI PARTY

Red Pepper Dip*
Chicken and White Bean Chili*
Beef and Black Bean Chili*

Warm flour tortillas
Cracked Pepper Cornsticks*
Mango Sorbet*

GARDEN LUNCHEON

Country Herb Soup*
Turkey Fruit Salad with
  Apricot Dressing*
Whole-wheat French bread

Mixed Berry Summer Pudding*
Iced tea with orange slices and
  fresh mint

AT THE SHORE

Chesapeake Bay Crab Cakes*
  with Red Pepper Tartar Sauce*
Summer Layered Vegetables*

Cabbage coleslaw with
  reduced-fat dressing
Blueberry Peach Honey
  Shortcakes*

NATURE HIKE LUNCH

Happy O's Trail Mix*
Whole-wheat sliced turkey
  sandwiches with sprouts

Sesame Wonton Chips*
Sliced cucumbers and tomatoes
Granola Bars*

MARDI GRAS

Spinach-Stuffed Mushrooms*
Seafood Creole*
Whole-wheat biscuits

Romaine lettuce with light
  vinaigrette
Praline Cookie Cups* filled with
  frozen lime yogurt and
  fresh berries

HARVEST THANKSGIVING

Lemon Turkey Tenders*
Garlic Mashed Potatoes*
Maple Pecan Squash*
Relish tray

Steamed green beans with
  fresh dill
Pumpkin Flan with Apple
  Walnut Syrup*

SUMMER DINNER IN 25 MINUTES

Pasta with Fresh Tomato
  Escarole Sauce*
Sliced cucumbers with
  fresh herbs

Broiled pita wedges with
  Parmesan
Sliced strawberries over frozen
  lemon sorbet

*See recipe.

WINTER DINNER IN 25 MINUTES

*Berry Good Turkey**
*Bulgur Pilaf**
*Steamed broccoli with lemon
  and herbs*

*Sliced banana and orange
  yogurt parfaits*

SUNDAY EVENING BLUE PLATE SPECIAL

*Lemon Mustard Meatloaf**
*Garlic Mashed Potatoes**
*Green and White Bean Medley**

*Apple Apricot Pandowdy**

AN EVENING WITH GOOD FRIENDS

*Tangy Eggplant Dip**
*Roasted Salmon with Pepper
  Herb Crust**

*Fresh Spinach Basil Salad**
*Confetti Couscous**
*Chocolate Crêpes with Berries**

BREAKFAST AT THE INN

*Denver Spaghetti Omelet**
*Lemon Ricotta Pancakes**
*Pineapple Upside-Down Muffins**

*Dried Blueberry Lemon Loaf**
*Peach Melba**

NEIGHBORHOOD GET-TOGETHER

*Cool Garden Pizza**
*Ginger and Spice Party Mix**
*Pulled Pork Barbecue**
*New Potato Salad with Dill**

*Southwest Three Bean Salad**
*Spring Green Pasta Salad**
*All-American Raspberry Brownies**
*New York Cheesecake**

SOUP FOR SUPPER

*Pinto Bean Tortilla Soup**
Warm cornbread

Spinach salad
*Winter Fruit Crisp**

FAMILY-TIME DINNER

*Alpine Swiss Steak**
*Twice-Baked New Potatoes**
*Settler Succotash**

Whole-grain dinner rolls
*Gingersnap Pear Tart**

CASUAL GET-TOGETHER

*Pita Party Pizza**
*Black Bean Lasagna**
Marinated vegetable salad

*American Harvest Loaf**
Praline Cookie Cups filled with
  lemon yogurt and fresh berries*

*See recipe.

BIRTHDAY BASH

Artichoke Bars*
Basil Chicken Rolls*
New York Waldorf Salad*
Halibut with Sweet
  Red Pepper Sauce*

Fettuccine tossed with lemon and
  fresh herbs
Spicy Vegetable Sauté*
Sweetheart Cherry Pie*

AMERICAN HERITAGE 4TH OF JULY

Oven-Fried Chicken*
Rainbow Vegetable Coleslaw*
Chow-chow relish

Corn-on-the-cob
Molasses Baked Beans*
Double Blueberry Tarts*

MIDWEEK MEATLESS MEAL

Eggplant Strata*
Mixed Winter Greens with
  Garlic Croutons*
Broccoli and cauliflower with
  diced red pepper

Rosemary Soda Bread*
Orange Poppyseed Loaf*

AN ELEGANT EVENING

Pear Slices with Smoked Trout
  and Basil*
Rumaki*
Maple-Glazed Pork Tenderloin*

Cranberry Rice*
Tossed romaine with endive
Easy Apricot Soufflé with
  Raspberry Sauce*

WORLD SERIES SUPPER

Philadelphia Steak Sandwiches*
Crispy Sweet Onion Rings*
Spiced Beets*

Fresh vegetable platter
Honey Jack Popcorn*

NEW YEAR'S BREAKFAST

Fresh-squeezed orange juice
Coconut Waffles with Ambrosia*
Low-fat turkey sausage links

Hot herbal tea or fresh-ground
  mocha coffee

*See recipe.

Index

Note: <u>Underscored</u> page references indicate boxed text. **Boldface** references indicate photographs.

marinated tomato salad

oven-roasted asparagus

1 bunch (12 to 14 ounces) asparagus spears
1 tablespoon olive oil
½ teaspoon salt
¼ teaspoon ground black pepper
¼ cup shredded Asiago or Parmesan cheese

1. Preheat oven to 425°F.

2. Trim off and discard tough ends of asparagus spears. Peel stem ends of asparagus with vegetable peeler, if desired. Arrange asparagus in shallow baking dish. Drizzle oil onto asparagus; turn stalks to coat. Sprinkle with salt and pepper.

3. Bake until asparagus is tender, about 12 to 18 minutes depending on thickness of asparagus. Chop or leave spears whole. Sprinkle with cheese.   *Makes 4 servings*

peach freezer jam

2 pounds peaches, peeled, pitted and coarsely chopped
1 package (1¾ ounces) no-sugar-needed pectin
1 to 1½ cups unsweetened apple juice
1 to 1½ cups EQUAL® SPOONFUL*

*May substitute 24 to 36 packets Equal® sweetener.

● Coarsely mash peaches in large bowl with potato masher or pastry blender (about 2½ cups).

● Gradually stir pectin into apple juice in medium saucepan. Heat mixture to a rolling boil (one that does not stop when being stirred) over high heat, stirring constantly; boil, stirring constantly, 1 minute.

● Stir hot mixture into peaches; stir in Equal®. Fill jars, allowing ½ inch headspace. Cool jam; seal and freeze up to 3 months.   *Makes 3 (½-pint) jars*